UTAH
Byways

Backcountry Drives
For The
Whole Family

By TONY HUEGEL

WILDERNESS PRESS
BERKELEY

First Edition 1996
Second Edition May 2000

Copyright © 2000 by Tony Huegel
Photographs by the author except where noted
Cover photo: *The southern end of the Lockhart Basin Road (Tour 44)*
Copyright © 2000 by Tony Huegel
Maps and book design by Jerry Painter

Library of Congress Card Catalog Number 00-024577
ISBN 0-89997-263-2

Manufactured in the United States of America

Published by   **Wilderness Press**
                      1200 5th Street
                      Berkeley, CA 94710
                      (800) 443-7227; FAX (510) 558-1696
                      mail@wildernesspress.com

Contact us for a free catalog
Visit our website at www.wildernesspress.com

Library of Congress Cataloging-In-Publication Data
Huegel, Tony.
    Utah byways : backcountry drives for the whole family / by Tony Huegel.
--2nd ed.
        p. cm.
    Includes bibliographical references (p.) and index.
    ISBN 0-89997-263-2 (alk. paper)
        1. Utah--Tours. 2. Automobile travel--Utah--Guidebooks. 3. Rural
roads--Utah--Guidebooks. 4. All terrain vehicle driving--Utah--Guidebooks.
I. Title.

F824.3 .H84 2000
917.9204'33--dc21   00-024577

Disclaimer

Utah Byways has been prepared to help you enjoy backcountry driving. It assumes you will be driving a high-clearance four-wheel drive vehicle that is properly equipped for backcountry travel on unpaved, sometimes unmaintained and primitive backcountry roads. *Utah Byways* is not intended to be an exhaustive, all-encompassing authority on backcountry driving, nor is it intended to be your only source of information about the subject. There are risks and dangers that are inevitable when driving in the backcountry. The condition of all unpaved backcountry roads can deteriorate quickly and substantially at any time. Thus, you may encounter road conditions considerably worse than what is described here. If you drive the routes listed in this book, or any other backcountry roads, you assume all risks, dangers and liability that may result from your actions. The author and publisher of this book disclaim any and all liability for any injury, loss or damage that you, your passengers or your vehicle may incur.

Exercise the caution and good judgment that visiting the backcountry demands. Bring the proper supplies. Be prepared to deal with accidents, injuries, breakdowns and other problems alone, because help will almost always be far away and a long time coming.

Acknowledgments

I am indebted to many people who helped me find, research and appreciate the tours in *Utah Byways*.

First and foremost are my wife, Lynn MacAusland, and our children, Hannah and Land. They have for years accompanied me on many of America's most rugged and remote backcountry byways, often enduring the kind of rudimentary conditions and hair-raising moments that adventure and exploration entail.

Jerry Painter, as always, has contributed greatly through his maps and other graphic elements.

I am grateful to the busy U.S. Bureau of Land Management, U.S. Forest Service, National Park Service and Utah Division of Parks and Recreation staffers statewide who helped me identify and describe the routes. They were helpful, courteous and professional, and their contributions cannot be overstated. Any errors or shortcomings that might still exist in this book are my responsibility, not theirs.

I also thank National Geographic Maps/Trails Illustrated and the Automobile Club of Southern California (AAA) for providing complimentary copies of their outstanding maps, which I can honestly recommend highly.

Michael Dobrin, of Michael Dobrin Public Relations, has my thanks for providing assistance, support and enthusiasm that helped make the months of field research possible. I am grateful as well to Toyota Motor Sales, Inc., for providing the sport-utility vehicles that I use for researching my *Byways* guides. Over thousands of punishing backcountry miles, my family and I have never had a backcountry breakdown in a Toyota.

Chris Moore provided information about Sego Canyon and vicinity.

Finally, I must recognize Wilderness Press, whose backpacking guides long ago made exploring and enjoying wildlands an integral part of my life.

Contents

Appendix

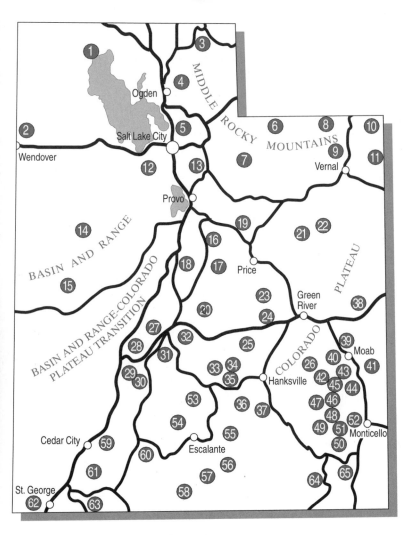

Author's Favorites

Transcontinental Railroad (Tour 1): Driving this National Back Country Byway is to relive one of the most legendary chapters in American history. The race to reach Promontory Summit and the drama of hammering in the "golden spike" there in 1869 is part of the American legend. Now you can drive the actual bed of this historic route across a remote stretch of the Great Basin, passing abandoned townsites, lonely cemeteries and crumbling trestles along the way.

Inspiration Point (Tour 4): This is an ideal road for sport-utility vehicles, with outstanding vistas. It culminates high in the dramatic Wasatch Range at a vista point with a truly breathtaking view. This route, too, is relatively close to Wasatch Front cities and towns.

Skyline Drives (Tours 5, 16, 17): The routes I call Skyline Drives I, II & III are utterly magnificent. The high-elevation scenery is unsurpassed. I also especially like the variety they offer, from easy graded two-lane dirt to narrow mountainside ledges. In addition to top-of-the-world views, Skyline Drive I is especially appealing because of its convenient proximity to Salt Lake City and other Wasatch Front population centers.

Pony Express Trail (Tour 15): This long and remote route also lets the adventurous motorist relive a legendary moment in American history. You'll really get to know the awesome expanse of the Great Basin as you follow the trail used by Pony Express riders and stagecoaches. Ruins of Pony Express and stage stations help bring it all back to life.

White Rim Road (Tour 42): This is my all-time favorite, in part because Canyonlands National Park and the surrounding area is where my family and I got started in backcountry touring. In my opinion, the White Rim Road's remoteness, the vast scale of its exotic red-rock scenery and the contrast between the powerful geology and the fragile ecology make it one of the most remarkable backcountry roads anywhere.

Map symbols

Point of interest	■	Parking	
Paved road		Hiking trail	
Easy dirt road		Forest or county road	3S01
Primitive road		Interstate highway	5
Camping	▲	U.S. highway	101
Lake		State highway	1
Stream		North indicator	N
Mountain			
Ranger station			
Picnic area			
City or town	○		

Tours in shaded background
Paved road
Easy dirt road
Primitive road

Guide to Tour Highlight Icons

Mt. biking

Rock art

Photo opportunities

Camping

Hiking

Arches

Picnicking

Restaurant

Historic sites

Wildlife viewing

Ruins

Rock hounding

How To Use Utah Byways

LOCATION: Where the drive is.

HIGHLIGHTS: What's best about the drive.

DIFFICULTY: This is subjective, since opinions and levels of experience will differ. Conditions can and do change, as well. I assume you are not a serious four-wheeler, but somebody traveling in a stock, high-clearance 4-wheel-drive (4wd) vehicle with all-terrain tires and a transfer case with high and low range. That said, the ratings are: *easy,* which means it's a cruise that probably won't require using 4wd unless conditions deteriorate; *moderate*, which means slower going using 4wd at least occasionally, with rough spots, possible stream fordings, ruts, etc., but little or no technical terrain; and *difficult*, which means at least some technical four-wheeling, rough and slow going in 4wd/low range, and the possibility that you will scrape the undercarriage or body panels.

TIME & DISTANCE: The approximate time it takes to complete the drive, excluding travel time getting to the starting point and stops you might make along the way. Since odometer accuracy varies among vehicles, your measurements of distances may differ from mine somewhat.

MAPS: Each tour description is accompanied by a general locator map, with the route highlighted in gray. They should not be used as your primary navigational map. For route finding, I list maps that provide greater detail. Choose one, and refer to it often along the way. These include maps produced by the U.S. Geological Survey (USGS), U.S. Forest Service (USFS), Bureau of Land Management (BLM) and National Geographic Maps/Trails Illustrated. *Indian Country*, by AAA affiliate Automobile Club of Southern California (ACSC), provides good coverage of southern Utah. *Recreational Map of Utah*, by GTR Mapping, is a good statewide map. The Utah Travel Council (UTC) publishes a series of five maps that I recommend as well. Rick Showalter's *Recreation Map of the San Rafael Swell & San Rafael Desert* is useful for that region. I also cite the page where the routes can be found in DeLorme's *Utah Atlas & Gazetteer*. I highly recommend *Grand Staircase-Escalante National Monument,* produced by the Public Lands Interpretive Association (PLIA; formerly called the Southwest Natural and Cultural Heritage Association). You can obtain the brochures and maps from the information sources listed, or from outdoor recreation supply stores, book and map retailers, AAA travel stores, Forest Service and BLM offices, and national park visitor centers. Sometimes I recommend other useful publications as well.

INFORMATION: An agency that may be able to provide current road conditions and other information. Telephone numbers, addresses and Internet Web sites are listed at the back of the book. This information tends to change over time.

SPECIAL NOTES: Rules, restrictions or recommendations to keep in mind.

GETTING THERE: How to reach the starting point. I typically describe routes going in a particular direction to help you locate and identify landmarks more easily. But many drives can be taken in the opposite direction.

REST STOPS: Places for a picnic, to camp, see a historic or cultural site, etc.

THE DRIVE: In this section I provide details of the trip, such as what turns to take, where you will end up, how far it is from here to there, and what you will see along the way. My geologic descriptions often include the abbreviation MYA, for million years ago.

ALSO TRY: A worthwhile route in the area that is not described in detail.

Transcontinental Railroad (Tour 1)

Swinging Bridge, Brown's Park (Tour 10)

Cottonwood Canyon's hunting scene, off Nine-Mile Canyon (Tour 21)

Strike Valley Overlook Road, in Upper Muley Twist Canyon (Tour 36)

Shafer Trail switchbacks and White Rim Road in winter (Tour 42)

INTRODUCTION

Dome (or Death) Canyon Pass, in the House Range (Tour 14)

Foreword

Hiking. Backpacking. Mountain biking. When I was younger, fitter and more footloose, I enjoyed them all. But life always seems to make more, not fewer, demands on our time. Thus, over the years work, family, lawn care and, I must admit, the passing of my physical prime took me away from those cherished modes of backcountry travel. As middle age appeared on the horizon, I worried that my days of wandering the wild were over.

Then I discovered that the West's most beautiful and remote regions, including some wilderness areas where mechanized travel is usually prohibited, are crossed by unpaved, often little-known backcountry roads. I learned that, with a factory-stock sport-utility vehicle equipped with high clearance and four-wheel drive, my family and I could have a wildland experience in the comfort and convenience of our family "car" anytime, whether for a few hours or a few days.

Bringing whatever amenities we wanted, we could explore soaring mountain ranges, high plateaus and remote desert canyons by day and then, if we didn't want to camp, relax at a motel at night. A child in diapers? No problem. No time to hike? I could drive. That bothersome foot? It would never hold me back again.

I'd broken free of the limitations of time, distance and physical ability. I'd learned that America's most spectacular wildlands were not just for the young, fit and free, or those who drive motorcycles, ATVs and highly modified 4x4s. Since many of the West's most rural backroads are relied on by people who live off the land, I found most to be easily driveable, while others were rough enough to provide exhilarating moments of adventure and challenge. I didn't need a winch, a lift kit or oversized tires and wheels. Our daily driver would do just fine.

Over the years, backcountry touring played a bigger and bigger role in my family's outdoor life and travel itineraries. We got to know the beauty and history of the West, as well as each other, in ways that would not have been possible for us otherwise.

Utah Byways, part of my multi-state series of backcountry touring guidebooks, will take you along many of the Beehive State's most beautiful and historic backways, which rank among the best in the West. Many of the tours are included in Utah's Scenic Backways program, which highlights some of the state's premier backcountry drives. Several are part of the U.S. Bureau of Land Management's National Back Country Byways program, which recognizes rural roads of particular scenic, historic and cultural value.

With its forested mountains, high-walled canyons, broad plateaus and pristine red-rock deserts, Utah offers extraordinary opportunities to escape the beaten path. Just turn these pages and see.

The Utah Experience
From the Precambrian to the Pioneers

"If you ever come this way it will scare you to death to look down it. It is about a mile from the top down to the river and it is almost straight down, the cliffs on each side are five hundred feet high and there is just room enough for a wagon to go down. It nearly scared me to death.

From a letter by Elizabeth Morris Decker, a Mormon pioneer with the 1879-1880 Hole-In-The-Rock expedition, which had to widen a crack in the sandstone wall of Glen Canyon before lowering their wagons almost 2,000 feet to the Colorado River.

U tah was a formidable frontier for the Latter-day Saints who made a home of it in the second half of the 19th century, pioneers like Elizabeth Morris Decker. While much of Utah has been tamed since her day, the wonder of the place in the 21st century is that so much of it is still wild, awe-inspiring, even intimidating at times. Four generations after the Hole-In-The-Rock Expedition braved the Utah wilderness, adventurous travelers can still find unspoiled wild-lands there, from pale desert basins and twisting slickrock canyons to snowy peaks 12,000 feet high and remote river gorges a thousand feet deep.

In theory, Utah's rectilinear borders give its two million residents 84,916 square miles in which to live, making it the 11th largest state. Yet 77 percent of Utahns live along the narrow, well-watered and thus heavily urbanized north-south corridor of Interstate 15, pinched between the vast Great Basin Desert immediately to the west and the towering escarpment of the Wasatch Range immediately to the east. About 65 percent of the land is federally controlled, some of it military preserves, some of it national forests, much of it rangeland. But there are also five national parks, two national recreation areas, a national historic site and seven national monuments. Among the latter is the new (1996) Grand Staircase-Escalante National Monument, at almost 1.9 million acres the largest in the Lower 48. Utahns have added 45 state parks to the mix. Altogether, these federal and state lands include some of the most spectacular, historic, geologically and ecolog-ically significant wildlands remaining in the contiguous states. There are still places where, even from a high vantage point on a moonless night, one might not see a single man-made source of light. Anxious words similar to Decker's could be spoken even now by a canyoneer descending into the magical labyrinths of the Escalante River, a hiker gazing across the Great Basin from high in the House Range, a rock climber about to rappel down a sheer red-rock cliff, or a backcoun-try traveler who peers at flooded Glen Canyon through the very same Hole-In-The-Rock that stalled the pioneers.

Whether one focuses on natural resource extraction, energy development, ranching, farming, outdoor recreation or wilderness, the land has always been a fundamental source of Utah's sustenance and identity. A once-remote place settled by persecuted Mormons seeking a place where they would be left alone, its famous parks, monuments, ski resorts and spectacular publicly owned wildlands today attract visitors by the millions. Now local folks, many of them descendants of the pioneers who settled this difficult land, and who've had some of the world's most beautiful places as their backyard all of their lives, find themselves in a tug of war with strangers from every corner of the country over how much of Utah should remain forever wild.

The story of Utah is long and complex. At the mouth of the Wasatch Range's Farmington Canyon (Tour 5), in what geologists term the Middle Rocky Mountains Province, one can drive past Precambrian rock that is some 2 billion years old, making it the oldest exposed rock in Utah. In the House Range (Tour 14), in the Basin and Range Province, one can dig for fossils of early invertebrates, extinct trilobites that crept along sandy seabeds half a billion years ago. On the Colorado Plateau Province, a 65-million-year-old uplift consisting of smaller plateaus, rivers, mountains and deeply incised canyons, varicolored layers of sedimentary rock tell of primordial tidal flats, vanished forests and vast deserts the likes of which no human has ever seen. And mountain slopes from the Wasatch Range far into the Great Basin remain notched by the varied shorelines of ice-age Lake Bonneville, which, after it began to form some 25,000 years ago, eventually inundated almost a quarter of Utah beneath as much as 1,100 feet of water.

Indian sites from the Paleolithic period (8,500 to 12,000 years ago) have been found in the Uinta Basin. If you visit Horseshoe Canyon (Tour 26), you will find large, ghostly pictographs, reddish anthropomorphs thought to have been painted on the canyon's walls during the Archaic period (8,500 to 2,500 years ago). On the walls of Nine-Mile Canyon (Tour 21) are thousands of images pecked and painted by Fremont Culture Indians, scattered bands who occupied the western Colorado Plateau and eastern Great Basin between about 400 and 1300 A.D. In Beef Basin (Tour 48) and throughout the Four Corners region are the abandoned structures of ancestral Puebloan people, the Anasazi, contemporaries of the Fremont who, like the Fremont, mysteriously abandoned the region some 700 years ago.

The first European known to enter Utah was the Spaniard Juan Maria Antonio de Rivera. Venturing northwest from Abiquiu, New Mexico, in 1765 he reached the Colorado River at the site of today's Moab. In 1776, Francisco Atanasio Dominguez and Silvestre Velez de Escalante, two Franciscan friars, passed through Utah in their unsuccessful search for a route from Santa Fe to Monterey, California. The 1800s brought fur trappers and explorers like Jedediah Smith, James Bridger, John C. Fremont and Maj. John Wesley Powell. In 1847, a party of Mormon emigrants led by Brigham Young descended from the Wasatch Range via Emigrant Canyon into a place they hoped to call their own. In the following decades, Mormons were called to settle beyond their base in Salt Lake City, spreading first throughout Utah, then throughout the West and even the world. In 1896, after the LDS Church renounced the practice of polygamy, Utah was granted statehood.

From its highest point (13,528-foot King's Peak, in the Uinta Mountains) to its lowest (2,350-foot Beaver Dam Wash, in Utah's southwestern corner), Utah is a place of countless contrasts. For example, driving to Golden Spike National Historic Site, where a pair of steam locomotives regularly re-enact the historic linkup of East and West in 1869, one passes Thiokol Propulsion's sprawling aerospace facility and outdoor rocket display. In colorful canyon country, mountain bikers, jeepers and hikers explore broad benchlands and narrow canyons on Cold War-era uranium prospecting and mining roads that followed old stock trails that followed old Indian trails. Thousands of motorists each day speed along Interstate 80 across the Great Basin, while more adventurous travelers journey along the old Pony Express and Overland Stage trail (Tour 15) to the south. Still others pilot rocket cars on the same forbidding salt flats once braved by pioneers in plodding wagon trains. In northeastern Utah, the state's highest mountains, the Uintas, extend east to west, in a region where mountain ranges typically trend north to south. As crowds of Utahns commute in stop-and-go traffic beneath smoggy skies, some no doubt view Salt Lake City's hosting of the 2002 Winter Olympics as proof of their arrival on the world stage. Yet it is canyon country's trendy little Moab, a former uranium mining town that has become an outdoor recreation Mecca, that buzzes with the babel of the world during vacation season.

Silently and continuously, the forces of nature that created Utah's semi-arid deserts, steep mountains, sprawling plateaus and serpentine canyons carry on. Often, as in the southwestern corner, where the Mojave Desert and Great Basin meet beneath the red-rock ramparts of the Colorado Plateau, the front lines of geologic change are so close that you can cross from one geologic, biologic or climatic zone to another in minutes. Just about everywhere, one sees the Earth's crust being ceaselessly uplifted, eroded, buckled and folded by relentless geologic forces. Whether one looks at the limestones of the Great Basin, where water finds no outlet to the sea, or walks across canyon country's layers of sedimentary rock, one is encountering a record of a planet in an unending state of change.

Utah may be most famous for the exotic landscapes of the Colorado Plateau, a region of epic scale and unparalleled beauty that includes most of eastern and southern Utah. Named for the river that drains it through a system of sinuous tributaries, it is renowned for its richly colored, labyrinthine canyons, towering cliffs and monoliths formed of primordial seabed sediments and ancient desert dunes. Here, one finds dramatic gorges scoured by the great Colorado River and its almost-as-great tributary, the Green, as well as such smaller branches of the Colorado River system as the Escalante, San Juan and San Rafael. In places, huge blocks of erosion-resistant igneous rock — the landmark La Sal, Abajo (a.k.a. Blue) and Henry mountains — stand like islands where, in their earlier molten form, they'd squeezed up through faults and pressed against the thick layers of more easily eroded sedimentary rock, forming great domes that were gradually worn away. Hardened and exposed now, these laccolithic mountains tower above expanses of sandstone that are being lifted and sculpted even now by the same forces that have shaped the Colorado Plateau for eons. In the vicinity of Moab, subterranean salt formations thousands of feet thick, the remains of a bygone sea, shift beneath the mass of overbearing sediments, leading, in partnership with erosion, to the creation of wonders like Arches National Park's sandstone statuary.

Through this country threads an alluring network of backcountry roads. Many are maintained county roads that even a passenger car can travel safely. Others are little-used single-lane roads. Still others are rudimentary two-tracks, the motoring equivalent of hiking trails, scratched across the land many decades ago by pioneers, ranchers, miners and loggers.

A great many of them offer the chance to enjoy scenic splendor and solitude. Others — the old Pony Express and Overland Stage trail, the original grade of the first transcontinental railroad, even the route of America's first transcontinental highway, the Lincoln Highway — are notable for the almost-mythical places they occupy in American history. Some are part of the U.S. Bureau of Land Management's network of National Back Country Byways. Many others are highlighted in the state of Utah's Scenic Backways program. Still others follow segments of the Great Western Trail, a multiple-use backcountry trail system that may one day stretch from Mexico to Canada.

The roads across Utah's outback offer the chance to experience some of the most unspoiled and historic places in the West. Whether you seek out sandstone canyons, mountain peaks, distant plateaus or prehistoric and historic sites, you will return from your journeys with a sense that Utah remains, in many ways, an American frontier.

Adventuring In Your SUV
Backcountry Touring 101

Utah Byways is intended to introduce the pleasures of backcountry touring to people who travel in factory-stock, high-clearance four-wheel drive sport-utility vehicles equipped for possibly rough off-highway conditions. Since relatively few people who drive SUVs take advantage of what their vehicles can do, I'm going to assume that your experience is limited, and provide some basic know-how. My hope is to help you have a safe and enjoyable experience while protecting Utah's natural environment as well as its historic and cultural sites for future generations.

Get to know your vehicle

Some automakers, eager to tap into the motoring public's yen for at least the visage of adventure, have begun to apply the label "sport-utility" to just about anything with wheels. Don't be fooled. Know what you're driving, and drive within the vehicle's limits as well as your own.

Familiarize yourself with your SUV's four-wheel drive system. Is it a full-time, part-time or automatic system? In a full-time, or permanent, 4wd system, all four wheels are continually engaged as driving wheels; there is no 2wd mode. Multi-mode systems do include a 2wd mode. Full-time 4wd systems have a center differential or viscous coupling to allow the front and rear axles to turn independently for typical daily driving. Some systems allow the driver to "lock" the center differential so that, in poor conditions, both axles will turn together for greater traction. Part-time systems use only the rear wheels as driving wheels until the driver shifts a console-mounted lever or pushes a button to engage 4wd. With part-time systems, you must disengage 4wd when you return to pavement to avoid excessive drivetrain stress. An automatic system is designed to sense on its own when 4wd should be engaged. All-wheel-drive (AWD) systems, such as those in some passenger cars, vans and even some station wagons, provide power to all four wheels much as a full-time 4wd system does. But such vehicles are usually designed for all-weather use, not rough off-highway, all-terrain use.

Does your vehicle have a transfer case? More than any other single feature, a transfer case identifies a vehicle suited to all-terrain travel. It sends power to the front axles as well as to the rear axles, and, acting as an auxiliary transmission, provides a wider range of gear ratios for a wider range of driving conditions. Use high-range 2wd for everyday driving in normal conditions, both on pavement and off. Use high-range 4wd when added traction is helpful or necessary on loose or slick surfaces, but when conditions are not difficult. Use low-range 4wd in difficult low-speed conditions when maximum traction and power are needed, and to keep engine revs high while moving slowly across rough or steep terrain.

Does the vehicle have all-season highway tires or all-terrain tires? Tires take a terrible beating in off-highway conditions, for which the latter are designed.

Find out where the engine's air intake is, and how high it is. This is important to avoid the devastating consequences of sucking water into the engine through the air intake while fording waterways.

Does the vehicle have steel "skid plates" protecting undercarriage components like the engine oil pan, transfer case and transmission? Skid plates are essential to avoiding expensive and very inconvenient damage that obstacles, particularly roadbed rocks, can inflict while traveling primitive roads.

Know where you're going

The maps in this book are general locator maps only. So you will need a good statewide map in addition to a detailed map illustrating the area you will be visiting and the route you'll be driving.

Each tour description recommends at least one map for route-finding (see p. 9). These maps often will include other useful information about the area's natural and human history, regulations, campgrounds, picnic areas and historic sites. They often differentiate between public and private lands as well. Since Utah is famous for its exposed geology, I enjoy using Lehi F. Hintze's *Geologic Highway Map of Utah*, published by the Department of Geology at Brigham Young University. Forest Service maps may be the best all-purpose maps. But some are out of date, and thus depict road numbers that no longer apply, campgrounds that have become picnic areas, and roads that are now closed or whose quality has changed. In some cases, different national forest maps will depict the quality of the same road differently. So be sure to buy the latest map available. Maps of various kinds can be purchased at Forest Service and U.S. Bureau of Land Management offices, bookstores, information centers and outdoor recreation equipment stores.

Go over your maps before you begin the drive. Become familiar with sights and landmarks to watch for along the way, and as you travel keep track of your progress to avoid missing important turnoffs, places of interest and side trips.

Don't expect to rely on road signs. The agencies that manage backcountry roads and the wildlands they cross do post signs, but they typically don't last long. Vandals, especially the gun-toting kind, often make short work of them. If you reach a point where there are several routes to choose from and none has a sign, it's usually best to follow what appears to be the most heavily used route.

Global Positioning System navigation units are increasingly popular. I'm sure some backroad travelers find them handy at times, especially when they're trying to pinpoint a hard-to-find destination. But I've not yet found a GPS unit to be necessary.

As you wander the wild, remember that the settlers, ranchers, miners and loggers who made these roads probably didn't have your safety in mind.

Weather and when to go

The backcountry driving season in Utah depends on a variety of factors, including time of year, how heavy the preceding winter's snowfall was, rainfall patterns, elevation and climatic zone.

High mountain roads will likely be closed in winter, and they can remain blocked by snow and mud into June, perhaps even July in some places. Generally, I suggest July through October for high-elevation areas. Winter, though, turns redrock deserts into a snow-veiled land of beauty and solitude, and while some lower-elevation roads are closed or impassable, others are not, and they can provide a unique and rare backcountry travel experience. But night comes early.

In early spring, say March and April, the desert areas will open up, green and fresh from precipitation. But the weather can be unsettled, windy and a bit cool, even wet. Streams may be running high and fast with runoff from melting snow and rain. Late spring is typically better.

Summer in the highlands, even high desert areas, can be pleasant. The lower-lying deserts, especially the southern deserts, can be buggy and hot, with temperatures reaching triple digits. Short, high-intensity storms, even storms that occur miles away, quickly fill normally dry desert washes and narrow canyons with torrents of water, rock and mud. Everything from ruts to washouts will occur on roads then. Pay attention to the sky, even the sky in the distance. Stay out of washes and narrow canyons if rain seems likely. When it rains, many dirt roads in Utah become dangerously slick, and are often impassable even with 4wd. The danger aside, driving on muddy roads leaves tracks that can erode into major ruts, so avoid them. If you do get caught in rain, it's often best to pull over and wait until it stops and the road dries out, which may not take very long.

Fall is the best season. Temperatures are mild to pleasantly cool, the weather is more stable, the deciduous trees are turning color and the sunlight is taking on its golden autumn hue. But the days are becoming shorter. You may want to avoid the mountains during the general hunting season, in October, when you can encounter bumper-to-bumper backcountry traffic.

Inquire locally for road conditions, which change. Check with local 4x4 rental shops, tour operators and visitor centers. The most knowledgeable people with the U.S. Forest Service and Bureau of Land Management often are out in the field, so accurate and current information may not be readily available from those agencies. Their ability to monitor conditions along remote backcountry roads and trails is limited, anyway. So don't be surprised if you find that up-to-date information is difficult or impossible to get. Often, you will have to go see for yourself.

Finally, don't get caught out there after dark. Unless a drive is a short one, get an early start. Don't drive at night.

Going alone

There is security in having more than one vehicle, and more than one source of ideas and labor if things go awry. It's also more fun to be with other people. But when you're on vacation, or venturing off for a few hours, a day or a weekend, you and yours will probably go alone, in a single vehicle. And that's OK, since so many of Utah's backways are actually pretty good roads. Just be sure that your vehicle is reliable, and that you're prepared to handle emergencies alone.

You won't always have the road to yourself. To the contrary, Utahns love their scenic and historic backroads. Tourists do, too. And exploring backcountry roads is becoming an increasingly popular pastime. So while the more remote roads may provide genuine solitude, others, such as those in Canyonlands National Park in spring and fall, can be quite busy with everything from jeepers to mountain bikers and hikers. Be considerate.

Rules of the road

Even in places where no one will be watching, there are rules to follow, and practices that help to preserve natural and historic areas. The intent behind them is simple: to keep you safe, to keep your vehicle operating reliably, and to protect fragile wildlands and cultural sites from abusive and destructive activities. Misconduct and mistakes can result in personal injury, damage to your vehicle, areas being closed and legal penalties.

Here are some things to keep in mind:

• Drive only on established roads. Never go "off-road," make a new route or follow in the tracks of someone who did. The same goes for hiking and mountain biking.

• A cardinal rule in Utah's desert areas is to avoid driving, riding or stepping on the delicate cryptobiotic crust that grows on Utah's desert soils. You will see it almost everywhere on the Colorado Plateau. It appears to be a thin, lumpy mineral crust that's almost invisible in its early stages, and reddish, brown or black when it matures. But it's actually a living, self-sustaining community of organisms. Its name, in fact, means "hidden life." It provides critical nutrients to plants, absorbs and holds water, and helps stabilize desert soils and prevent erosion. One footstep can destroy decades of growth. Once the crust is damaged or destroyed, it can take 50 to 250 years to recover. Meanwhile, however, other people are likely to follow in your footsteps or tracks. Vegetation will not regenerate, loose sand will take the place of the living biological unit, and dunes and gullies will begin to form. So stick to the rock (called slickrock in canyon country), dry washes and designated roads and trails.

• In many places in canyon country you will see exposed rock marked by numerous depressions, or potholes. They appear to be nothing more than dirty little basins when dry. In reality, though, many tiny crustaceans, larvae, tadpoles and snails lie dormant in that dirt until precipitation fills the potholes with water. Then, they literally teem with life. So don't step in them, and, to avoid contamination, don't touch the water.

• Do not disturb archaeological or historic sites or artifacts. They are not replaceable, and are protected from theft and vandalism by federal laws. Do not touch the Native American rock art that you will see in many places. Again, they are an irreplaceable cultural treasure, often thousands of years old, and they are easily destroyed or damaged. Never enter, climb on or even walk close to an ancient rock structure unless it is designated for tours, because doing so, again, can destroy it or degrade it over time. View them from a distance. If you find an artifact, prehistoric or historic, don't disturb it. Moving it might damage it, and its exact location and position can provide critical information for archaeologists. Report it to a ranger. Do the same if you see someone vandalizing a site or removing artifacts.

• Do not use archaeological or historic sites for picnics or camping unless they are developed for those purposes, because the more time people spend at them, the more they are degraded.

• Your vehicle must be street legal to take these drives. Obey traffic laws and regulatory signs, wear your seat belt and keep the kids buckled up.

• If you get lost or stuck, stay with your vehicle unless you are certain help is nearby. A vehicle will be much easier for searchers to find than you will be if you're out there wandering aimlessly. In summer, if you do attempt to walk out, don't do so during the heat of day.

• Many of the places you will visit remain honeycombed with old mines that pose many dangers, from radon gas to unstable, abandoned dynamite, rotting timbers and collapsing structures. Avoid them, or view them from a distance.

• Be especially careful on blind curves, which are common.

• Mechanized travel of any kind, including motorcycles and mountain bikes, is not allowed in designated wilderness areas and wilderness study areas unless a legal corridor exists.

• Desert soils lack the micro-organisms that help break down solid human waste and toilet paper, an increasingly serious problem as visitation increases in desert areas. So bring a portable, washable toilet for overnight trips. In fact, some places included in *Utah Byways* will require you to have one. As with most things, you can spend as much as you want on a portable toilet. But you really don't need to spend much, and it doesn't need to be elaborate. A plastic pail with a tight lid will do. If you want to buy something more sophisticated, check your favorite outdoor equipment supplier, or an RV supply store. Toilets can be emptied at RV dump stations, or into fixed toilets once you get back to town. If you don't have a toilet, dig a hole six to ten inches deep (if possible, in the more organic soil beneath a pinyon pine or juniper, where the fragile cryptobiotic soil crust may not be present) at least 300 ft. from a water source, sandy wash or trail. Carry out toilet paper in a sealed container.

• If you camp, use minimum-impact practices and try to leave no trace of your stay. Camp on more resilient mineralized soils (never on the cryptobiotic crust or vegetation), and only in established campsites or areas that show previous use. Bring your own water (even many developed campgrounds are dry), and camp at least 300 feet from the banks of streams, ponds and lakes to avoid damage and pollution, and to allow access by wildlife. Never camp in washes or narrow canyons, especially in summer when the desert's inability to absorb sudden down-pours creates flash floods that can instantly sweep you and your vehicle away. Clean up the campsite before you leave, and take your trash with you.

• In southeastern Utah's red-rock deserts, wood fires cause ecological damage and leave the ground unnaturally blackened. Cook with a gas stove. If you want to have a fire where it is legal and appropriate, bring your own wood (there's very little in the desert, and wood collecting tramples the cryptobiotic soil crust), use a fire pan and haul out the ash. In some places, particularly national parks, wood fires are prohibited in the backcountry.

• In some areas, pets are prohibited in the backcountry, or are restricted to road corridors and must be kept on leashes. Find out before you go. Dogs are the real problem. They foul campsites, and if they run loose, they trample the soil's crust and chase wildlife. Some have even dug up archaeological sites, thereby destroy-ing the knowledge that could have been gained from artifacts and their locations. So leave Fifi and Fido at home.

• You will cross a lot of grazing land. Leave gates as you find them. Don't dis-turb wildlife or livestock.

• Don't drink the water in the streams, which can be contaminated by that longtime bane of backpackers, the parasite giardia.

• Avoid parking on grass, because hot exhaust systems can ignite fires.

• Avoid steep hillsides, stream banks and boggy areas.

Go prepared

Things can and will go wrong out there, so always go prepared to spend a night or two, and to handle problems alone. Here's a basic checklist of some things to bring.

• A topped-off fuel tank. Fill up before every backcountry drive, every time. You will use your vehicle's low gears much of the time, which will mean higher fuel consumption than during on-highway driving. Unless you're traveling for an extended period in a particularly remote area, like Canyonland's Maze District, it shouldn't be necessary to carry extra fuel. If you do, strap a full can to the exterior of the vehicle, preferably the roof. Fill the can, so that dangerous fumes won't build up inside.

• A shovel. Mine has been a life-saver, and is the single most useful tool I carry. Yours will be, too.

• A good first-aid kit, food and drinks, and clothing for inclement weather.

• Good all-terrain tires, a good (and properly inflated) spare and jack, a small board to support the jack on dirt, a couple of cans of pressurized tire sealant (avail-able at department stores), a small electric air compressor (the kind that plugs into the cigarette lighter, also available at department stores), a tire pressure gauge and tire chains. A warning: Old mine sites and ghost towns are often littered with old, rusty nails.

• Some basic tools, including a folding saw, jumper cables, duct tape, electri-cal tape, baling wire, spare fuses, multipurpose knife, high-strength tow strap, fire extinguisher, and a plastic sheet to put on the ground. An assortment of screws, washers, nuts, hose clamps and such could come in handy as well, especially if you're driving an older or modified (meaning trouble-prone) vehicle.

• Maps, compass, extra eyeglasses and keys, binoculars, trash bags, flashlight or head lamp with extra batteries, matches, watch, hats, sunscreen, insect repellent.

Except for the food, I keep much of this stuff ready to go in a large plastic storage container, like Rubbermaid's ActionPacker. It's also important to tie it all down so it doesn't get tossed about on rough terrain.

Sometimes I bring my mountain bike as a backup vehicle. Since I do a lot of exploring, I also use it to check out places that I don't want to drive to. Think about getting a CB radio, even though transmitting range is limited. These days, a cellular telephone can be handy, although I've found they often don't work in the wild.

Off-highway driving

Most of the time simply driving more slowly and cautiously than you do on paved roads will get you where you want to go and back again. But when the going gets rough, as it will, you will need to apply some specialized techniques.

Uphill traffic has the right of way, if practical, because it's usually easier and safer to back up to a pullout, using gravity as a brake, than to back down a slope while fighting the pull of gravity.

Think ahead. If you have a part-time 4wd system, engage it before you actually need it to stay out of trouble.

When in doubt, scout. If the road ahead seems dicey, walk it and see.

Air down in sand, deep mud and rough terrain. While standard tire pressure usually will suffice, deep mud and soft, dry sand may require temporarily airing down (letting air out) to 15-18 psi or even lower to expand the tire's "footprint" for greater flotation. Dampening dry sand with water can make it more firm. On rocky terrain, airing down will soften the ride and lessen the punishment the roadbed inflicts on the suspension. On especially rocky and steep terrain, airing down also will allow the tires to conform to the rocks so they can grip better.

Remember to re-inflate the tires before driving at speed or on pavement, using a small electric air compressor.

As I've mentioned, the soil in many places in Utah instantly becomes something akin to grease as soon as rain hits it, and even 4wd won't help you. (Tire chains can. Though heavy, they are easy to pack, and can save the day. Carry them.) Because of the range of problems that driving in mud poses (roadbed damage, vehicle damage, transporting biological organisms from one ecosystem to another), I say avoid it. If it rains, pull onto firm ground and let the storm pass. Then wait an hour or so to let the road dry out.

If you begin to lose traction in mud, turn the steering wheel rapidly one way and then the other, back and forth. That can help the tires get a grip. Shallow mud can be underlain by firm ground, so normal tire inflation or even over-inflation can help tires penetrate to terra firma. If you do get stuck, dig out the sides of the tires to relieve suction. Then pack debris around the tires for traction.

Dust storms and flash floods. Blinding dust storms can kick up suddenly in the desert. Do not attempt to drive through one. Instead, pull over to a safe place, turn off the engine to avoid clogging the air filter and wait it out, keeping windows and doors closed.

In spring, and during and after summer storms, you are likely to encounter flooded roads.

In spring, check the depth and speed of the water before fording. If it's fast and deep, stay out and come back in a few weeks if you can.

Summer, especially late summer, is thunderstorm season, and heat aside, that is a dangerous time in the desert. And a great deal of Utah is desert of one kind or another. Sooner or later you will encounter a road or canyon that is flooded by storm runoff. Stay out of it. The murky water is usually moving very fast (it can easily wash you and your vehicle away), is carrying rocks and debris, and is rapidly eroding the roadbed away. If you get caught in an area where and when a flood is likely, get to the highest ground possible as quickly as possible. You may be able to just wait until the water has subsided, but after a flash flood, quicksand, mud, rocks, debris and deep ruts can block the way. Stay out of Utah's beautiful, serpentine "slot" canyons in summer. They provide little or no chance of escaping a sudden rush of water and mud.

Maintain steady forward momentum in sand, mud and snow. Often, stopping can be the worst thing to do, so go as slow as you can, but as fast as you must. Higher gears can be more effective than lower gears.

Stick to the high points. When the going gets particularly rough, shift into low range, go slow and steady, and keep the tires on the high spots, thus keeping the undercarriage high and away from obstacles that can damage the differentials, or so-called "pumpkins," or other components. Let the tires roll over the rocks. Do not let large rocks pass directly beneath the vehicle.

All thumbs? You won't be for long if you forget to keep them on top of the steering wheel. Otherwise, the wheel's spokes can badly injure your thumbs if a front wheel is suddenly jerked in an unexpected direction. If the steering wheel is being rocked back and forth by the terrain, keep your hands loose on the wheel, at 10 and 2 o'clock.

Another tip for rough terrain: Lean forward, keeping your back away from the seat back, and ride as though you're in a saddle. That way you won't be tossed about so much.

Straddle ruts, letting them pass beneath the vehicle. If you must cross a rut, do so at an angle, easing one tire at a time across it. Do the same for depressions, dips, ledges or "steps," and ditches. If you get stuck, raise the vehicle with a good jack (not the bumper-mounted kind) and fill in the space beneath and around the affected wheels with dirt and debris until you've created a ramp (it can help to make it high enough so that the wheel's on a downslope).

To get over a nasty ledge, either use the rock ramp that is likely to be there already, or use a few nearby rocks to build one. You may need to put one wheel over at a time.

A word about earth-moving: If you've had to build a rudimentary ramp to get over an obstacle or out of a rut, afterwards put the dirt and rocks back where you found them. Don't leave an excavation site behind.

Deadfall. Once in a while you may encounter a fallen tree or limb in the road. It might be possible to drive across it, crossing at an angle and putting one wheel at a time over it. If you carry a folding saw, as I do, cut it away. If the obstacle is too large to cut or move by hand, consider using your tow strap to pull it out of the way.

Have someone act as a spotter to help you maneuver through difficult places, and use low range and a low gear for better control.

Try not to spin your tires, which tears up the road and can get you stuck, or stuck worse than you already are. Some new SUVs have sophisticated 4-wheel electronic traction-control systems that are intended to eliminate wheel spin by instantly transferring power from spinning wheels to the wheel or wheels with traction. A few, like Toyota's 4Runner and Land Cruiser, can be purchased with locking differentials, a.k.a. "lockers." These mechanisms vastly improve your ability to get through or out of nasty off-highway situations by equalizing power to the driving wheels and eliminating the differential's tendency to transfer power to the wheel with the least traction. I recommend them.

If your SUV gets high-centered, that is, the undercarriage is hung up atop an obstacle like a rock, jack it up and see if the obstacle can be removed. Or build small ramps, using dirt and rocks, beneath the tires so you can drive off the obstacle.

Before climbing a steep hill, learn what's at the top and on the other side. Depending on how steep it is and how much power your vehicle has, shift into first or second gear/low range. Drive straight up, accelerate as you climb, keep moving, then slow down as you near the top.

Some hills will be badly chewed up by the spinning tires of vehicles that lack locking differentials or traction control systems. If you encounter such a hill, shift into low range and keep your wheels on the high spots between the holes.

If the engine stalls on a hill, stop and immediately set the parking brake hard and tight. Here, an automatic transmission can help you get going again easily. Just shift into "park" and turn the key. If you have a manual transmission, you may be able to compression-start the engine if you're facing downhill. If you're facing uphill, try shifting into first gear/low range. Turn the engine over without clutching, and let the starter motor move things along a bit until the engine restarts and takes over. Otherwise, you'll have to work the clutch, hand brake and accelerator simultaneously to get going again without rolling backward. Modern clutch-equipped vehicles require the driver to depress the clutch pedal to start the engine. However, some SUVs have clutch bypass switches that let you start the engine without depressing the clutch, a great help when stalled on a climb.

If you can't make it up a hill, don't try to turn around. Stop, and put the transmission in reverse/low range. If the vehicle has exterior mirrors that are easily adjusted, tilt them so you can see what the rear tires are doing. Then slowly back straight down. Never descend in neutral, relying on the brakes. If you must apply the brakes, do so lightly and steadily to avoid losing traction and going into a slide. Go straight down steep inclines, using low range and the lowest driving gear so the engine can help brake. But remember that automatic transmissions, which I think are best overall, don't provide as much engine-braking ability as manual transmissions.

Avoid traversing the side of a steep hill. Occasionally, though, mountain roads do cross steep slopes, sometimes tilting the vehicle "off-camber," or toward the downhill side. It's almost always an unnerving experience for me, especially if the road has become wet and perhaps a bit slick. Lean heavily (no pun intended) toward caution under such circumstances. You might want to remove cargo from the roof to lower your vehicle's already-high center of gravity. Then go slow. It might help to turn the front wheels into the hill. If you decide not to continue, do not attempt to turn around. Tilt the exterior mirrors so you can watch the rear tires, shift into reverse/low range for greater low-speed control, and slowly back up until you reach a spot where you can turn around safely.

Avoid crossing waterways if you can. Fording streams and shallow rivers is fun, to be sure. But many living things reside in or otherwise depend on streams. They can be harmed by careless and unnecessary crossings, which can stir up sediment and erode stream banks. If you must cross, use an established crossing point. Check the depth with a stick, comparing the depth to your vehicle, or walk across first. Don't cross if the current is very fast and deep, or if a desert wash is flooding. Check for deep holes. Often, a somewhat fast-moving perennial stream will be safer to cross than a sluggish one, because the moving water prevents sediments from settling, keeping the bed rocky and firm. Slow-moving or still water, on the other hand, lets sediment and mud build up.

A slow, steady crossing will stir up less sediment, and will make less of a bow wake, thus minimizing streambank erosion. (In particularly deep water, however, a bow wake can create a beneficial air pocket for the engine.)

Be aware of where your engine's air intake is. It may not be high enough to ford deep water. If it isn't, it could suck water into the engine, causing severe damage.

In deep crossings, it's also possible for water to be drawn into your vehicle's gear boxes unless the differential vents have been raised to a point that will keep them above the water. (To avoid that, I've extended my 4Runner's front and rear differential vents up into the engine compartment, using long sections of hose. This also helps to keep them clear of dust and dirt, which can clog them, causing interior pressure to build up and seals to leak.) I try to avoid water that is higher than the wheel hubs.

Once across, stop and inspect the vehicle. The brakes will be wet, so use them a few times to dry them out. The tires also will be wet, and may not grip the roadbed as well.

SUVs, accessories and such

Properly equipped sport-utility vehicles are built to take people to places that sedans, vans and station wagons either cannot go, or shouldn't. Despite their comforts, they are rugged and reliable transport — backcountry or frontcountry. They can go from the showroom straight into the hills without modifications.

One of my family's two Toyota 4Runners has a 5-speed manual transmission and a stock 4-cylinder engine, which I've found to be adequate even when it's loaded with the four of us and our camping gear. The other has a relatively fuel-frugal V6 and automatic transmission. I've never felt any need for a large, thirsty V8.

Manual transmissions have advantages. They are more responsive and tend to provide slightly better fuel mileage. They are better at engine braking on steep terrain. But many clutch-equipped vehicles require the driver to fully depress the clutch pedal when starting the engine, a problem on a steep hill. However, on a steep incline you can put the transmission in first gear/low range and let the starter motor start the engine while it simultaneously pulls the vehicle forward. It's also possible to compression-start the engine if the starter or battery dies.

I prefer automatic transmissions. I find them easier to use on rough terrain, where having a manual transmission can require three feet: one for the brake, one for the clutch and one for the accelerator, all working pretty much simultaneously.

I've learned to appreciate options that I once dismissed as unnecessary. Easily adjusted electric side mirrors, for example, will pay for themselves the first time you have to back up a narrow shelf road with a killer drop-off. When I'm exploring Utah's narrow, high-walled canyons, a sunroof/moonroof is handy option indeed.

There is a huge four-wheel-drive accessories market. Are those add-ons necessary? It depends on how much, and what type, of adventure motoring you plan to do. The requirements of serious four-wheeling on technically challenging routes differ from those of backcountry touring. The former can require extensive vehicle modifications, which can degrade on-highway performance and reliability. The latter does not. Still, if you enjoy traveling the West's vast network of backcountry roads, there can be real benefits to adding extra lights, sturdier tires, a more versatile roof carrier, heavier skid plates, perhaps even an after-market locking differential to your SUV. (In case you're wondering, I've never owned a winch.)

Maintenance. Backcountry roads are hard on all vehicles, so follow the recommendations in your owner's manual for dusty, wet and muddy conditions.

Check the tires often, because no part of your SUV will take a greater beating. If you pass through an old mining area, expect to pick up a nail now and then. Always travel with a good spare, because you will need it.

Wash your vehicle when you return to town to prevent rust and corrosion. You also don't want to carry home the mud, dirt and debris that has collected underneath, because transporting spores, insects and other organisms to disparate geographic regions via off-highway vehicles can spread pests and diseases.

Have fun

Exploring backroads is an outstanding addition to the list of outdoor recreation opportunities found in Utah. If you're particularly interested in preserving the privilege of exploring backcountry byways, you might join Tread Lightly!, Inc., a nonprofit organization founded to promote responsible use of off–highway vehicles. It is based in Ogden, Utah. Call 1-800-966-9900.

And as you travel, tell me what you've found, whether it's mistakes, or trips and tips you'd like to see added to future editions. You can write to me in care of Wilderness Press, 1200 Fifth St., Berkeley, CA 94710.

Salt Creek Canyon (closed beyond Peekaboo Camp)

Making It Fun For All

Trying to keep kids, especially teenagers, happy on car trips is always tough. But there are some things you can do to make touring the backcountry fun and interesting for them, too.

Probably the best advice I can give is this: Don't just drive. Stop, and stop often. Watch for wildlife, especially early in the morning or evening. Try to identify and interpret the geologic features you will see. In canyon country, scanning cliffs for ancient rock art and structures can be a rewarding game. Just remember the rules about preserving these national treasures: never touch rock art, or enter or in any way disturb ancient structures.

Recreational rock collecting with hand tools is permitted on most lands managed by the U.S. Bureau of Land Management (Grand Staircase-Escalante National Monument is a prime exception), but not on lands managed by the National Park Service. Inquire with the appropriate agency before you dig. Don't forget to bring a magnifying glass.

If Utah is about anything, it's about geology and Western history. Bring some good reference books along so you can enjoy Utah's human and geologic story. I think it's especially interesting to know the story behind place names. Get some good books on identifying wildflowers, birds, insects, vegetation and animals in the region as well. They're all available at bookstores and visitor centers.

Make a photocopy of the area on the map where you'll be going. Get each child an inexpensive compass. Let them help you navigate and identify peaks, creeks, historic sites and other landmarks. Let each child pack his or her favorite books and toys, but don't cram the car with stuff. And don't forget the sunscreen.

Bring at least one personal cassette player. Before leaving, go to your local public library and check out some children's cassette tapes. Better yet, buy some. You'll make good use of them for years to come.

Books on tape, something I listen to myself on long highway drives, are great diversions for children. Many video rental stores carry them.

Other items that have brought quiet and good humor to the back seat are an inexpensive point-and-shoot camera the kids can use, and inexpensive binoculars. When he was younger, my son, Land, liked to have his own notebook and pencil so he could pretend that he was taking notes about our journeys just like Dad.

If you have a responsible, licensed teenage driver on board, let him or her drive now and then. The sooner a teen learns backcountry driving skills, the longer he or she will remain an eager participant. And someday you may need a capable co-pilot.

Bring snacks, preferably the nutritious, non-sticky kind, and drinks. There will be plenty of bumps on your adventures, so be sure cups have secure tops that you can poke straws through. Plastic garbage bags, paper towels, changes of clothing, wet wipes and pillows for the sleepy are good to have along as well.

Safety is always a concern. Hazards exist. In many places you'll come across old mine sites. Don't let children anywhere near them. For that matter, adults should stay clear of them, too. If you want a closer look, use your binoculars. Never attempt to get close to wildlife, either.

Whether you travel with children or not, make the drive part of a day that draws on the huge range of experiences Utah has to offer. Plan a picnic. See the sights. Hike to a hilltop. Ride your mountain bikes. And do something civilized when you get back to town: Go out to dinner.

Buckhorn Draw Road (Tour 23)

THE
DRIVES

Transcontinental Railroad

LOCATION: This National Back Country Byway crosses the desert north of the Great Salt Lake, from Golden Spike National Historic Site almost to the railroad siding at Lucin, east of the Nevada-Utah line.

HIGHLIGHTS: The meeting at Promontory Summit of the eastbound Central Pacific Railroad and the westbound Union Pacific Railroad on May 10, 1869, may have been the most important event in America's westward expansion. It linked east and west, opened up access to vast regions, provided easy access to new markets and cut coast-to-coast travel time from months to days, but hastened the end of Native American culture as it had existed for centuries. On this tour, you will drive on the final segment of railroad grade built by the CPRR's Chinese laborers before the historic linkup with rail laid by the UPRR's Irish crews. Signs interpret former townsites, cemeteries and sidings. At GSNHS, replicas of the two steam locomotives that met on that historic day, the CPRR's *Jupiter* and the UPRR's *No. 119*, operate daily May 1 through the first weekend of October. "Last Spike" re-enactments are held each May 10, and during the annual Railroader's Festival on the second Saturday in August. A visit to GSNHS is the perfect way to begin this byway, the last segment that remains surrounded by largely unchanged scenery. An alternative to the byway is GSNHS's 9-mile "Promontory Trail" auto tour, which follows a portion of the "Old Line." Removing artifacts is illegal.

DIFFICULTY: Easy, on high-clearance 2wd roads. 4wd can be required in the vicinity of Peplin Mountain. Expect mud in early spring. There are no services or facilities. Avoid old trestles and culverts, and watch out for badly eroded spots. Spring and fall are best.

TIME & DISTANCE: 8 hours; 90 miles.

MAPS: UTC's *Northern Utah*. DeLorme pp. 58-59, 63.

INFORMATION: BLM, Salt Lake Field Office. GSNHS. Get a copy of the BLM's *Rails East to Promontory: The Utah Stations*. A good Web site is www.utah.com/destin/greatb/gbpublic/blmcprr.htm.

GETTING THERE: Take exit 368 from I-15 at Brigham City. Take Utah Hwys. 13 and 83 northwest for 18.7 miles. Turn left (west) onto 7200 North Road. The GSNHS visitor center is about 9.3 miles farther. I start just west of the visitor center, at the gravel road.

REST STOPS: GSNHS (no camping).

THE DRIVE: From Promontory Summit, the route parallels the old railroad grade for 7.5 miles through little-changed high-desert scenery. Imagine gazing from the window of a sooty rail car as it rolled across the vast expanse. You will begin driving on the CPRR grade itself beyond the Back Country Byway sign. Signs explain how busy the Promontory Branch was until 1904, when it was bypassed by the shorter and more economical Lucin Cutoff across the Great Salt Lake. As traffic on the Promontory Branch dwindled, towns at Kelton (1869-1942) and Terrace (1869-1910) died out. The line was abandoned in 1938; in 1942 the rails were removed. At mile 16.6 from the visitor center, keep right at the Y, leaving the grade where it's washed out. Go left at the next two Ts. At a bend 0.4 miles beyond the second T, take the two-track to the left to return to the grade. About 3 miles from Kelton go left toward (but not to) the Hogup Mountains. In 3.3 miles go right (west) on a two-track past Peplin Mountain, toward the site of Terrace. The byway ends about 22 miles from there, at an intersection near the site of today's Lucin. From the intersection, it's 52 miles to I-80 near Wendover. Or go right to reach Hwy. 30 in 5 miles.

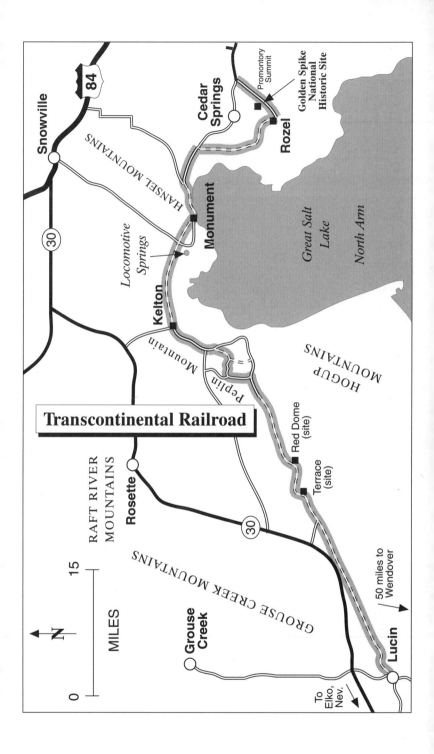

Transcontinental Railroad

Silver Island Mountains Loop

LOCATION: In the Great Salt Lake Desert northeast of Wendover, and just north of the Bonneville Salt Flats near the Nevada border.

HIGHLIGHTS: This BLM National Back Country Byway loops around the base of an "island" range of jagged volcanic peaks. It's a convenient side trip off I-80, and is particularly beautiful in the golden light of late afternoon. 4wd roads spur from the main loop road into Jenkins, Cave, Silver Island and Donner canyons. From these spurs, hikers can access trailless ridges that lead to the main peaks. It's best in spring and fall.

DIFFICULTY: Easy on a dirt-and-gravel road.

TIME & DISTANCE: 2.5 hours; 54 miles. Longer if you explore side routes.

MAPS: Recreational Map of Utah. UTC's *North Central Utah*. DeLorme pp. 50, 58.

INFORMATION: BLM, Salt Lake Field Office.

GETTING THERE: Take the Bonneville Speedway exit from I-80 about 2.7 miles east of Wendover. Follow the signs for the speedway. Where the paved road angles right toward the speedway, go left onto Leppy Pass Road. There may be a sign for the Silver Island Mountains. Soon you will see the road branch off to the right. Set your odometer at 0 here.

REST STOPS: There are many primitive campsites. Vehicle camping is permitted within 100 feet of the road.

THE DRIVE: Made of uplifted limestone sediments from the bottom of a vanished primordial sea, the Silver Island Mountains were partially submerged by the melting ice-age glaciers that created Lake Bonneville, whose shoreline can still be seen etched on the mountain slopes in the region. After the limestone layers were raised high above sea level to form the mountains, volcanic activity covered them with lava flows, such as those seen at Leppy Pass and Volcano Peak. The presence of Native Americans, who were able to take advantage of Lake Bonneville's fish and waterfowl, has been traced back 10,300 years. In the 19th century mountain men, explorers and pioneers crossed these mountains on their way west. Pilot Peak, a 10,716-foot sentinel 11 miles to the northwest in Nevada, was a beacon for them. In 1846, the ill-fated California-bound Donner-Reed Party abandoned their wagons in the soft mud east of the range, and crossed these mountains via the pass at the north end of the byway. At mile 11 you will see the left turn to Silver Island Pass, which bisects the range. By mile 25, you're angling west. At 33.4 you may see a signpost marking the Hastings Cutoff, a pioneer route. At mile 55 the road rejoins Leppy Pass Road. Go left to return to I-80 and Wendover.

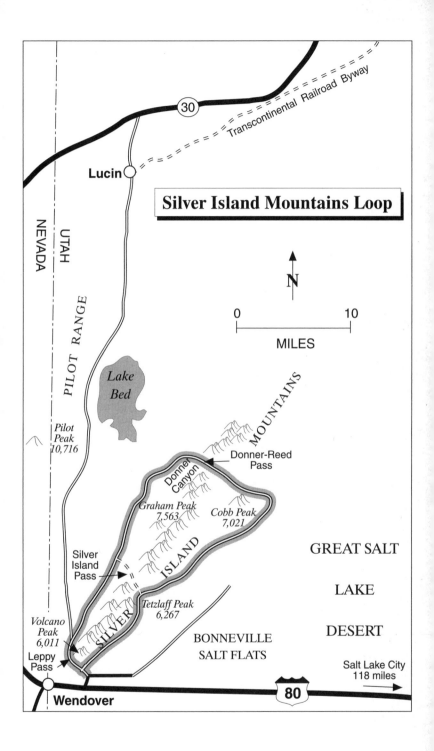

Silver Island Mountains Loop

N

0   10
MILES

NEVADA
UTAH

PILOT RANGE

Transcontinental Railroad Byway

30

Lucin

Lake Bed

Pilot Peak 10,716

MOUNTAINS

Donner-Reed Pass

Donner Canyon

Graham Peak 7,563

Cobb Peak 7,021

Silver Island Pass

SILVER ISLAND

GREAT SALT

LAKE

DESERT

Tetzlaff Peak 6,267

Volcano Peak 6,011

Leppy Pass

BONNEVILLE SALT FLATS

Salt Lake City 118 miles

Wendover

80

Hardware Ranch Road

LOCATION: Wasatch Range southwest of Bear Lake.

HIGHLIGHTS: This tour offers views of fascinating canyons, pastoral valleys, rolling hills, and stands of aspen and pine. If you're lucky, you will see wildlife as well. It ends at Bear Lake Summit, on U.S. 89. It's best in summer and fall.

DIFFICULTY: Easy to moderate. You are likely to encounter at least one stream crossing, possibly more during spring runoff. It can be very slick and perhaps even impassable when it rains.

TIME & DISTANCE: 2.5 hours; 41 miles.

MAPS: Wasatch-Cache National Forest's *Ogden and Logan Ranger Districts* (1994). DeLorme pp. 61, 63.

INFORMATION: Logan Ranger District.

GETTING THERE: From Hyrum, take Utah Hwy. 101 between the steep walls and cliffs of Blacksmith Fork Canyon for 15.5 miles to Hardware Ranch, where the asphalt ends. Watch for a Utah Scenic Backway sign.

REST STOPS: There are a number of campgrounds along U.S. 89.

THE DRIVE: Hardware Ranch, once owned by Brigham City hardware dealer Alonzo Snow, is now a largely state-owned wildlife management area where elk feed in winter. At Hardware Ranch the road, No. 054 (a.k.a. Bear Lake Road), turns to hard-packed dirt, and is rocky and rutted in places as it bends north through rolling hills of grass, sagebrush, pinyon pines and junipers. About 6.8 miles beyond the pavement, shortly before reaching a slope of loose rock at a bend in the road, turn left onto road No. 105. Follow this narrow, winding road, Danish Dugway, down a canyon. After 1.2 miles, cross Saddle Creek and veer right (north). If the creek seems too high and fast, you can return to 054 and go through Strawberry Valley for 4.1 miles, turning left at a Y toward Saddle Creek Spring, where you will reach road 105 after 2.3 miles. If you cross Saddle Creek, follow it up a canyon lined with rock spires. Continue north at the intersection you will reach after about 3.5 miles, passing through Hell's Hollow and Log Cabin Hollow, and groves of pines and large aspens. Not far from U.S. 89 the road passes an open meadow marked by sinks caused by water seepage and erosion.

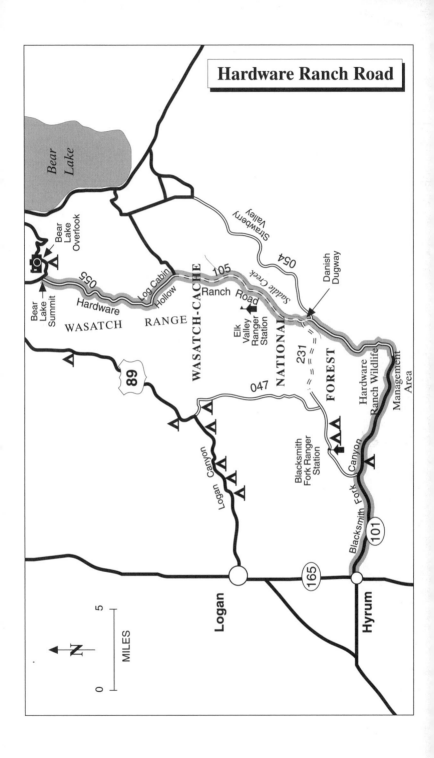

Hardware Ranch Road

Inspiration Point

LOCATION: In the Wasatch Range, east of I-15 and south of U.S. 89/91 and Mantua Reservoir; between Ogden and Brigham City. Wasatch-Cache National Forest.

HIGHLIGHTS: As you climb more than 4,000 feet, this route, which the state of Utah has designated the Willard Scenic Backway, provides superb high-elevation scenery, from shady forests to the spine of the Wasatch Range, the Salt Lake Valley and the vast Great Basin. It ends at aptly named Inspiration Point, on 9,422-foot Willard Mountain, named for Richard Willard, a counselor to Mormon leader Brigham Young. It's usually open mid-July to early October.

DIFFICULTY: Easy to moderate. Late-season snow drifts can block the road in places. Watch for all-terrain vehicles (ATVs).

TIME & DISTANCE: 5 hours; 30 miles with spurs.

MAPS: Wasatch-Cache National Forest's *Ogden and Logan Ranger Districts*. DeLorme p. 60.

INFORMATION: Ogden Ranger District, Union Station Information Center. Seasonal road-opening and closing dates can vary due to weather, so call ahead.

GETTING THERE: In Mantua, about 4 miles east of Brigham City on U.S. 89/91, zero your odometer and follow Main Street south through town. Keep left at the Y at a small city park. Keep right at the Mormon church.

REST STOPS: Box Elder Campground, at the start of the drive. Waterless (although there's a spring nearby) Willard Basin Campground, about 2 miles before Inspiration Point. You'll see a park and playground at the city building in Mantua. There is also a small park at the Y on South Main.

THE DRIVE: Two-lane, dirt and gravel Willard Peak Road (084) narrows to a single lane that is quite rocky and rutted as it climbs through shady forest, providing fine views of valleys east of the Wasatch Range. About 7.3 miles from Mantua the road crosses a saddle, then dips down the other side and becomes rougher. Keep left. The right fork goes a short distance down some moguls to a pond. Eventually you will reach a pass at 9,300 feet There should be a sign for Willard Basin, up ahead. Uncontrolled fires and abuse of the land denuded this basin earlier this century, causing destructive floods. Environmental restoration work in the 1930s has stabilized it and restored its beauty. (Note the terracing on the slopes.) The road angles left of the sign. (Some of the spurs that go short distances to the north and south are worth exploring.) The main road loops around Willard Basin, passing the campground at the site of a Depression-era Civilian Conservation Corps camp. In a couple of miles, the road climbs to Inspiration Point, on 9,422-foot Willard Mountain, where the views stretch from the Wasatch Range across the expanse of the Great Basin to the west. Hardy souls can hike and scramble to the nearby summit of Willard Peak (about 1.5-2 hours).

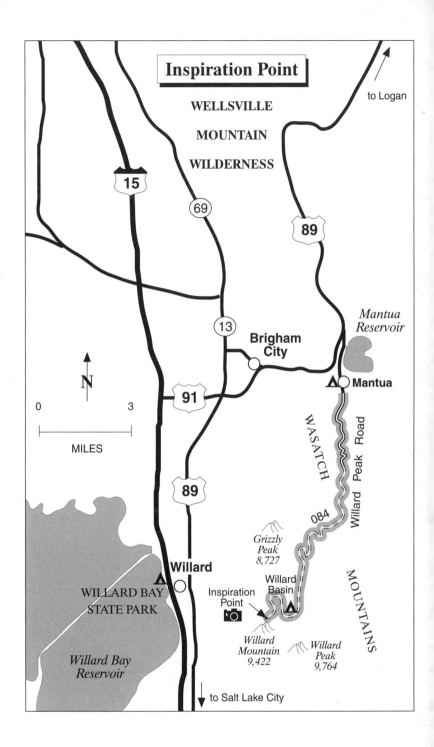

Inspiration Point

WELLSVILLE
MOUNTAIN
WILDERNESS

to Logan

15

69

89

Mantua
Reservoir

13

**Brigham
City**

91

Mantua

WASATCH

Willard Peak Road

0   3

MILES

N

89

084

*Grizzly
Peak*
8,727

Willard
Basin

Willard

WILLARD BAY
STATE PARK

Inspiration
Point

MOUNTAINS

*Willard
Mountain*
9,422

*Willard
Peak*
9,764

*Willard Bay
Reservoir*

to Salt Lake City

Skyline Drive I

LOCATION: East of I-15 on the crest of the Wasatch Range, between Bountiful and Farmington.

HIGHLIGHTS: You will constantly be distracted by awesome vistas from atop the Wasatch Range, across the Great Salt Lake and into the Great Basin. This is a magnificent, convenient and thus popular drive close to major urban centers. Try it in summer and fall.

DIFFICULTY: Easy. It's a good, narrow and serpentine 2wd dirt and gravel road. But it is rocky in places, and there are many blind curves and some narrow sections.

TIME & DISTANCE: 2-3 hours depending on how much time you spend enjoying the views; 25 miles.

MAPS: Wasatch-Cache NF's *Salt Lake, Kamas, Evanston and Mountain View Ranger Districts* (1994 edition). DeLorme p. 53.

INFORMATION: Wasatch-Cache National Forest, Salt Lake Ranger District. Seasonal road-opening and closing dates can vary due to weather, so call ahead. It's usually open from early July to mid-October.

GETTING THERE: You can take this north-south route starting at either Bountiful and going north, or at Farmington and going south. (Both are off I-15.) **From Bountiful** (the way I describe below): Follow 400 North east toward the mountains. Turn left (north) onto 1300 East (Skyline Drive). Skyline Drive will wind uphill through a residential area, ending at a dirt parking area north of Bountiful's Mormon Church temple. As you exit the residential area, Skyline Drive immediately angles left (north). There may be a sign listing campgrounds and a Utah Scenic Backway sign. **From Farmington:** Take Burke Lane east to 600 North (Main Street). Go right onto 600 North, and drive toward the mountains. Watch for a brown Scenic Backway sign on the right side of the street. Where Main bends south (right), go left (east), following 600 North up a hill to 100 East (North Skyline Drive). This is a mile from I-15. Turn left here, and soon you will see a Skyline Drive sign. Now you're on your way to beautiful Farmington Canyon.

REST STOPS: There are many vista points along the way, as well as campgrounds at the north end. Do not park on the narrow segments.

THE DRIVE: The views to the west of the Great Basin's pale desert flats and waves of mountain ranges are just spectacular. At mile 3.4 is Ward Canyon Overlook, the first of a number of scenic pullouts. At about mile 7.2, a parking area will be on the right, where the Sessions Mountains Road (805) angles south along the eastern slope, providing excellent views of valleys and ranges to the east. In another 3.5 miles is Bountiful Peak Overlook, with an inspiring view of the Great Basin and Wasatch Range from almost 9,000 feet. The road descends steadily from here through stands of aspen and pine. Go left at the intersection where a sign says Farmington Flats is to the right. At mile 14.6, where the road bends left, the road to the right (No. 600, Francis Peak Road) is closed. It goes to an electronic site atop Francis Peak. Your tour winds down Farmington Canyon. At the mouth of the canyon are the oldest exposed rocks in Utah, the 2 billion-year-old Farmington Complex. The road is paved by mile 21.3. Beyond the campground signs, go right, onto 600 North, which will get you to I-15 in a mile.

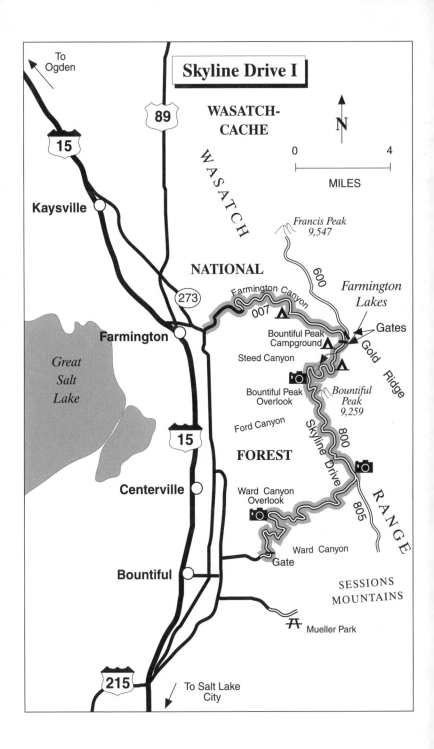

Skyline Drive I

To Ogden

WASATCH-CACHE

N

0   4
MILES

Kaysville

Francis Peak
9,547

NATIONAL

Farmington Canyon

Farmington Lakes

600

007

Gates

Bountiful Peak Campground

Gold Ridge

Farmington

Steed Canyon

Great
Salt
Lake

Bountiful Peak
Overlook

Bountiful
Peak
9,259

Ford Canyon

Skyline Drive

800

FOREST

Centerville

Ward Canyon
Overlook

805

RANGE

Ward Canyon

Bountiful

Gate

SESSIONS
MOUNTAINS

Mueller Park

To Salt Lake
City

North Slope Road

LOCATION: South of the Wyoming border on the north slope of the Uinta Mountains. Wasatch-Cache National Forest.

HIGHLIGHTS: This drive is high and remote, with historic ruins, lush meadows, lakes, streams and wildlife. I recommend going in summer and fall.

DIFFICULTY: Easy. It's closed in winter.

TIME & DISTANCE: 6 hours; about 90 miles.

MAPS: Wasatch-Cache National Forest's *Salt Lake, Kamas, Evanston and Mountain View Ranger Districts*. DeLorme/Utah pp. 54-55, and DeLorme/Wyoming pp. 16-17.

INFORMATION: Evanston and Mountain View ranger districts. The Bear River Ranger Station is south of the starting point on Utah Hwy. 150.

GETTING THERE: From Utah Hwy. 150 at East Fork and Bear River campgrounds, take 058 east toward Black's Fork River, named in the 1820s for Arthur Black of the Ashley Fur Co.

REST STOPS: There are many campsites, and a toilet at the start. Bear River Service, north of the starting point, has supplies.

THE DRIVE: For 11 miles the road is exceptionally good as it takes you through forest toward 10,235-foot Elizabeth Pass, passing fantastic vistas of canyons, cliffs and peaks salted with snowfields. At mile 14 is an old log building, the remains of one of the area's early-20th-century logging camps where "tiehackers" cut railroad ties. At 16.2 Little Lyman Lake Campground will be to the left; a short distance farther, road 063 branches right to the West Fork of the Black's Fork. This side trip passes through a gorgeous valley with some private land. It ends in 6.7 miles at a trailhead after you ford the West Fork. Continuing on 058, about 8.2 miles from the West Fork turnoff is road 073, initially a more rudimentary road, on the right. You will take it later, but for now go toward Meeks Cabin Reservoir. Soon you'll see a cluster of log ruins, the old Black's Fork Commissary, a lumber camp (1870-1930) and government commissary. Road 073 is rough as it climbs among lodgepole pines, passing more log ruins. In about 5.5 miles road 074 branches north to Suicide Park (2.5 miles), where three tiehackers who are believed to have committed suicide are buried. 073 improves greatly from here. When you reach 075 you can go north to Mountain View (27 miles) or continue to China Meadows (where the road becomes 072) and Stateline Reservoir. About 2.5 miles beyond the reservoir, road 017 branches right. You can continue to Mountain View, 22 miles north, or go right to Lonetree, 20 miles away.

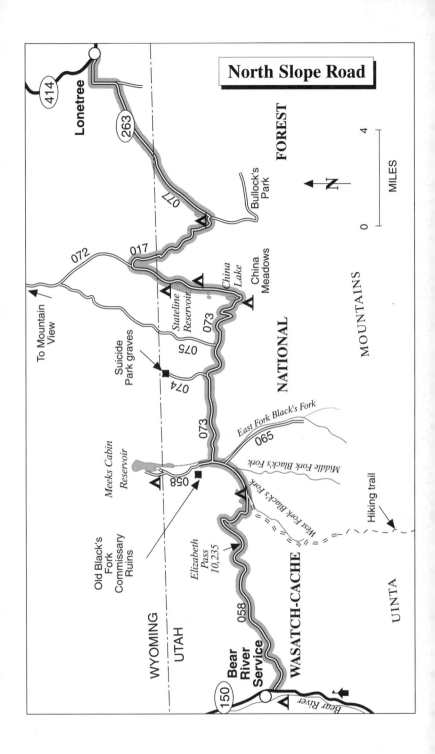

North Slope Road

FOREST

NATIONAL

MOUNTAINS

WASATCH-CACHE

UINTA

N

MILES

0   4

Lonetree

414

263

077

017

072

To Mountain
View

075

074

073

073

058

090

065

Bullock's
Park

China Lake

China Meadows

Stateline Reservoir

Suicide
Park graves

Meeks Cabin
Reservoir

Old Black's
Fork
Commissary
Ruins

East Fork Black's Fork

Middle Fork Black's Fork

West Fork Black's Fork

Hiking trail

Elizabeth
Pass
10,235

WYOMING

UTAH

Bear
River
Service

150

Bear River

Broadhead Meadows

LOCATION: East of Kamas off Utah Hwy. 150, in Wasatch-Cache National Forest.

HIGHLIGHTS: This fun, pretty and convenient loop off scenic Hwy. 150 follows a rudimentary forest road along the edge of a high, pristine Alpine meadow, named after a local settler. Try this route in summer and fall.

DIFFICULTY: Easy to moderate.

TIME & DISTANCE: An hour or less; 5 miles.

MAPS: Wasatch-Cache National Forest's *Salt Lake, Kamas, Evanston and Mountain View Ranger Districts.* DeLorme p. 54.

INFORMATION: Kamas Ranger District.

GETTING THERE: Take Hwy. 150 about 21.6 miles east of Kamas. The turnoff for Murdock Basin Road, No. 137 on the right (east) side of the highway, is well-marked.

REST STOPS: The right at the Y takes you to a pretty place to stop for lunch, or to walk through the meadow. Upper Provo Bridge Campground is along the highway between where you go in and where you come out. Provo River Falls overlook is about 2.4 miles north of where you rejoin the highway.

THE DRIVE: 1.4 miles after you turn off the highway, onto an old logging road through second-growth lodgepole pine forest, rough and narrow road 416 branches left to Broadhead Meadows. There might be a sign. (The rough Murdock Basin Road continues to a basin with high Alpine lakes.) Road 416 is a somewhat rocky, undulating one-lane road through shady forest. 1.3 miles later it reaches a Y. You might see on a tree a small arrow pointing right. This spur goes a short distance to the edge of a lush meadow protected by a rustic log fence and traversed by a pretty creek. Continuing on the main road, you will soon see a pond, and the peaks of Murdock Mountain, which rise to 11,212 feet. (The meadows are at about 9,600 feet.) From there, the road crosses a brook, then begins to descend to the highway.

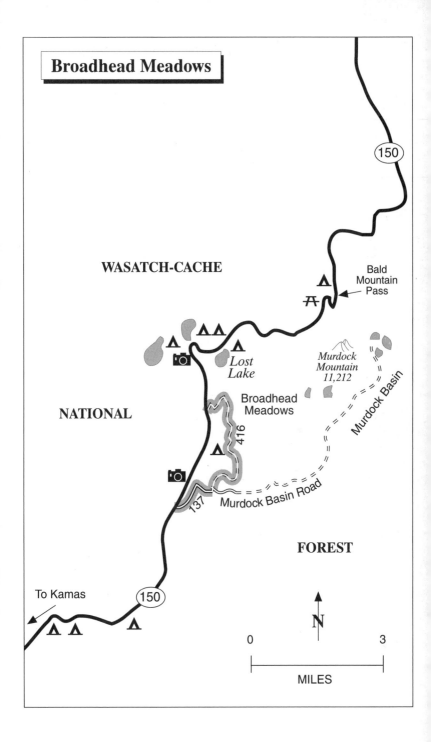

Broadhead Meadows

WASATCH-CACHE

NATIONAL

FOREST

Bald Mountain Pass

Murdock Mountain 11,212

Murdock Basin

Lost Lake

Broadhead Meadows

416

137

Murdock Basin Road

150

To Kamas

150

N

0   3

MILES

Sheep Creek Loop

LOCATION: In the Uinta Mountains west of Flaming Gorge National Recreation Area.

HIGHLIGHTS: Aspen and pine forest (much of it clearcut, however), Honslinger Draw and the Sheep Creek Canyon Geologic Area. Go in summer or fall.

DIFFICULTY: Easy, on a good, mostly two-lane dirt and gravel road. The road down into Honslinger Draw is one lane.

TIME & DISTANCE: 2.5 hours; 48 miles. Add an hour and 13 miles for the geologic area.

MAPS: Ashley National Forest. Trails Illustrated's No. 704 (Flaming Gorge/Eastern Uintas). DeLorme/Utah p. 56, and DeLorme/Wyoming p. 17.

INFORMATION: Ashley National Forest, Flaming Gorge District. For the geologic area tour, get the brochure *Wheels of Time*.

GETTING THERE: You can go in either direction, starting off Utah Hwy. 44 south of Manila and heading west, or off Utah Hwy. 43 at McKinnon, Wyo., going south, then east. I do the latter.

REST STOPS: Refer to your map for campgrounds. Spirit Lake Lodge has cabins, a cafe, row boats, horse rides, pack trips. There are picnic sites along the geologic tour, where the road is paved.

THE DRIVE: From the store at McKinnon, go south through farmlands on a good road (it becomes forest 221) into the forested Uintas. After 6 miles the road climbs through aspens and pines to enter Uinta National Forest at about mile 6.7. At 13.2, after the road bends east, you will see on the right the turnoff for Spirit Lake, road 001. It passes meadows and logged areas for 5.8 miles to end at about 10,000 feet elevation, at a small lake set against a beautiful amphitheater of iron-colored mountains. There's a campground, and you'll be charmed by homey Spirit Lake Lodge. On road 221, continue east past areas of former lodgepole pine forest, both logged and burned. Almost 36 miles from the Spirit Lake spur you can go right on road 005 to visit restored Ute Mountain Lookout, a national historic site. When the road comes to an intersection, you can go left to the fantastic Sheep Creek geologic tour, which exposes a billion years of multicolored rock strata. But go right, on narrow road 539, for the plunge into Honslinger Draw, where there's a campground. To take the geologic tour after reaching the highway at the end of this drive, go north on Hwy. 44 for 3.2 miles to the turnoff.

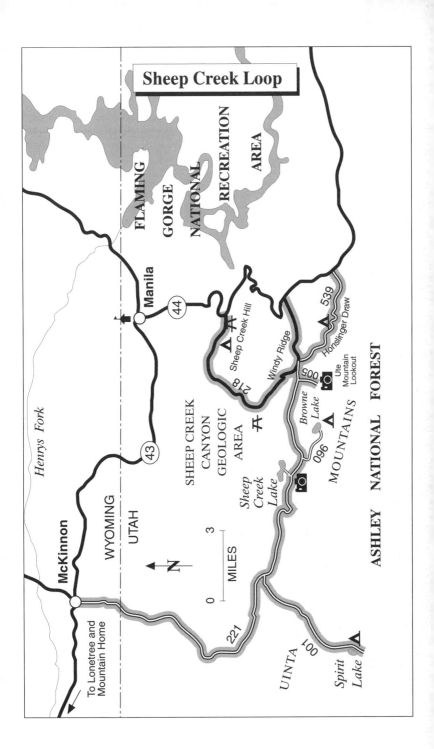

Red Cloud Loop

LOCATION: Uinta Mountains north of Vernal.

HIGHLIGHTS: This tour offers great vistas, pretty meadows and canyons, lodgepole pine forest (there's been much clearcutting, however), wildlife and the extraordinary McConkie Ranch petroglyphs. Summer and fall are best.

DIFFICULTY: Easy, on a good dirt-and-gravel road. Watch out for logging trucks.

TIME & DISTANCE: 4-5 hours and 60 miles, including the sidetrip to Horseshoe Park and visits to the petroglyphs.

MAPS: Ashley National Forest. Trails Illustrated's No. 704 (Flaming Gorge NRA/Eastern Uintas). DeLorme p. 56.

INFORMATION: Ashley National Forest, Vernal Ranger District. Get the *Indian Petroglyphs* and *Red Cloud Loop* brochures, available at local motels and at the Northeastern Utah Visitor Center, in the Field House of Natural History on East Main Street.

GETTING THERE: You can go in either direction, starting in Vernal. To go the way I describe, take U.S. 191 north for about 18 miles. Turn west on road 018, Red Cloud Loop, and set your odometer to 0. Or take Hwy. 121 (West 500 North) west from downtown. In about 3.5 miles there should be a sign on the right for Dry Fork Canyon/Red Cloud Loop, and a Scenic Byway sign. Turn right (north) here, onto 3500 West, which becomes Dry Fork Canyon Road.

REST STOPS: There are a number of campgrounds along the way. You can also stop at the Dry Fork Picnic Area and Remember the Maine County Park, both near the end in Dry Fork Canyon. A $2 parking fee gets you access to the amazing prehistoric rock art at privately owned McConkie Ranch, also in Dry Fork Canyon. But the crude foot trail among the rocks where the figures are found is not handicapped-accessible or for unsteady individuals.

THE DRIVE: At the start, look south across the Uinta Basin, beyond the uplift of the uniquely east-west trending Uinta Mountains. Follow the paved road 3.4 miles, then go left at the sign for the Red Cloud Loop. The road becomes graded gravel, meandering through hills of aspen, grass and sagebrush. Turn left again at mile 4.1. Soon you will pass lodgepole pine forest and lush meadows. At mile 9.1 is Kaler Hollow CG. About 4 miles farther is the turnoff to a somewhat better one, Oak's Park. Go left in another 3.3 miles, toward Dry Fork. Soon you will see a small, more appealing campground on the North Fork of Ashley Creek. Beyond Lily Pad Lake is Dry Fork Overlook, where you can gaze across the Uinta Basin. From there, the road winds down through scenic Brownie Canyon. 8 miles from the overlook turn right onto road 031, which goes up Dry Fork Canyon toward Horseshoe Park. In 1.7 miles you will pass the Dry Fork Nature Trail. At an open area, a small road branches left, and goes through a gate. Just beyond it, scan the cliffs on the right for a small arch. A short distance farther, also on the right, is a small, interesting cave you can easily climb to. Back on 018, continue through magnificent Brownie Canyon. When the asphalt resumes, you've left the national forest. Go left at a T. Watch for the sign on the left for McConkie Ranch, which has outstanding Fremont Culture rock art that was painted and etched onto the rock 1,000 years ago, maybe longer. Vernal is 10 miles farther.

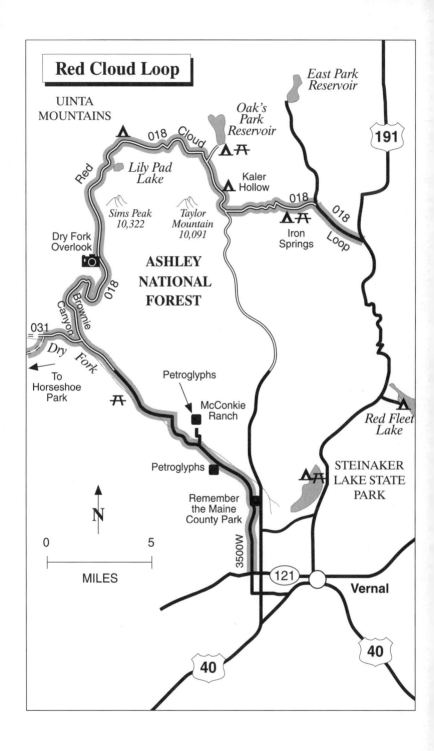

Red Cloud Loop

UINTA MOUNTAINS

East Park Reservoir

Oak's Park Reservoir

191

Red

018 Cloud

Lily Pad Lake

Kaler Hollow

018 Loop

018

Sims Peak 10,322

Taylor Mountain 10,091

Iron Springs

Dry Fork Overlook

ASHLEY NATIONAL FOREST

018

Brownie

Canyon

031

Dry Fork

To Horseshoe Park

Petroglyphs

McConkie Ranch

Red Fleet Lake

Petroglyphs

STEINAKER LAKE STATE PARK

Remember the Maine County Park

3500W

N

121

Vernal

0   5

MILES

40

40

TOUR 10

Brown's Park

LOCATION: This route is just west of the Colorado border, and southeast of Flaming Gorge National Recreation Area.

HIGHLIGHTS: The list includes great vistas, scenic Crouse Canyon, the narrow (9 ft. 8 in.) "swinging bridge" across the Green River, migratory waterfowl (best seen in spring and fall) at Brown's Park National Wildlife Refuge (along the river on the Colorado side), and the John Jarvie Historic Property. Brown's Park, a 40-mile-long valley shared by Utah and Colorado (with some of it extending into Wyoming), was a refuge for Wild West outlaws between jobs.

DIFFICULTY: Easy, although rain can make the roads very slick.

TIME & DISTANCE: 3 hours; 78 miles starting at Vernal.

MAPS: Recreational Map of Utah. DeLorme pp. 56-57. Get the brochure *Flaming Gorge, Brown's Park, Diamond Mountain Loop* at the Northeastern Utah Visitor Center in Vernal.

INFORMATION: BLM, Vernal Field Office. Jarvie Historic Property (BLM). Brown's Park National Wildlife Refuge.

GETTING THERE: I start at Vernal. Take Vernal Avenue (U.S. 191) north about a half-mile from Main Street. Turn right, onto East 500 North, toward Diamond Mountain, Jones Hole and Brown's Park. Set your odometer to 0. About 3 miles farther keep left, continuing north on Diamond Mountain Road.

REST STOPS: There are campgrounds at the north end of the swinging bridge and off the road on the north side of the river (both are waterless with pit toilets). Near the Jarvie site are two campgrounds. It offers tours 7 days a week, May-October, 10 A.M. to 5 P.M.

THE DRIVE: From Vernal, the narrow paved road climbs to Diamond Mountain Plateau, providing a panorama of geologic turmoil. At a Y 7.7 miles from U.S. 191/Vernal Avenue, take the left branch, toward Diamond Mt. The right goes to Rainbow and Island Parks (Tour 11). In about 18 miles you'll be on the plateau's rim, at about 7,500 feet. In about 7 more miles is the left turn to Brown's Park. It's a good dirt road through a vast landscape with a sweeping view of Utah's restless geology. Continue through sorrel mountains and rolling valleys. 5.6 miles from where the dirt began is the turnoff to Crouse Reservoir. In 8 miles, descend into Crouse Canyon, named after settler Charlie Crouse, on a one-lane road between high red cliffs. You will emerge into Brown's Park. Snaking through the valley is the Green River. Ute and Shoshone Indians, mountain men, explorers and settlers were drawn to the remote valley by its mild winters and abundant game, grass and water. Outlaws like The Wild Bunch appreciated its proximity to three state borders. The road enters Colorado, passes through the refuge, then crosses the river on a rare one-lane suspension bridge. At a paved stretch of Hwy. 318, go west toward the Jarvie site (10 miles). Dirt resumes at the Utah line. The Jarvie property, home of settler and community leader John Jarvie, was an important trading and social hub for 100 miles around from 1880-1909. Beyond it the road climbs up Jesse Ewing Canyon, also named for a settler, then crosses an underground natural gas storage facility at Clay Basin. The last 8 miles to U.S. 191 are paved. Some folks want the 17 unpaved miles of Brown's Park Road paved as well.

ALSO TRY: The refuge has a 9-mile self-guided auto tour on the north side of the river. There is also an 8-mile-long two-track along the south side of the river. Bring binoculars for viewing wildlife.

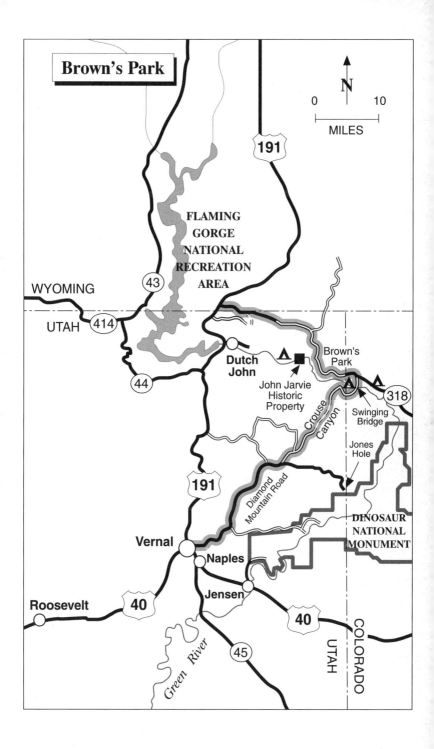

Brown's Park

N

0 — 10
MILES

191

FLAMING
GORGE
NATIONAL
RECREATION
AREA

WYOMING

UTAH

43

414

44

Dutch
John

Brown's
Park

John Jarvie
Historic
Property

Crouse Canyon

Swinging
Bridge

318

Jones
Hole

191

Diamond
Mountain Road

DINOSAUR
NATIONAL
MONUMENT

Vernal

Naples

Jensen

40

40

Roosevelt

Green River

45

COLORADO

UTAH

Rainbow and Island Parks

LOCATION: Dinosaur National Monument.

HIGHLIGHTS: Gaping Split Mountain Canyon, the fantastic prehistoric petroglyphs at McKee Spring and historic Ruple Ranch. Spring and fall are best.

DIFFICULTY: Easy, although the roads can become impassable when wet. You will encounter wash crossings (don't attempt to cross if they're flooding), dips and blind curves.

TIME & DISTANCE: 2.5 hours; about 42 miles round-trip starting at the road to Jones Hole.

MAPS: Trails Illustrated's No. 220 (Dinosaur National Monument). Recreational Map of Utah. Get Dinosaur National Monument's flyer, *Island Park and Jones Hole Areas*. DeLorme pp. 56-57.

INFORMATION: Dinosaur NM; BLM, Vernal Field Office.

GETTING THERE: From Vernal, take U.S. 191 north from Main Street. Turn right (east) at 500 North, toward Jones Hole, Diamond Mountain and Brown's Park (Tour 10). In about 8 miles go right, onto a small road. (If you miss this turn, there's another just ahead that will get you where you need to go.) Reset your odometer to 0. You can also reach this route from the road to the Quarry Visitor Center north of Jensen (It's 26 miles to Rainbow Park from the quarry.)

REST STOPS: There are two shady but waterless campsites at Rainbow Park (carry out your trash).

THE DRIVE: The narrow road winds through badlands to connect with Brush Creek Road, which takes you south. In a couple of miles go left (east), onto the road to Island Park and Rainbow Park (there may or may not be a sign). From here, the drive north of Split Mountain's dramatic anticline presents fascinating color contrasts, with the pale greens and yellows of high-desert vegetation, the tans of the soil, and reds and grays of the massive uplifts. The road will take you past The Reef, a sharp line of up-thrusted rock, then into the monument at about mile 12. Just beyond the monument boundary, the road winds down into the low, brushy canyon at McKee Spring. Drive slowly through it, scanning the cliffs for anthropomorphic and geometric shapes. (Watch for places where people have been pulling to the side of the road.) About 0.6 mile from the park boundary, there are some good petroglyphs on a rock face above the road to the right. But just as you exit the canyon, there will be a small pullout area and, on the left (north) side of the road, a short hiking trail that leads to fantastic anthropomorphs pecked into the rock in what's called the Classic Vernal style. Beyond McKee Spring you will reach the turnoff to Rainbow Park, a mile to the right at the Green River. There you can peer into the maw of Split Mountain Canyon, where the river has scoured a high-walled passage through Split Mountain. From the turnoff to Rainbow Park continue 5 miles to Island Park. But after 1.5 miles detour to the right up a hill, to Island Park Overlook. At Island Park are the remains of historic Ruple Ranch. The Ruples were the first whites to settle in the area, in the 1880s. (Historic sites and artifacts are protected by federal law. Don't disturb or take anything.)

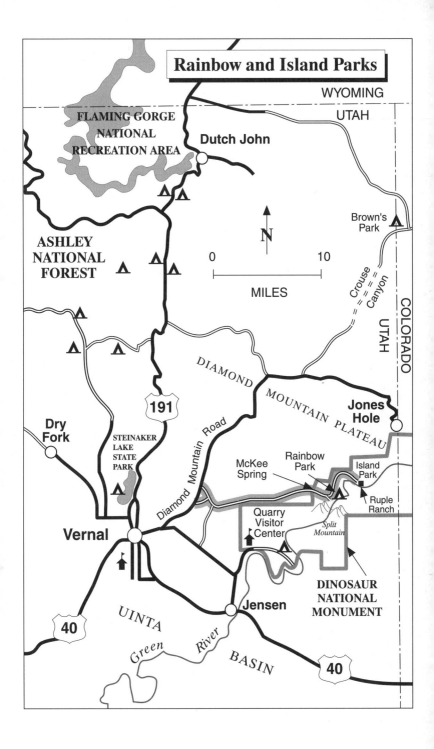

Rainbow and Island Parks

WYOMING
UTAH

FLAMING GORGE NATIONAL RECREATION AREA

Dutch John

Brown's Park

ASHLEY NATIONAL FOREST

N

0   10

MILES

Crouse Canyon

UTAH
COLORADO

DIAMOND MOUNTAIN PLATEAU

Jones Hole

191

Dry Fork

STEINAKER LAKE STATE PARK

Diamond Mountain Road

McKee Spring

Rainbow Park

Island Park

Ruple Ranch

Quarry Visitor Center

Split Mountain

Vernal

DINOSAUR NATIONAL MONUMENT

40

UINTA

Green River

BASIN

Jensen

40

Middle Canyon Road

LOCATION: In the Oquirrh Mountains, between Tooele and Riverton.

HIGHLIGHTS: After climbing 3,800 feet you will reach an overlook above the world's largest open-pit copper mine, Kennecott's 2.5-mile-wide, half-mile deep Bingham Canyon Mine, a National Historic Landmark. The drive also provides great views across the Salt Lake Valley to the Wasatch Range, and south to Utah Lake.

DIFFICULTY: Easy, but possibly hazardous in bad weather. There are some sharp, steep and blind turns. The road is closed in winter. Summer and fall are best.

TIME & DISTANCE: 1.5 hours; 26.5 miles.

MAPS: Recreational Map of Utah. DeLorme pp. 52-53.

INFORMATION: Tooele County Road Department.

GETTING THERE: You can go in either direction. I start in the town of Tooele, at Main and Vine. Set your odometer at 0, and drive east on Vine.

REST STOPS: There are picnic spots with tables along the way, east of Tooele. The overlook is the best place to stop.

THE DRIVE: As you drive the paved, two-lane road east from Tooele you will see up ahead a deep gash in the mountains. That's Middle Canyon. The mountains' name, Oquirrh, is a Goshute Indian word with several meanings, including "wooded mountain." Indeed, they once were heavily wooded, but have since suffered from deforestation caused by logging and smelter fumes. By mile 2.7 the road has entered narrow Middle Canyon. Its lower reaches are forested with box elder and maple, its higher reaches with fir and aspen. At mile 3.7 there will be some picnic spots on the right. At mile 6.8 the pavement ends, and the graded but washboarded dirt road narrows to a little more than one lane. The road begins to climb fairly steeply, and you will encounter some switchbacks and possibly some eroded spots. At mile 8.3 the road crosses Butterfield Pass, at about 8,400 feet. Ahead, where it drops down the eastern side, is a long view toward the Wasatch Range. Go left here, driving 2.5 miles to a vista point high above the mammoth Bingham Canyon Mine. The elevation here is about 9,400 feet. If you listen carefully, you can hear the low hum of the operation. Watch your speed on the winding descent from Butterfield Pass. At mile 17.6 pavement resumes at the Butterfield Reclamation Area, at the base of a huge tailings pile. In a couple of more miles you will be in Riverton.

ALSO TRY: South Willow Road, 5 miles south of Grantsville (northwest of Tooele), is a lovely 14.8-mile (round-trip) drive through forest and high-walled narrows in the Stansbury Mountains. There are pleasant campgrounds as well.

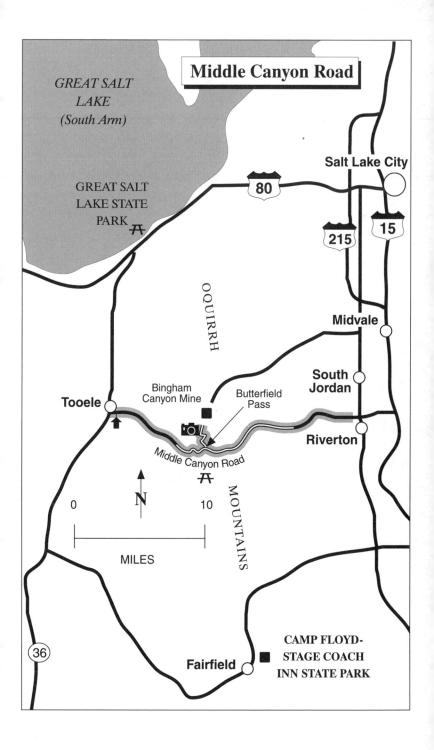

Middle Canyon Road

Cummings Parkway

LOCATION: Wasatch Range. Wasatch Mountain State Park.

HIGHLIGHTS: This drive takes you to the crest of an 8,000-foot-high ridge with views of 11,750-foot Mt. Timpanogos. The park itself has many amenities. Cascade Springs, where fast-flowing water pours out over rocks, is an interesting sight as well. Little Deer Creek Campground has water and flush toilets. The easy drives (on good dirt and gravel roads) to Park City and Brighton are beautiful as well. It's best in summer and fall.

DIFFICULTY: Easy to moderate.

TIME & DISTANCE: 2.5 hours; 26 miles.

MAPS: *Wasatch Mountain State Park & Vicinity* flyer, available from the park. Wasatch-Cache National Forest's *Salt Lake, Kamas, Evanston and Mountain View Ranger Districts.* Trails Illustrated's No. 701 (Uinta National Forest). DeLorme pp. 53-54.

INFORMATION: Wasatch Mountain State Park.

GETTING THERE: This north-south road (No. 220 on some maps; shown on the Forest Service map as No. 317 at the southern end and 085 at the northern end) can be taken in either direction. It's arguably more scenic going north to south, but then one must go up a particularly rocky stretch. So I go south to north, starting south of Midway. From Utah Hwy. 113, turn west onto Tate Lane. Go right after a half-mile onto Stringtown Road, then left onto Cascade Springs Drive (also No. 220). Reset your odometer.

REST STOPS: Wasatch Mountain State Park, Utah's most developed, has just about every amenity you could want, from hot showers to a 27-hole golf course and a pond where the kids can fish for rainbow trout. Cascade Springs has water and restrooms, but no tables. Take a 20-minute walk around the springs, which daily produce more than 7 million gallons of water that flows over travertine ledges and through a series of pools.

THE DRIVE: Cascade Springs Drive, a good dirt-and-gravel road bordered by a rustic fence of lodgepole pine, crosses picturesque farmland as it approaches the ramparts of the Wasatch Range. As it climbs to Decker Pass, you will have an expansive view of Heber Valley. At mile 5.6 is Cascade Springs. Here the road becomes paved. In another 0.4 mile, at a sharp left bend in the road, turn right (north) onto a dirt road, toward Little Deer Creek CG and Wasatch Mountain State Park. In 2.75 miles, before you reach the campground, you will see your route branch off to the right. Watch for a sign saying Tibble Fork jeep trail and Snake Creek. This is Cummings Parkway. The road switchbacks up to a ridge, providing excellent views of Mt. Timpanogos, to the southwest. Drive north on the crest of the ridge. About 5.7 miles from where you turned, the Tibble Fork jeep trail, road 085, branches to the left. (I've not yet been on it, but I've been told it's moderate overall, with a difficult rocky stretch through some narrows. It's 11 miles to Tibble Fork Reservoir.) Go right, toward Midway. In 2.5 miles the road will become very rocky. It would be a rough uphill stretch in the opposite direction, but it's only about 150 yards long. At paved Snake Creek Road, go right toward the visitor center, 2 miles farther.

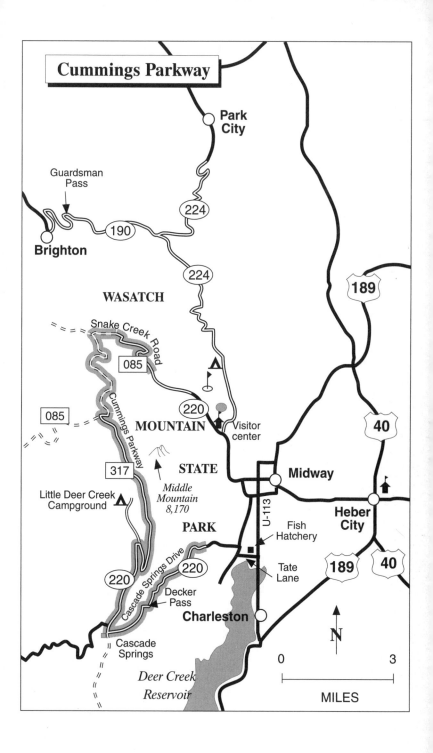

Cummings Parkway

Park City

Guardsman Pass

224

190

Brighton

224

189

WASATCH

Snake Creek Road

085

085

220

MOUNTAIN

Visitor center

317

STATE

40

Midway

Middle Mountain 8,170

Little Deer Creek Campground

Cummings Parkway

PARK

U-113

Heber City

Fish Hatchery

189

40

220

Cascade Springs Drive

220

Tate Lane

Decker Pass

Charleston

N

Cascade Springs

0   3

Deer Creek Reservoir

MILES

House Range

LOCATION: In the Great Basin, west of Delta.

HIGHLIGHTS: Marjum and Dome (or Death) Canyon are beautiful. The 4,000-foot-plus western face of 9,655-foot Notch Peak has a sheer, roughly 2,000-foot vertical face. Top-of-the-world views are found at the Sinbad overlook and, for hikers, the summits of Notch and Swasey peaks. (Bristlecone pines, among the oldest living things on Earth, grow on both.) The range is noted for fossils of trilobites, primitive hard-shelled marine invertebrates that were extinct before dinosaurs existed. Recreational collecting is allowed. Spring and fall are best.

DIFFICULTY: Easy, on 2wd roads. No fuel or services.

TIME & DISTANCE: There are various options. Generally, allow 5-6 hours or longer and plan on 50 to 100 miles or more off-highway.

MAPS: BLM's *Tule Valley*. Also see the BLM's *House Range & Warm Springs Recreation & Vehicle Guide*. DeLorme p. 35.

INFORMATION: BLM, Fillmore Field Office. U-Dig Fossils.

GETTING THERE: Take U.S. 6/50 west from Delta. Almost 32 miles from the bridge in Delta, turn north at the sign for U-Dig Fossils (20 miles), Death Canyon (21 miles) and Marjum Pass (21 miles). Or continue west on the highway for another 10.2 miles toward Skull Rock Pass. At milepost 46, turn north at the Scenic Backway and "Old HWY 6 & 50" sign. This is a starting/ending point for Utah's Notch Peak Loop Scenic Backway, so it's where I start. Feel free to chart your own course.

REST STOPS: There is primitive camping, and water at Antelope Springs. U-Dig Fossils is a fun place to dig. Call for rates and to make arrangements. Their season is April 1 to Oct. 15.

THE DRIVE: The limestone and shale reveal a Paleozoic record dating back to the Ordovician and Cambrian periods 438-570 MYA, when trilobites left their imprints in primordial seabed. At mile 4.3 is the left branch toward Miller Canyon. (For the 3 to 3.5-hour hike to Notch Peak, the BLM says, turn here and drive toward Miller Canyon, but go left at the sign for Sawtooth Canyon. Drive to the old stone cabin, then go another half-mile. Hike up the bottom of Sawtooth Canyon to a saddle on the east side of Notch Peak, then scramble up the last quarter-mile to the summit.) The tour continues north toward 9,678-foot Swasey Peak and Antelope Springs. At about mile 15.1 pass the left (west) turn to Marjum Pass, part of old U.S. 6/50 until it was bypassed by the paved highway in 1950. There's a four-way intersection at about mile 19.9. Go northwest toward Swasey Peak, Antelope Springs and Dome Canyon (or Death Canyon, perhaps named after pioneers said to have frozen to death there). Soon you will see U-Dig Fossils, a commercial trilobite quarry. A bit farther is another junction. To the left is Dome/Death Canyon. The road to the right ends at Sinbad Overlook, with a fantastic view of Tule Valley. The road down Dome/Death Canyon descends west between cliffs. At the hulk of an old truck, go left (south). In 6.8 miles is the left to Marjum Canyon. Continue south to reach the highway in about 14 miles, or drive 3.2 miles up Marjum. At that point, on the left (north), is a two-track up a side canyon. From its end walk about 150 yards to a cliff dwelling occupied by Robert Stinson from 1920-1945. Continue over Marjum Pass to the road on the east side, which will return you to the highway. Or backtrack from Marjum and drive to U.S. 6/50 along the range's west side.

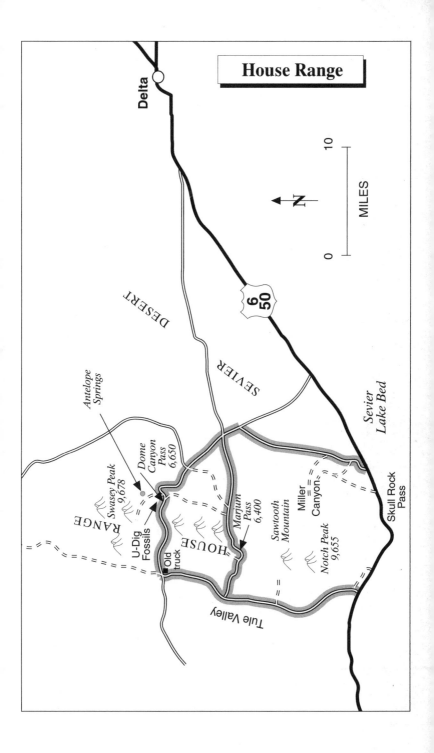

House Range

Delta

N

MILES
0   10

6 50

DESERT

SEVIER

Sevier
Lake Bed

Antelope
Springs

Dome
Canyon
Pass
6,650

Swasey Peak
9,678

RANGE

U-Dig
Fossils

Old
truck

HOUSE

Marjum
Pass
6,400

Sawtooth
Mountain

Miller
Canyon

Notch Peak
9,655

Skull Rock
Pass

Tule Valley

Pony Express Trail

LOCATION: In the Great Basin, between Camp Floyd-Stagecoach Inn State Park (at Fairfield) and the hamlet of Ibapah.

HIGHLIGHTS: This National Back Country Byway retraces the Pony Express and the Overland Stage route, as well as a leg of the Lincoln Highway, the nation's first coast-to-coast auto road. Interpretive sites and ruins help you relive the Pony Express' 19 months of operation, in 1860-61, and stagecoach travel. You can view wildlife year-round at Fish Springs National Wildlife Refuge.

DIFFICULTY: Easy, on graveled 2wd roads. There are no services. Prepare for desert travel. Flash floods are possible during storms.

TIME & DISTANCE: 6 hours; 133 miles.

MAPS: Recreational Map of Utah. BLM's *House Range & Warm Springs Recreation & Vehicle Guide*. DeLorme pp. 42-43, 44, 50, 52-53.

INFORMATION: BLM, Salt Lake and Fillmore Field Offices. Camp Floyd-Stagecoach Inn State Park. Fish Springs NWR.

GETTING THERE: South of Salt Lake City, take Utah Hwy. 73 to Camp Floyd-Stagecoach Inn State Park, which is west of Utah Lake.

REST STOPS: There's a BLM fee campground at Simpson Springs (no water Oct. 15-March 1), and a dry but free primitive campground 4 miles south of Callao. There are picnic areas at Camp Floyd (fee), Lookout Pass (just a table) and Fish Springs. Generally, the best times to view waterfowl at Fish Springs are mid-April and mid-September. Recreational rock collecting is allowed at Dugway Geode Beds.

THE DRIVE: From Camp Floyd-Stagecoach Inn, take Hwy. 73 southwest to Five-Mile Pass, then turn left onto Faust Road. At mile 18.9 you will come to Hwy. 36. Go left (south) on the highway for a half-mile, then right at the sign onto a graveled road that climbs to 6,192-foot Lookout Pass. On the pass is a cemetery where a stagecoach station operator's beloved dogs lie buried beside three people who died along the trail. At mile 45.2 is the reconstructed Simpson Springs Pony Express Station. From here, cross the Dugway Range, and at about mile 70 the road passes the Dugway Geode Beds. At about mile 82, the road enters marshy Fish Springs, which has an 11-mile auto tour route. Just as you enter the refuge, note the red, white and blue "L" painted on a fence post. Here, the Lincoln Highway, begun in 1913, joined the old Pony Express and Overland Stage route. Extending between New York City and San Francisco, in many places it was just a single-lane dirt road, yet it helped establish automobile travel as adventure. Continue to isolated Callao, at the base of the Deep Creek Range, which rises to more than 12,000 feet. (About 1.7 miles south of the T-intersection at Callao is a small road that ascends the benchlands of these uniquely well-watered Great Basin mountains. The upper reaches are a wilderness study area.) The tour goes right (north) from the T. In 5.2 miles go right at the Y, and the road will become a single lane. On a strategic knoll at the entrance to Overland Canyon are the remains of Overland, or Round, Station, an Overland Stage outpost built after Indians in 1863 killed the agent and four soldiers and burned the original buildings. 5.9 miles farther go left at another T. (6 miles to the right is the Gold Hill ghost town.) The tour ends at the paved road to Ibapah and U.S. 93A. Head north to Wendover and I-80.

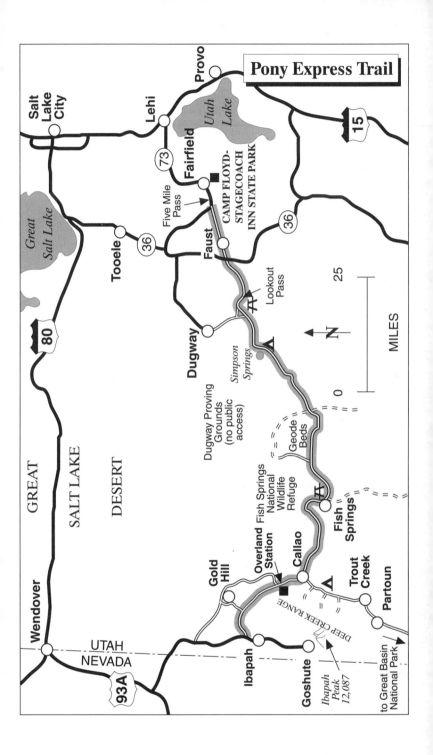

Pony Express Trail

Skyline Drive II

LOCATION: Southeast of Provo, between U.S. 6 and Utah Hwy. 31.

HIGHLIGHTS: This is a scenic high-elevation cruise atop the Wasatch Plateau, with endless vistas of mountains, valleys and deserts. It will take you through stands of aspen and pine, and broad Alpine meadows. There are many good places to pull off the road and enjoy the view. This also is a leg of the multiple-use Great Western Trail and Adventure Highway. Depending on the weather, you may encounter a midsummer wildflower display. Autumn is pretty, too.

DIFFICULTY: Easy, on a good 2wd dirt and gravel road.

TIME & DISTANCE: 1.5 hours; 28 miles.

MAPS: Manti-La Sal National Forest's *Sanpete, Ferron and Price Ranger Districts.* DeLorme p. 46.

INFORMATION: Sanpete Ranger District; and the Ferron/Price Ranger District's Price Office.

GETTING THERE: This north-south route can be taken in either direction, beginning or ending on U.S. 6 southeast of Spanish Fork. I go south. Take U.S. 6 to the Tucker rest area, 30 miles southeast of I-15. Drive between the picnic area and the building, angling left. Reset your odometer. Follow road 150.

REST STOPS: Tucker rest area has shady picnic sites, and there are many undeveloped campsites along the way in addition to developed Gooseberry Campground. There's fishing at Lower Gooseberry Reservoir, near the end of the drive.

THE DRIVE: The Left Fork of Clear Creek is on your left as you follow a one-lane road among cottonwoods, pines and aspens. At mile 2.7, where the road enters Manti-La Sal National Forest, the road begins climbing to the top of the Wasatch Plateau. You were at about 6,200 feet elevation at the rest area. By mile 10, you will be over 10,000 feet, meandering south among rolling, pastoral mountaintops that melt into plateau country to the east. To the west lie the gray mountains and alkali flats of the Great Basin. To the north rises the dramatic escarpment of the Wasatch Range and the uplift of the uniquely east-west trending Uinta Mountains. The road is two lanes in sections, and well-maintained. Do watch your speed, because the gravel tends to cause tires to lose their grip. At mile 28.2 the road is paved. A short distance farther is Hwy. 31, a designated scenic byway. If you want more high-elevation adventure, try rougher, longer Skyline Drive South, which I call Skyline Drive III (Tour 17). Go left (southeast) on Hwy. 31, then right (south) after 4.9 miles where road 150 resumes.

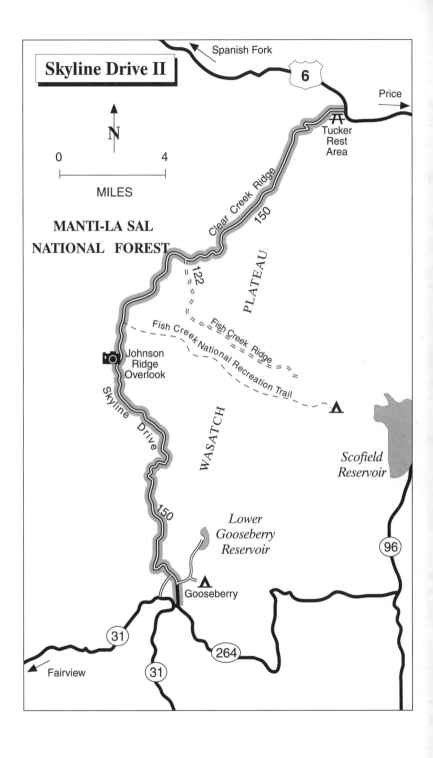

Skyline Drive II

MANTI-LA SAL
NATIONAL FOREST

N

0   4

MILES

Spanish Fork

6

Price

Tucker Rest Area

Clear Creek Ridge

150

122

PLATEAU

Fish Creek Ridge

Fish Creek National Recreation Trail

Johnson Ridge Overlook

Skyline Drive

WASATCH

150

Scofield Reservoir

Lower Gooseberry Reservoir

Gooseberry

96

31

264

31

Fairview

Skyline Drive III

LOCATION: North of I-70, between U.S. 89 and Utah Hwy. 10.

HIGHLIGHTS: There are awesome vistas, stretching from the Great Basin to the Colorado Plateau. Road conditions vary, and include some narrow ledges. That adds to the fun of reaching 10,900 feet on the Wasatch Plateau. The mountain biking opportunities are good as well. Summer and fall are best. This road is also known as Skyline Drive South.

DIFFICULTY: Easy to difficult depending on where you start. The north end can be muddy and rutted. At mile 23 the road crosses a north-facing slope that can be blocked by snow well into summer.

TIME & DISTANCE: 6 hours; 76 miles.

MAPS: Manti-La Sal National Forest's *Sanpete, Ferron and Price Ranger Districts*. Fishlake National Forest, Richfield Ranger District. DeLorme pp. 37-38, 46.

INFORMATION: Manti-La Sal National Forest, Sanpete Ranger District; Ferron/Price Ranger District's Price Office and Ferron Office; Fishlake National Forest, Richfield District. Get the brochure, *Auto Tour: Great Basin Experimental Range,* from the Sanpete Ranger District.

GETTING THERE: If the weather has been dry for some time, letting the road dry out, you can start on Hwy. 31 at the Sanpete Valley Overlook and drive south. Expect severe ruts. Easier accesses are the serpentine, 15-mile gravel road (Forest Hwy. 8) from Ephraim east up Ephraim Canyon; or the 37-mile drive from Castle Dale, on Utah Hwy. 10 and west on Utah Hwy. 29/FH 8 past Joe's Valley Reservoir. I start at Utah Hwy. 31, from which you can drive the entire route.

REST STOPS: Twelve-Mile Flat Campground.

THE DRIVE: This leg of road 150 is more rugged and even more spectacular than the route I call Skyline Drive II (Tour 16), which starts 4.9 miles farther north on Utah Hwy. 31. The route begins high above Sanpete Valley. You will pass a number of lush, U-shaped glacial basins, and at about mile 20 the road takes you past North and South Tent Mountains, both of which exceed 11,200 feet. At mile 22.3 cross a sharp divide at about 10,600 feet, and a short distance farther cross the ridge. The road improves from here, though it's still one lane as it crosses an exposed, rocky landscape of rolling mountaintops and Alpine meadows. At mile 43.9 you will reach Hightop, the highest point on the drive. The sign says it's 10,897 feet; the map says 10,904 feet. Descend to Twelve-Mile Flat, and go left at the campground toward Gunnison Valley. 10.3 miles farther road 290 angles right (west), descending toward Mayfield. Follow the two-track that continues ahead into the woods. Soon it enters Fishlake National Forest, where road 150 becomes road 001. In 6 miles road 001 (from here scenic Willow Creek Road) goes right (west) 25 miles toward U.S. 89. Skyline Drive, road 009, continues south down Salina Canyon to I-70 (13 miles).

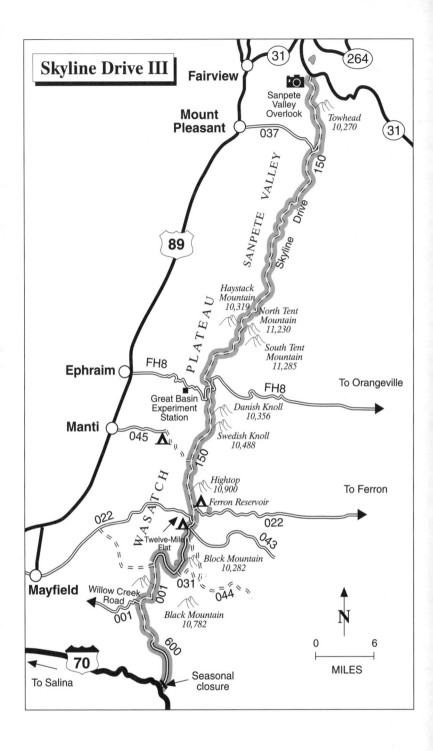

Skyline Drive III

Chicken Creek

LOCATION: In the San Pitch Mountains south of Nephi, east of Levan. This tour is in a part of Uinta National Forest that is administered by Manti-La Sal National Forest.

HIGHLIGHTS: This is an excellent drive through a narrow, rugged canyon with exposed rock and forested with pine, aspen, maples and other deciduous trees. You will see some side canyons that invite a hike, and many fine views. Make it a summer or fall drive.

DIFFICULTY: Easy.

TIME & DISTANCE: 1.5 hours; 16 miles.

MAPS: Manti-La Sal National Forest's *Sanpete, Ferron and Price Ranger Districts.* DeLorme p. 45.

INFORMATION: Manti-La Sal National Forest's Sanpete Ranger District.

GETTING THERE: You can take this east-west route in either direction, beginning or ending at Levan or Wales. I start at Levan, on Utah Hwy. 28 south of Nephi and east of I-15. In Levan, turn east off Hwy. 28 (Main Street) onto First South Street. My mileages begin here.

REST STOPS: Chicken Creek Campground.

THE DRIVE: As you follow the paved road toward the mountains you will see the canyon ahead. At mile 1.5 there is a Y; left goes to Pigeon Creek, so go right, toward Wales. Here the road surface becomes dirt and gravel, just a bit more than one lane, although you will travel over short paved segments. Note the exposed, yellowish sedimentary rock on the canyon's north wall. At mile 4.2 look ahead and to the right, and you will see a small waterfall. At 4.5 the road, now No. 101, enters Uinta National Forest. By 5.2 the roadbed becomes somewhat rougher, though it remains a good road. At 5.8 Chicken Creek Campground is on the right, with water and toilets. From here the road climbs steadily, and becomes rockier. At 6.7, the canyon's walls reveal that these mountains are composed of a jumble of rocks, stones and sediment called conglomerate, mostly lakebed deposits laid down in the Mesozoic era (66-208 MYA). At mile 8.2, a trail on the left goes up pretty Reddick Canyon. Continue straight at mile 12, where road 157 to Wales branches right, heading down Wales Canyon toward a magnificent view of Sanpete Valley and the Wasatch Plateau. The scene soon will be framed by the rock walls of a gap that the road takes you through. At mile 16 asphalt resumes, at the hamlet of Wales.

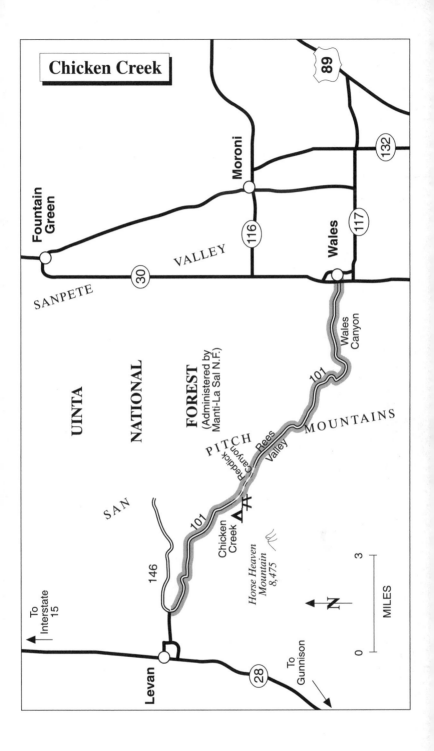

Chicken Creek

Reservation Ridge

LOCATION: Between U.S. 6 & U.S. 191 north of Helper.

HIGHLIGHTS: This is a beautiful drive along a high ridge, on a road of varied quality and remarkable vistas. It's particularly appealing because of its proximity to three highways. It also has a perfect mix of pine and aspen forest, meadows and distant vistas, and glimpses of wildlife early in morning or evening. If you begin or end at U.S. 40, you can take in Strawberry Pinnacles, sedimentary formations at the confluence of Strawberry River and Red Creek. Summer is nice, but fall is great.

DIFFICULTY: Easy to moderate. The road can be severely rutted, and extremely slick when wet. It's best in summer and early fall.

TIME & DISTANCE: 2 hours; 27 miles.

MAPS: Ashley National Forest. DeLorme pp. 46-47.

INFORMATION: Uinta National Forest, Spanish Fork District. Ashley National Forest, Duchesne/Roosevelt Ranger District, Duchesne and Roosevelt Offices.

GETTING THERE: You can go several ways. I begin off U.S. 6 near Soldier Summit, and end at U.S. 191. The turnoff for Uinta National Forest road 081 is on the east side of U.S. 6, 0.7 mile south of the summit. Another option: From U.S. 40 about 3 miles west of Hwy. 208, go south on Red Creek Road, a.k.a. Strawberry Pinnacles Road. Go south to the pinnacles, then west on road 149 up Timber Canyon to the ridge.

REST STOPS: There are many primitive campsites, as well as developed Avintaquin Campground.

THE DRIVE: This tour quickly becomes very pretty, especially in the coppery light of a late autumn afternoon, as you drive through hills of grass and sagebrush toward mountains forested with aspen and pine. The road forks at mile 0.6; keep right. It narrows to a single lane as it winds up a canyon through stands of aspen that promise autumn color. By mile 7.6, the view west down the canyon you've come up extends across range after distant range. A mile more and you're on Reservation Ridge, at about 8,800 feet. To the east, beige hills roll toward the Strawberry River drainage in the Uinta Basin and the West Tavaputs Plateau. To the south and west, forested mountains and valleys spread like a rumpled woolen blanket to the horizon. Road 147 south on the crest of the ridge provides a relaxing cruise among mountaintops and through more aspen groves, although the undulating one-lane road can be rough in spots. By mile 17 the road has climbed to 9,700 feet, and then it begins the gradual descent to Avintaquin Campground, at 25.5. U.S. 191 is a couple of miles farther.

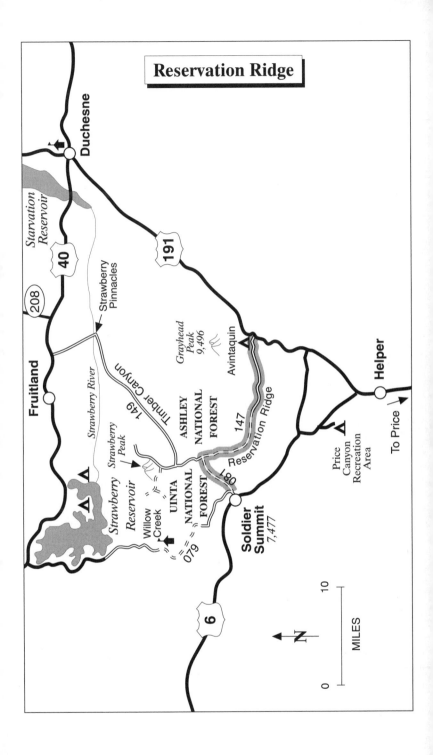

Reservation Ridge

Mayfield to Ferron

LOCATION: On the Wasatch Plateau between U.S. 89 and Utah Hwy. 10. Manti-La Sal National Forest.

HIGHLIGHTS: On this drive, you will climb a mile to Skyline Drive III (Tour 17). The vistas are outstanding, and Ferron Canyon adds scenic value as well. It ends at Millsite State Park, which has showers, campsites and a golf course. Summer and fall are best.

DIFFICULTY: Easy. Watch for logging trucks.

TIME & DISTANCE: 2.5 hours; 47 miles to the park.

MAPS: Manti-La Sal National Forest's *Sanpete, Ferron and Price Ranger Districts*. DeLorme pp. 37-38.

INFORMATION: Sanpete Ranger District. Ferron/Price Ranger Districts, Ferron Office.

GETTING THERE: Begin this east-west route at Mayfield or Ferron. I start at Mayfield, near Gunnison. From Main Street, turn east onto Canyon Road near the post office and City Hall, toward Skyline Drive. Reset your odometer.

REST STOPS: There is camping at Twelve-Mile Flat, Ferron Reservoir, Ferron Canyon and Millsite State Park. Sky Haven Lodge has a cafe, gas and cabins.

THE DRIVE: Canyon Road goes through pinyon- and juniper-covered hills, and at mile 1.7 the pavement ends. At mile 3.6 the road enters the national forest, where it becomes No. 022, and in a couple of more miles it enters the Twelve-Mile Recreation Area. Here, switchbacks climb steeply, and broad vistas of canyons, basins and mountains appear, with a particularly beautiful view at mile 11. You will begin to see many exceptionally large aspens, and by about mile 15 you will pass the Grove of the Aspen Giants Scenic Area, where the normally slight trees reach 30 inches in diameter. In another 3 miles or so the road comes to Twelve-Mile Flat, where there is a fine campground at 10,120 feet. Turn left here onto road 150/022, part of superlative Skyline Drive III (Tour 17), and 1.7 miles farther road 022 resumes to the right, descending toward Ferron. If you've not been on this leg of Skyline Drive before, go north a short distance to Hightop. At about 10,900 feet, it is Skyline Drive's highest point. (Mayfield is at 5,660 feet.) Here, you are on the divide between the Great Basin to the west and the Colorado River drainage to the east. Road 022 winds down through a basin, and passes Ferron Reservoir and Sky Haven Lodge. As you descend, trading forested mountains for desert, you will have tremendous vistas of the badlands, sandstone cliffs and canyons of plateau country. At mile 36 is the turnoff to Ferron Canyon overlook, which gives you a preview of the spectacular canyon leading to Millsite State Park and Ferron.

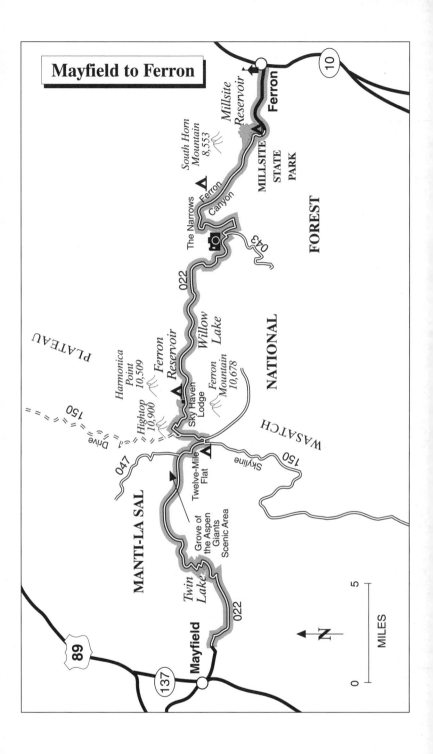

Mayfield to Ferron

Nine-Mile Canyon

LOCATION: Between Wellington and Myton.

HIGHLIGHTS: Nine-Mile Canyon is actually a 40-mile-long trough between the Bad Land Cliffs and the West Tavaputs Plateau that drains into the Green River. The name is from a map prepared by the 1872 government expedition led by Maj. John Wesley Powell, which used the canyon as the site of a nine-mile survey triangulation. Its human history goes back 8,000 years, from the prehistoric Archaic, Fremont and Ute Indian cultures to homesteaders and ranchers. It is a gallery of Native American rock art, with petroglyphs and pictographs created by all three Indian groups (interspersed with 19th-century names and dates). It's most famous for abundant Fremont Culture rock art, created by the various native groups included in that somewhat generic label. The Fremont occupied the western Colorado Plateau and eastern Great Basin from roughly 400 to 1300 A.D., then disappeared along with their Puebloan contemporaries, the Anasazi. Many figures are visible from the road (bring binoculars). Fremont dwellings and granaries can also be seen. The original road was built in the 1880s by the African-American 9th U.S. Cavalry to link Fort Duchesne with Price. You'll pass old stagecoach stops, settlers' cabins, even iron telegraph poles. The 23-mile Harmon Canyon-Prickly Pear Canyon loop is popular for mountain biking. **Note:** Do not touch or disturb archaeological sites, which are protected by federal law.

DIFFICULTY: Easy when dry, though possibly dusty. Rain can make the roads impassable even with 4wd, and summer storms can cause floods. Spring and fall are best. Be careful on the blind curves.

TIME & DISTANCE: Plan to spend all day; 80-100 miles.

MAPS: The Castle Country Travel Council has a very good brochure with a detailed self-guided tour. Also get the booklet, *The Pioneer Saga of the Nine Mile Road.* DeLorme pp. 47-48.

INFORMATION: BLM's Price and Vernal Field Offices. Castle Country Travel Council. Be sure to check out the BLM's detailed Nine-Mile Canyon Web site: www.blm.gov/utah/price/9mile.htm.

GETTING THERE: From U.S. 6/191: Go north at Walker's Food & Fuel, on Soldier Creek Road, at the east end of Wellington. You will reach the canyon in about 20 miles. **From U.S. 40/191:** 1.4 miles west of Myton turn south onto 5550 West toward Sand Wash. Drive south 31 miles to Nine-Mile Canyon. I start at U.S. 6/191.

REST STOPS: There's no fuel for 78 miles between Wellington and Myton. There's a picnic area 4 miles west of Argyle Canyon. Nine-Mile Ranch has campsites, a store and tours. Bring food and drinks.

THE DRIVE: The pavement ends about 12.5 miles from U.S. 6/191, at Soldier Canyon Mine. The winding, maintained dirt road climbs to a summit, then descends into the canyon. It's difficult to explain the location of the many rock art sites, so refer to the Web site and brochure noted above. Go slow and look for places where others have stopped (avoid trespassing). At milepost 17, watch for a balanced rock on the north side of the road and the excellent petroglyphs near it. Almost 39 miles from U.S. 6/191 is Price-Myton Road, which goes north through Gate Canyon to Myton. About 6.5 miles farther down Nine-Mile Canyon is a Y. The left branch ends in 5.2 miles at a locked gate and the rocky, moderately difficult 4wd washbottom route up North Frank's Canyon. It connects to Wrinkle Road (Tour 22) in about 5 miles. Take the right branch of the Y across the bridge to Cottonwood Canyon. 1.2 miles from the Y you will see a rock face above and to the right. It bears the "hunting scene" shown on p. 12.

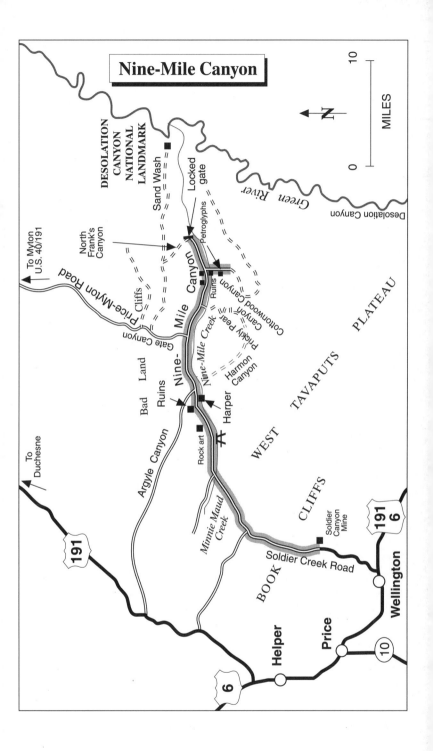

Nine-Mile Canyon

Sand Wash

LOCATION: On the West Tavaputs Plateau, south of the Uinta Basin and north of Nine-Mile Canyon (Tour 21). Sand Wash itself leads to the Green River southeast of Myton.

HIGHLIGHTS: This tour includes towering cliffs, a great vista from an overlook above the Green River, and historic Sand Wash, upriver from remote Desolation Canyon. You can combine this drive with Nine-Mile Canyon, famous for Native American rock art.

DIFFICULTY: Easy when dry, but these roads can become treacherous when wet, and may be impassable even with 4wd. Runoff from the cliffs cause many small ruts, making for slow going at times. Sharp stones can cause flats. Summer storms can cause flash floods, so I suggest going in spring and fall.

TIME & DISTANCE: 3.5 hours; 63 miles.

MAPS: Recreational Map of Utah. DeLorme pp. 47-48.

INFORMATION: BLM, Price and Vernal field offices.

GETTING THERE: There are several ways to take this tour. You can make an 85-mile loop from U.S. 40/191, beginning and ending southwest of Myton. Or start out the same way but end at Nine-Mile Canyon. In this description, I start at Nine-Mile Canyon, and take you east to Sand Wash and then north to U.S. 40/191 near Myton.

REST STOPS: Sand Wash has a waterless campground, nature trail and historic buildings.

THE DRIVE: Deep in Nine-Mile Canyon is a major T intersection. The road north, Price-Myton Road, is a well-maintained dirt and gravel road that passes through Gate Canyon at its southern end, and continues north to U.S. 40/191 southwest of Myton. Etched in the sandstone at the southern entrance to the canyon is Fremont Culture (300-1250 A.D.) rock art. You will also see names and dates from the 1880s. Almost 5 miles from Nine-Mile Canyon, a sign signals the right (east) turn to Sand Wash, on Wrinkle Road. It will take you along Myton Bench, which drops off in the distance where the Green River, perhaps most notably its Desolation Canyon, separates the West and East Tavaputs plateaus. Lofty sandstone cliffs dominate the bench, and now and then the road edges to the brink of a tributary of the river canyon. To the southeast, the river flows through Desolation Canyon, named in 1869 by John Wesley Powell, who led the first exploratory float trip down the Green and Colorado rivers. In 1969, Desolation Canyon was designated a natural historic landmark because, of all the canyons Powell explored, it has changed least. About 12 miles from the Price-Myton Road you will see on the right the rocky and ledgy, moderately difficult 4wd route down North Frank's Canyon, which ends in 5 miles in Nine-Mile Canyon. About 8 miles farther a spur branches right (east), past an airstrip to a spectacular viewpoint at the edge of the bench. The road down to Sand Wash is about a mile farther, again to the right (east). Once a ferry crossing, Sand Wash is now an entry point for floaters heading down Desolation Canyon. Back at Wrinkle Road, go right, and climb onto a bench, then drive northward. Some 25 miles from Sand Wash, keep left at an intersection and continue north. In 9.7 miles you will reach Price-Myton Road. Go right (north) to U.S. 40/191, or left (south) to Nine-Mile Canyon and U.S. 6/191 at Wellington.

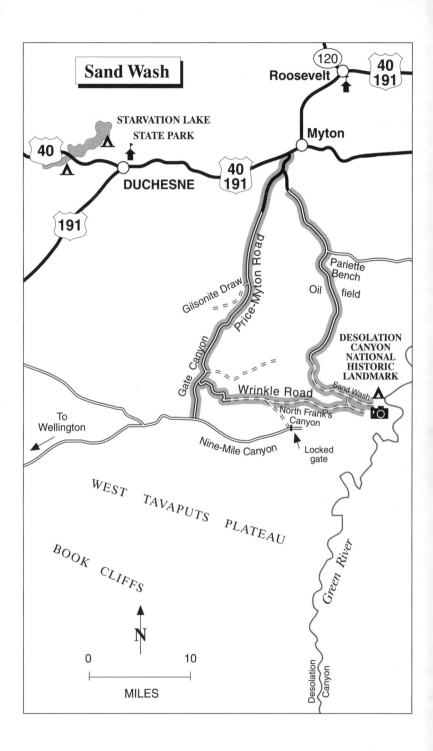

Sand Wash

STARVATION LAKE
STATE PARK

40

DUCHESNE

40
191

191

Roosevelt

120

40
191

Myton

40
191

Gilsonite Draw

Price-Myton Road

Gate Canyon

Pariette
Bench

Oil

field

DESOLATION
CANYON
NATIONAL
HISTORIC
LANDMARK

Wrinkle Road

Sand Wash

To
Wellington

North Frank's
Canyon

Nine-Mile Canyon

Locked
gate

WEST   TAVAPUTS   PLATEAU

BOOK   CLIFFS

Green River

N

0   10

MILES

Desolation
Canyon

Wedge Overlook/Buckhorn Draw

LOCATION: San Rafael Swell, between Hwy. 10, I-70, U.S. 6/191.

HIGHLIGHTS: This tour (best in spring or fall) goes through outstanding sandstone scenery in the San Rafael Swell, a massive blister in the Earth's crust and one of Utah's most dramatic geologic features. The Little Grand Canyon, viewed from the Wedge Overlook, ranks among Utah's most spectacular sights. You also can see prehistoric roadside rock art and, if you take the full scenic loop around Jackass Benches, gaze down into the San Rafael River's awesome Lower Black Box, an exceptionally narrow, dark gorge.

DIFFICULTY: Easy, mostly on graveled 2wd roads. You will encounter many washes, but don't attempt to cross if they're flooding. The Jackass Benches spur follows a 2wd, high-clearance dirt road, but the spur to the Lower Black Box is quite rocky in places. Avoid these roads if they're wet and slick. The intersections may be signed.

TIME & DISTANCE: It's 13 miles from Castle Dale to the turnoff to the Wedge Overlook, and just over 6 miles to the overlook; allow about 45 minutes one-way travel time. It's another 32.3 miles from the Wedge Overlook turnoff to I-70; allow about an hour. The Jackass Benches loop, with the optional and easy 2-mile or so (one-way) hike to the Lower Black Box of the San Rafael River, adds about 26 miles; allow about 4 hours. The Jackass Benches loop without the Lower Black Box segment is 18.4 miles; allow an hour.

MAPS: Recreation Map of the San Rafael Swell & San Rafael Desert. Trails Illustrated's No. 712 (San Rafael Swell). Recreational Map of Utah. Also refer to the brochure, *Recreation Guide to the San Rafael Area.* DeLorme pp. 38-39.

INFORMATION: BLM, Price Field Office.

GETTING THERE: From Castle Dale: Take Hwy. 10 north for 1.4 miles. Turn east at the sign for Buckhorn Wash and the Wedge Overlook. **From I-70:** Take exit 129, about 17.5 miles west of the junction with Hwy. 24. Buckhorn Draw Road is north of the interstate.

REST STOPS: There's primitive camping at the Wedge Overlook, and a free but dry campground at San Rafael Bridge Recreation Site.

THE DRIVE: The San Rafael Swell is an 80-mile by 30-mile bulge in the Earth's crust that has been sculpted over millions of years by wind, water and geologic forces. Today, its network of backroads provides views of deep river canyons, slickrock domes, towering buttes and spires. North of the San Rafael River, the road follows the long sandstone meanders of spectacular Buckhorn Draw, noted for a roadside rock art site with figures dating back perhaps 2,000 years. About 13 miles from Castle Dale, turn south toward the Wedge Overlook. Drive about 6 miles through pinyon-juniper woodland to the dizzying rim of Utah's Little Grand Canyon, where the San Rafael River courses through a gorge more than 1,200 feet below. South of the river, you will pass through picturesque rangelands. About 5.7 miles from I-70, Buckhorn Draw Road passes through Sinkhole Flat, site of a sinkhole just east of the road. Here is the spur for the Jackass Benches loop (and the rough west end of Black Dragon Wash; see Tour 24). 9.2 miles down this road (keeping left at several forks) it will take you to the optional but recommended spur for Swazey's (a.k.a. Swazys) Leap and the Lower Black Box. It ends in 3.8 miles. You can hike to the edge of the Lower Black Box, an incredible sight, and down to the river at Swazey's Leap, where a Sid Swazy is said to have leaped across the river on his horse long ago.

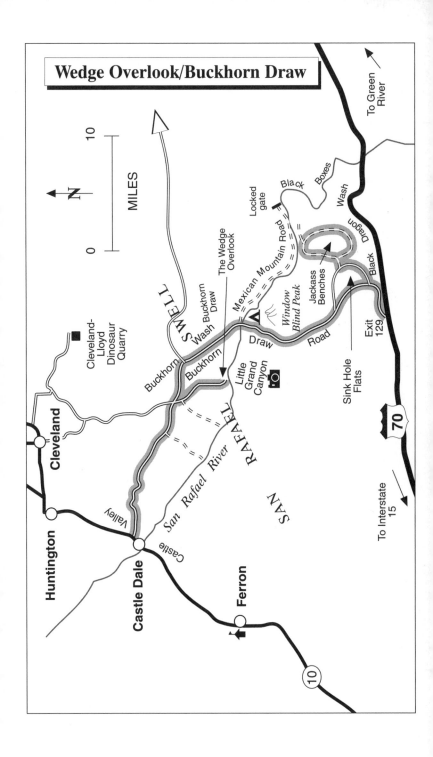

Wedge Overlook/Buckhorn Draw

Black Dragon Wash

LOCATION: In the San Rafael Swell's "reef," west of Green River.

HIGHLIGHTS: You'll enjoy the San Rafael Reef's colorful rock, prehistoric rock art and high-walled Black Dragon Wash (named for a pictograph that resembles a winged dragon). The 4wd trail (not shown on most maps) west of the rock art site is popular for mountain biking.

DIFFICULTY: It's easy to the canyon of Black Dragon Wash, where the road is rocky but not difficult. Beyond the rock art site there, which is as far as I take you, the scenic but unmaintained 4wd trail to Jackass Benches is potentially difficult, rocky in places and possibly washed out, but it does go to I-70 via Buckhorn Draw Road (Tour 23). Floods can block or damage the tunnel under I-70, referred to below.

TIME & DISTANCE: I cover two approaches. One is 3.4 miles round-trip and about an hour. The other is about 18 miles and 3 hours.

MAPS: Recreation Map of the San Rafael Swell & San Rafael Desert. Trails Illustrated's No. 712 (San Rafael Swell). DeLorme p. 39. The brochure *Recreation Guide to the San Rafael Area.*

INFORMATION: BLM, Price Field Office.

GETTING THERE: For the long tour, the way I take you: From Utah Hwy. 24 about 7.4 miles south of I-70, turn west just south of milepost 154, onto a graded dirt road. Set the odometer to 0, and continue toward the reef. For the short tour: Take I-70 to the San Rafael Reef, the up-tilted wall of the San Rafael Swell west of Green River. At 2.2 miles west of Hwy. 24, just west of milepost 145, watch for a dirt freeway median crossing. Directly across from it, on the north side of the freeway, is a gate. Go through it. (This access may eventually be closed.) The road soon angles left to cross the wash near the concrete passageway beneath I-70 that is used for the longer option (stay out of the wash if it's flooding). A mile from I-70, go left at the sign. Follow the wash into the canyon and to the fenced rock art site.

REST STOPS: There are no facilities. Dispersed camping is allowed on BLM lands except in the canyon of Black Dragon Wash, due to flood danger.

THE DRIVE: The San Rafael Swell, an eroded blister in the Earth's crust 80 miles long and 30 miles wide, is one of canyon country's most dramatic geologic features. Pioneers found the eastern side's north-south line of up-tilted sandstone plates, similar to others in Utah, an obstacle to east-west travel akin to ocean reefs. From Hwy. 24, the graded road heads directly toward the reef. At mile 1.7, it bends north and runs parallel to the reef as it enters sandy Greasewood Draw. At about mile 4, a two-track spurs to the west, toward the reef. Take it. When it forks in 2 miles, keep left, and continue to the boundary of the wilderness study area, where mechanized travel is not allowed. Walk along the creekbed to the canyon's mouth, and you will see petroglyphs pecked into the sloping canyon floor and north wall, near a small cave. (Do not step on or touch them.) The main road continues north. At I-70 is an underpass with two tunnels. Before entering, see if one lane or the other has been washed out. The washbottom route will connect with the shorter access to Black Dragon Wash. On the canyon's north wall are three groups of pictographs. To the left, above the talus slope, are several tall, ghost-like Barrier Canyon-style anthropomorphs, perhaps 2,000 to 4,000 years old. To the right are the "dragon" and "praying dog." There are other figures in an alcove farther right.

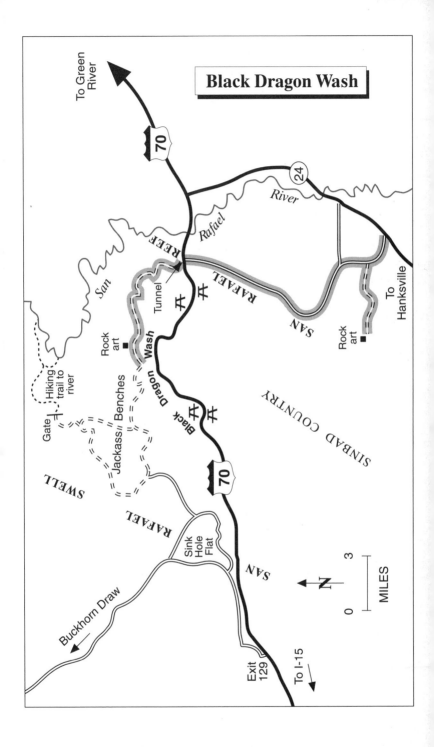

Black Dragon Wash

Reds Canyon/Hondoo Arch

LOCATION: In the San Rafael Swell, south of I-70 and west of Green River.

HIGHLIGHTS: This tour goes deep into the primitive, spectacular and relatively little-known San Rafael Swell. It passes through beautiful Reds Canyon to Hondoo Arch and Temple Mountain. Historic Swasey Cabin is worth the short side trip, and there are spurs to explore. At the south end are some ancient Barrier Canyon-style pictographs, which are thousands of years old, and the bizarre rock figures at Goblin Valley State Park. If you have the time, consider the optional visit to Little Wild Horse Canyon, where there is a popular canyon hiking trail and a road to Muddy Creek, through a varicolored moonscape of bentonite hills. Spring and fall are best.

DIFFICULTY: Easy, but the roads can be impassable when wet. The road to Little Wild Horse Canyon has sandy and washbottom segments. Old mines in the area are dangerous, so avoid them.

TIME & DISTANCE: 6 hours; 90 miles or more with spurs.

MAPS: Trails Illustrated's No. 712 (San Rafael Swell). Recreation Map of the San Rafael Swell & San Rafael Desert. Recreational Map of Utah. The flyer *Recreation Guide to the San Rafael Area*. DeLorme pp. 28-29, 38-39.

INFORMATION: BLM, Price Field Office. Goblin Valley SP.

GETTING THERE: You can begin at the south end, near Goblin Valley State Park, and go north to end at I-70 at exit No. 129, or vice-versa. My description begins on I-70 at exit 129, about 28 miles west of Green River. Watch for directional signs. Reset your odometer to 0.

REST STOPS: Swasey Cabin. Goblin Valley State Park. There's a pit toilet at the Little Wild Horse Canyon hiking trailhead.

THE DRIVE: From I-70, follow the road across rangeland toward the buttes, cliffs and canyons of Sinbad Country, named after scenes in *The Arabian Nights*, the centuries-old collection of folk tales from Arabia, Egypt, Persia and India. At mile 3.9 take the road on the right. At 4.1 go right again. A mile farther, as you drive among pinyon pines and junipers, go right again, through a gate. At mile 11 the main road continues straight, but go right to historic Swasey Cabin, built by ranchers in 1921. On the main road, at mile 19 you will reach a T at Taylor Flat. Go right for the Reds Canyon loop through a magnificent red-rock gash in the Earth's crust. By mile 33, as you approach towering Tomsich Butte, scan the skyline ahead for Hondoo Arch, named for its resemblance to a lariat's slip knot. The road will fork, right to the bottoms at Muddy Creek below Hondoo Arch, left to climb out of Reds Canyon and continuing the tour. Beyond Reds Canyon, return to Taylor Flat. Then it's on toward Temple Mountain, said to resemble the Mormon temple at Manti. About 0.2 mile after reaching pavement you will see reddish ghost-like anthropomorphs painted in an alcove to the left. Just beyond the Goblin Valley turnoff, a dirt road goes left (north) for a mile to another left turn that leads up narrow Temple Wash. It goes 3 miles to old uranium mines on Temple Mountain (watch out for nails). Hwy. 24 is 5.1 miles farther east. To get to Little Wild Horse Canyon, turn south toward Goblin Valley. Just after you cross the park boundary, turn right (west). The hiking trailhead is 5.4 miles; Muddy Creek is about 16.5 miles.

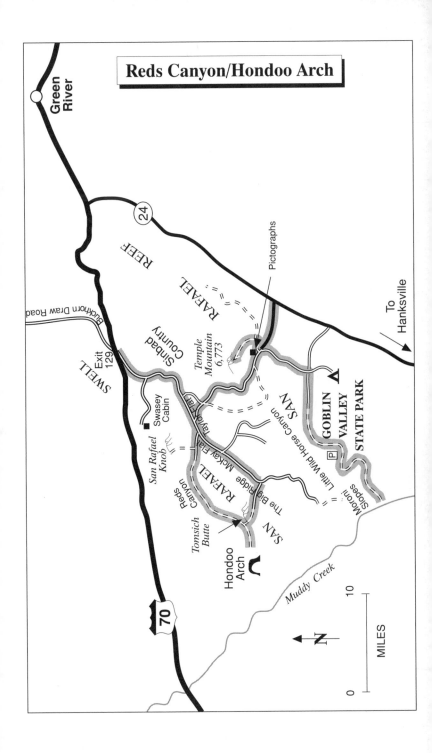

Reds Canyon/Hondoo Arch

Horseshoe Canyon to Hite

LOCATION: Between Hwys. 24 and 95, in Glen Canyon NRA's Orange Cliffs Unit and Canyonlands NP's Horseshoe Canyon Unit.

HIGHLIGHTS: This tour crosses one of Utah's most isolated and undeveloped vehicle-accessible regions, formed by eons of geologic uplifting and sediment deposition and sculpted by erosion into a spectacular landscape. The Great Gallery's famous Barrier Canyon-style pictographs are estimated to be 2,000-4,000 years old.

DIFFICULTY: Easy overall, with moderately difficult spots. The Flint Trail's switchbacks can be difficult. Summer storms can make the roads impassable. There are no services or potable water. Intersections are signed. The hikes into Horseshoe Canyon from the west and east rims involve a strenuous descent/ascent of some 800 feet. (There's an easier trail near Sugar Loaf Butte.) Be self-sufficient. Bring food, water, fuel, a portable toilet and emergency supplies.

TIME & DISTANCE: A day-and-a-half to two days; 145 miles. The Great Gallery is a 6.5-mile, 3- to 6-hour round-trip hike from the west rim. From the remote east rim, the hike is about 2 hours and 3 miles round-trip, plus time spent at the canyon's rock art sites.

MAPS: Trails Illustrated's No. 246 (Canyonlands Maze District; Northeast Glen Canyon). DeLorme pp. 29-30.

INFORMATION: Hans Flat Ranger Station. Inquire about restrictions and prohibitions on pets, fires, toilets, etc. before you go.

GETTING THERE: From I-70: Take Hwy. 24 south 24.6 miles. Just past the Goblin Valley turnoff (west), turn east onto a graded road marked by mileage signs. **From Hanksville:** Take Hwy. 24 north for 16.7 miles from the Dirty Devil River. Take the graded road east. **From Hite:** Take Hwy. 95 north across the Colorado River. 0.9 mile from the river, turn right onto Orange Cliffs Road. I start at Hwy. 24.

REST STOPS: There are primitive designated campsites; reservations are advised for April, May and October. The BLM allows camping at Horseshoe Canyon's west rim trailhead, where there is a toilet. There's also a toilet at Hans Flat. In the Orange Cliffs Unit and the Maze District, camp at designated sites. (A $25 fee is charged for a permit; you must bring a toilet.) No camping in Horseshoe Canyon.

THE DRIVE: From Hwy. 24, the graded road crosses undulating desert, climbing gradually until it reaches Hans Flat in about 46 miles. Here, amid the pinyon-juniper woodland atop the Orange Cliffs, is the Hans Flat Ranger Station, at the boundary for Glen Canyon NRA. Take the 4wd road that angles left, or north, along a high peninsula called The Spur, which provides great vistas. 12.2 miles from Hans Flat the road enters BLM land. 0.7 farther it forks; go left, toward Deadman's Trail. This segment is rougher, and ends in 4.8 miles at the foot trail to Horseshoe Canyon. Follow the cairns into the canyon (formerly called Barrier Canyon), which Barrier Creek has cut in Cedar Mesa sandstone. The Great Gallery's ghostly pictographs are in a south-facing amphitheater a bit down-canyon. (There are other sites as well.) From Hans Flat, drive 12.5 miles south to Flint Trail, which snakes down the Orange Cliffs. 2.6 miles farther is the turnoff for the Maze Overlook, 13 miles to the left (north). The road to Hite continues south along a shelf between cliffs and a canyon before descending toward Waterhole Flat. South of the Hite/Land of Standing Rocks/Sunset Pass junction, it parallels the Colorado River's Cataract Canyon (to the east) and crosses Andy Miller Flats. It improves after meandering around Rock Canyon on its way to Hwy. 95.

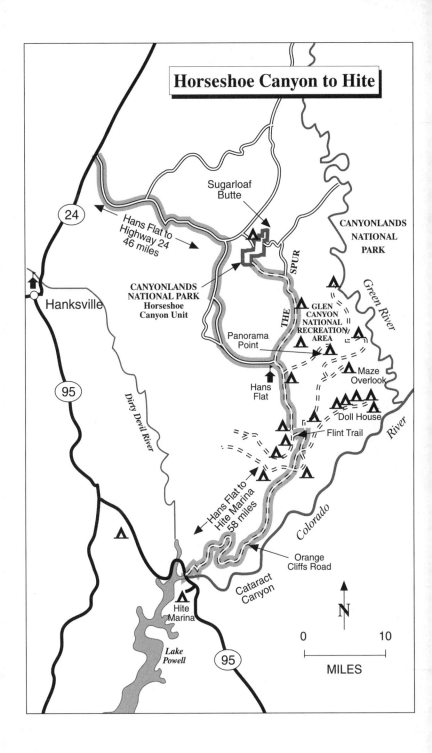

Horseshoe Canyon to Hite

Sugarloaf Butte

24

Hans Flat to
Highway 24
46 miles

CANYONLANDS
NATIONAL
PARK

Green River

CANYONLANDS
NATIONAL PARK
Horseshoe
Canyon Unit

THE SPUR

GLEN
CANYON
NATIONAL
RECREATION
AREA

Hanksville

Panorama
Point

Maze
Overlook

95

Hans
Flat

Doll House

Dirty Devil River

Flint Trail

Colorado River

Hans Flat to
Hite Marina
58 miles

Orange
Cliffs Road

Cataract
Canyon

N

Hite
Marina

0   10

95

Lake
Powell

MILES

Pahvant Range Traverse

LOCATION: In the Pahvant (also spelled Pavant) Range between Fillmore and Richfield. Fishlake National Forest.

HIGHLIGHTS: The scenic beauty is relentless along the crest of a high ridge between the Great Basin and Utah's plateau country. You might also visit the old territorial statehouse in Fillmore. Completed in 1855, it is Utah's oldest governmental building. I recommend a summer or fall visit.

DIFFICULTY: The first 6.7 miles are easy, and I rate the remainder moderate. There is some real four-wheeling along the way. The road can be muddy.

TIME & DISTANCE: 3.5 hours; 43 miles.

MAPS: Fishlake National Forest's *Fillmore, Richfield, Beaver and Loa Ranger Districts*. Trails Illustrated's No. 708 (Paiute ATV Trail). DeLorme pp. 36-37.

INFORMATION: Fishlake National Forest, Fillmore and Richfield ranger districts.

GETTING THERE: I start at Fillmore, on I-15, and end at Richfield, on I-70. But you can go in the opposite direction. From Main Street in Fillmore, take East 200 South Street (Chalk Canyon Road) east, following the U.S. Forest Service picnic area signs. 2.8 miles from Main Street the road enters Fishlake National Forest, and turns to dirt. Set your odometer to 0 here.

REST STOPS: The picnic areas along Chalk Creek, which have toilets, tables and fishing, are pleasant. Fillmore and Richfield have nice parks as well.

THE DRIVE: The one-lane dirt road, No. 100, climbs up rugged Chalk Creek Canyon into mountains of ancient lakebed sediments. The views west across the Great Basin are excellent. Between 5.4 and 6.4 miles from the forest boundary, the road passes four pretty picnic areas. It bends left at 6.7 miles, and becomes a 4x4 route as it winds up the side of the canyon. By mile 10 the serpentine track is a mere canyonside shelf. Soon it's quite rough; use 4wd. By mile 14.8 you're at about 9,200 feet, with endless vistas eastward across restless plateaus and, to the south, the Tushar Mountains, which reach 12,169 feet. By mile 17.8, at over 9,000 feet., road 100 reaches north-south road 096, the Richfield Pioneer Road, part of the popular Paiute ATV trail. Go right (south). It will be a struggle to keep your eyes on this rough road instead of the awesome scenery. By about mile 10 you will reach 9,500 feet, where the panorama stretches from the Colorado Plateau to the east across the pale Great Basin to the west. Stay on 096 for another 7.9 miles, then follow it left toward Richfield, where it meets road 500. The road improves some as you descend past rainbow-colored rock toward Richfield, staying on road 096.

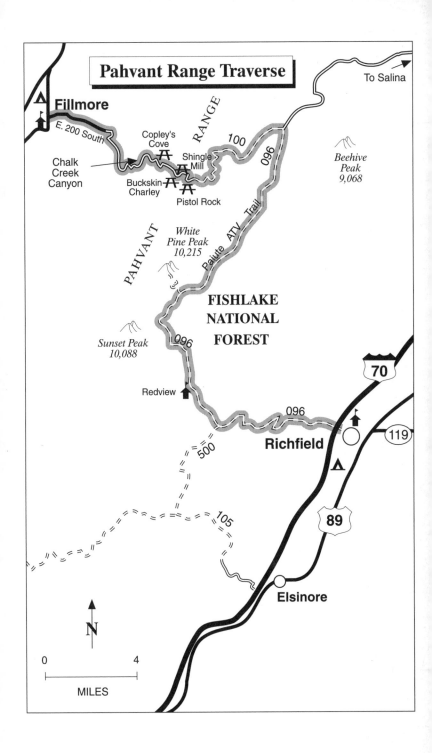

Pahvant Range Traverse

To Salina

Fillmore

E. 200 South

RANGE

100

096

Beehive
Peak
9,068

Copley's
Cove

Shingle
Mill

Chalk
Creek
Canyon

Buckskin
Charley

Pistol Rock

PAHVANT

White
Pine Peak
10,215

Paiute ATV Trail

FISHLAKE
NATIONAL
FOREST

Sunset Peak
10,088

096

70

Redview

096

500

Richfield

119

105

89

Elsinore

N

0   4

MILES

Kanosh Canyon

LOCATION: South of Kanosh, in the Pahvant (also Pavant) Range between I-70 and I-15. Fishlake National Forest.

HIGHLIGHTS: This is a pretty and relaxing summer or fall cruise through pastoral hills and scenic Kanosh Canyon.

DIFFICULTY: Easy.

TIME & DISTANCE: 1.5 hour; 24 miles.

MAPS: Fishlake National Forest's *Fillmore, Richfield, Beaver and Loa Ranger Districts*. Trails Illustrated's No. 708 (Paiute ATV Trail). DeLorme pp. 26, 36.

INFORMATION: Fillmore Ranger District.

GETTING THERE: You can take this north-south drive in either direction. I go south, ending near I-70 between Cove Fort and Fremont Indian State Park. In Kanosh, take East 300 South Street east off Main Street toward Kanosh Canyon, where the road becomes No. 106. Reset your odometer.

REST STOPS: Though it's beside the dirt road, Adelaide Campground is still very pretty. Visit Cove Fort, the best-preserved of Utah's 19th-century forts; and Fremont Indian State Park, where you can picnic and see prehistoric rock art and artifacts. You can camp at Castle Rock Campground, near the park.

THE DRIVE: The pavement will end in less than a mile, and in less than 2 more miles it enters Fishlake National Forest. Then the road continues up narrow Kanosh Canyon, along Corn Creek, taking you into the Pahvant Range. These mountains consist of lake deposits that are closely related to the brilliant pink deposits at Bryce Canyon National Park and Cedar Breaks National Monument. At mile 5.8 you will pass Adelaide Campground. The hills are vegetated with grass, sagebrush, pinyon pines and junipers, scrub oak and creekside cotton-woods. By about mile 14.3 the road crosses a low summit, at about 7,000 feet, as you follow the course of an undulating valley. As you continue south, descending gradually through rolling hills and knobby mountaintops, you will have fine views of the Tushar Mountains, which soar to 12,169 feet at Delano Peak (Tours 29 & 30 take you through them.) By mile 24.3, after passing through a rocky flat called Devil's Dance Floor and then Mud Spring Hollow, you will come to Utah Hwy. 4. I-70 is about 2 miles to the right (west), but I recommend going east to visit Fremont Indian State Park.

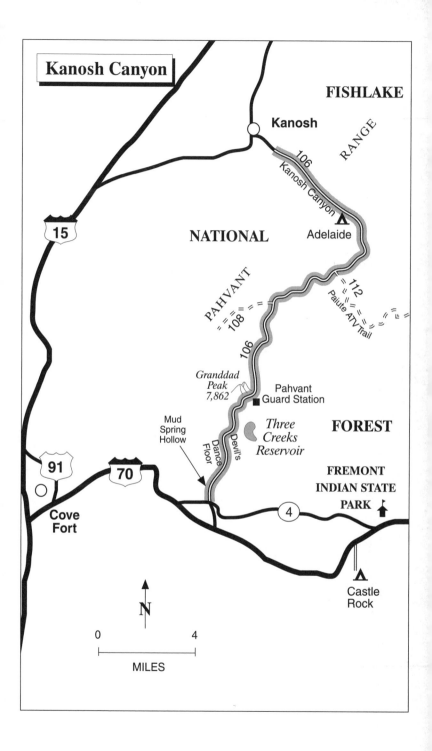

Kimberly-Big John Road

LOCATION: In the high, volcanic Tushar Mountains, northeast of Beaver and south of I-70. Fishlake National Forest.

HIGHLIGHTS: This is a thrilling summer or fall drive to over 11,400 feet. It will take you through Alpine meadows splashed with the colors of summer wildflowers, and past soaring peaks. At Fremont Indian State Park you can view prehistoric rock art and artifacts.

DIFFICULTY: Easy to moderate. Much of the land along the way is privately owned, so avoid trespassing.

TIME & DISTANCE: 2.5 hours; 30 miles.

MAPS: Fishlake National Forest's *Fillmore, Richfield, Beaver and Loa Ranger Districts*. Trails Illustrated's No. 708 (Paiute ATV Trail). DeLorme p. 26.

INFORMATION: Fishlake National Forest, Beaver Ranger District.

GETTING THERE: At Beaver, on I-15, take Utah Hwy. 153 east for about 16 miles. Turn left (north) on forest road 123, about 2.8 miles before Elk Meadows Ski Area. This is the way I go. To begin at I-70: Take road 113 off Hwy. 4 a mile west of the visitor center at Fremont Indian State Park. The southbound road passes beneath I-70. Another access is on Hwy. 153's beautiful, unpaved eastern leg from Junction, on U.S. 89.

REST STOPS: There are many primitive campsites. There are toilets at Big John Flat, developed campsites at Castle Rock Campground, and picnic sites and outstanding prehistoric rock art at Fremont Indian State Park.

THE DRIVE: You're at about 8,600 feet where you turn onto road 123. Follow the sign for Big John Flat. The somewhat rough road climbs gradually at first, through pines and aspens and open grassy areas. At Big John Flat (9,954 feet), a meadow ringed by high peaks, you will see a trailhead for the Skyline National Recreation Trail. Be sure you're in 4wd from here. The rough one-lane road switchbacks to a gap at mile 8.1, providing an inspiring view of Mt. Baldy (12,122 feet) and Mt. Belknap (12,137 feet) ahead, and Delano Peak (12,169 feet) to the southeast. You're above 11,400 feet here. The road soon edges along a hair-raising ledge at the base of exposed peaks. (More ledges are to come.) At mile 16.1 the road splits and becomes No. 113. Go left, descending toward I-70. The road, still on a ledge high above a deep canyon, improves some as you pass beneath forest canopies. At about mile 20.7 the road passes Winkler Point, which offers another great vista. In a couple of miles you will begin to see mine ruins as you pass through the sites of Upper and Lower Kimberly, late-19th- and early-20th-century camps where gold, silver, lead and copper were mined. Eventually you will see the cliffs of Red Narrows down below. Before long the road will take you through them, then beneath I-70 and into the state park.

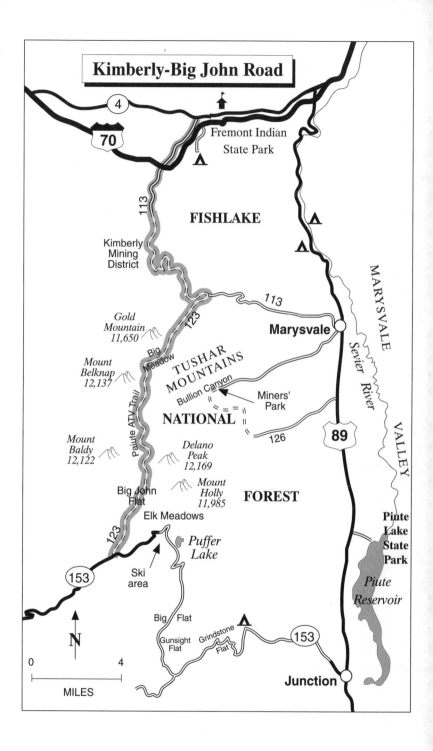

Kimberly-Big John Road

70

4

Fremont Indian
State Park

113

FISHLAKE

Kimberly
Mining
District

113

Marysvale

Gold
Mountain
11,650

123

Big
Meadow

**TUSHAR
MOUNTAINS**

Mount
Belknap
12,137

Bullion Canyon

Miners'
Park

Paiute ATV Trail

NATIONAL

126

89

Sevier River

MARYSVALE

Mount
Baldy
12,122

Delano
Peak
12,169

Mount
Holly
11,985

FOREST

123

Big John
Flat

Elk Meadows

Piute
Lake
State
Park

153

Ski
area

Puffer
Lake

Piute
Reservoir

VALLEY

Big Flat

Gunsight
Flat

Grindstone
Flat

153

N

0   4

153

Junction

MILES

Canyon of Gold

LOCATION: In the Tushar Mountains, southwest of Marysvale.

HIGHLIGHTS: This convenient tour will take you to 11,000 feet on a loop that has history, magnificent scenery and the thrill of high-elevation driving. You'll enjoy the *Canyon of Gold Driving Tour* in Bullion Canyon, and the Miners' Park historic site. Bullion Falls add to the scenic appeal. Best summer and fall.

DIFFICULTY: It's an easy 2wd road to Miner's Park, but Cottonwood Canyon is rougher, and I rate it moderate, especially if you go in the opposite direction from the way I describe.

TIME & DISTANCE: 3 hours; 23 miles.

MAPS: Fishlake National Forest's *Fillmore, Richfield, Beaver and Loa Ranger Districts.* Trails Illustrated's No. 708 (Paiute ATV Trail). DeLorme p. 26.

INFORMATION: Beaver Ranger District.

GETTING THERE: In Marysvale, turn west off U.S. 89 onto Bullion Avenue, a.k.a. Center Street. Set your odometer to 0.

REST STOPS: Picnic at Miners' Park. Hike to Bullion Falls, about a mile (one-way) from the Bullion City site. Much of the land along the drive is privately owned, so avoid trespassing.

THE DRIVE: Follow the signs for Bullion Canyon, a historic gold mining area. Soon you will see the canyon ahead. About 4.1 miles from town, the road, No. 126, enters Fishlake National Forest. Then you will see a decorated ore car on the right that announces the "Canyon of Gold" tour. Take a guide booklet from the box and put a dollar in the pipe. The booklet explains sites along the 2.5-mile drive up Pine Creek to Miner's Park. I'll let the booklet describe what you'll see, which will include a streamside *arrastra,* or grinding stone possibly used by early miners, maybe even Spaniards, to mill gold-bearing rock. At the site of Bullion City you will see where single-lane road 126 makes a left to Cottonwood Canyon. (It's 16 miles to Hwy. 89.) Bullion City once had some 1,600 people and was, for a time, the Piute County seat. Here, the official tour's end, is a wonderful historical park with old buildings and artifacts. The road to Cottonwood Canyon has turnouts that provide excellent views across Marysvale Valley to the Sevier Plateau. About 4.5 miles from the Bullion City site, the road narrows and becomes rougher with steep switchbacks. In another mile it crosses a saddle beneath 11,650-foot Edna (also Aetna) Peak. Soon it reaches a ledge at about 10,950 feet, with vistas across waves of mountains and valleys. You will see some mine trash as you approach a fork in the road, where the road makes a hard left. Descend along Cottonwood Canyon on a rough roadbed that would make for a bumpy climb in the opposite direction. Things improve, though, as you near the highway.

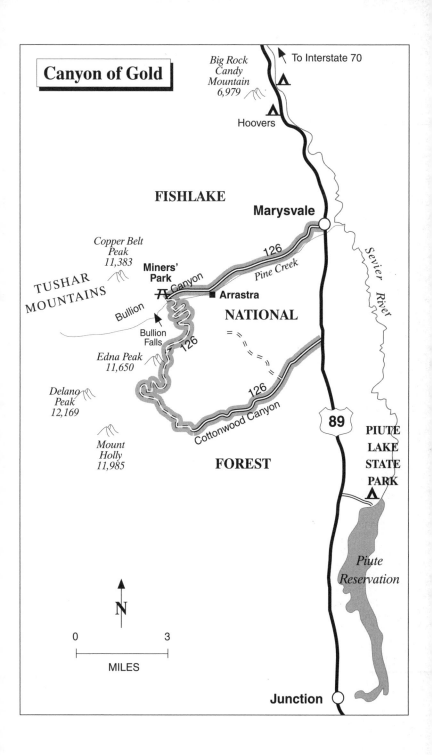

Canyon of Gold

Big Rock
Candy
Mountain
6,979

To Interstate 70

Hoovers

FISHLAKE

Marysvale

126

Pine Creek

Copper Belt
Peak
11,383

**Miners'
Park**

Canyon

Arrastra

TUSHAR
MOUNTAINS

Bullion

NATIONAL

Bullion
Falls

126

Edna Peak
11,650

Delano
Peak
12,169

126

Cottonwood Canyon

Mount
Holly
11,985

FOREST

Sevier River

89

**PIUTE
LAKE
STATE
PARK**

Piute
Reservation

N

0   3

MILES

Junction

Cove Mountain Road

LOCATION: Southeast of Richfield, on the Sevier Plateau.

HIGHLIGHTS: You will climb almost 5,000 feet through high valleys and aspen forests that promise brilliant autumn color. Best summer and fall.

DIFFICULTY: Easy to moderate. Rocky and rutted in places.

TIME & DISTANCE: 2 hours; 36 miles.

MAPS: Fishlake National Forest's *Fillmore, Richfield, Beaver and Loa Ranger Districts*. Trails Illustrated's No. 708 (Paiute ATV Trail). DeLorme pp. 27, 37.

INFORMATION: Fishlake National Forest, Richfield Ranger District.

GETTING THERE: In Richfield, take 300 North (Hwy. 119) east off Main Street. You will come to a Y where Hwy. 119 goes right toward Fishlake and Capitol Reef National Park. Take Hwy. 119 for about 4 miles, then turn right at the sign for Cove Mountain and Glenwood. In Glenwood, turn left at the stop sign at the town hall. You will come to another Y at the Glenwood Fish Hatchery. Cove Mountain Road is to the right. Set your odometer at 0.

REST STOPS: There is primitive camping at Milo's Kitchen, 1.9 miles from the intersection of roads 068 and 076.

THE DRIVE: The dirt and gravel road winds through hills of grass and sagebrush, boulders and rocks. At mile 2.8 you will reach a T. Go left, on what will become road 068 in Fishlake National Forest. The climb from the T provides fine views to the north of the Wasatch Plateau and the valleys of the Sevier and San Pitch rivers, as well as the Great Basin to the west. At about mile 4.5 the road surface becomes quite rocky. In another half-mile it crosses into the national forest, then runs along Bell Rock Ridge at about 7,400 feet. Continue climbing across broad Cove Mountain through gullies, ravines and hollows that separate slopes forested with aspens and pines. At mile 10.8, at over 8,000 feet, the road enters Hunter's Flat. Mile 13.2 will find you at Big Lake, in a basin at 9,000 feet. Continuing on 068, keep left at the next Y, where 080 branches right to Annabella Reservoir and Deep Lake. Soon you will soar to 10,200 feet and cross Magleby Pass. Descending toward Koosharem (an Indian word for a red clover, or an edible tuber that grows in the valley), you will have a view of the mountains and valleys to the east. At mile 27 is the right turn to Koosharem Guard Station, built in 1910. Two miles farther, road 068 meets road 076. Take road 076 to Koosharem, 7.4 miles farther.

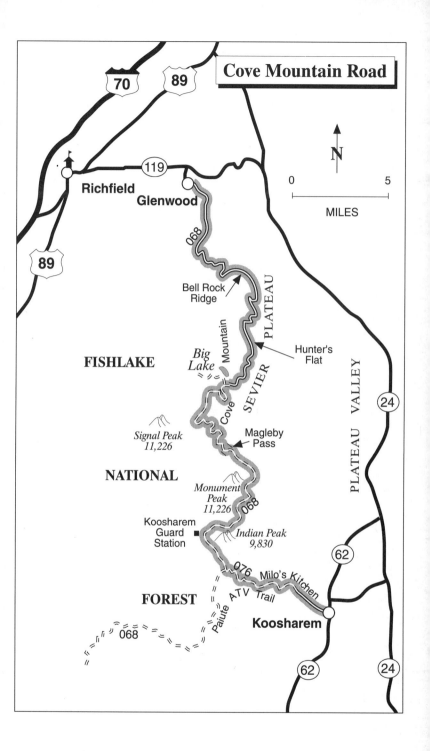

Cove Mountain Road

70 **89**

N

0 | | 5

MILES

119

Richfield

Glenwood

068

Bell Rock
Ridge

89

FISHLAKE

*Big
Lake*

Cove Mountain

SEVIER PLATEAU

Hunter's
Flat

*Signal Peak
11,226*

Magleby
Pass

NATIONAL

*Monument
Peak
11,226*

068

Koosharem
Guard
Station

*Indian Peak
9,830*

PLATEAU VALLEY

24

076 Milo's Kitchen

FOREST

Paiute ATV Trail

62

068

Koosharem

62

24

Gooseberry-Fremont Road

LOCATION: On Fishlake Plateau southeast of Salina, between I-70 and Johnson Valley Reservoir. Fishlake National Forest.

HIGHLIGHTS: The valley along Sevenmile Creek is one of the prettiest mountain valleys I know of, with wildflowers, wildlife and fine vistas. Soldier Canyon, at the north end, is beautiful as well. I suggest going in summer or fall.

DIFFICULTY: Easy, on a graded 2wd road. It can be very dusty.

TIME & DISTANCE: 1.5 hours; 30 miles.

MAPS: Fishlake National Forest's *Fillmore, Richfield, Beaver and Loa Ranger Districts*. DeLorme pp. 27, 37.

INFORMATION: Fishlake National Forest, Richfield Ranger District.

GETTING THERE: Take this north-south route in either direction. I start at Johnson Valley Reservoir and go north to I-70. About 4 miles north of Fremont, on Utah Hwy. 72, turn north onto Utah Hwy. 25 at the sign for Johnson Valley Reservoir and Fishlake National Forest. The highway, also designated road No. 036 on the Forest Service map, follows the Fremont River. 13.2 miles from Hwy. 72, turn north (right) onto dirt road No. 640. **From Salina:** Take East Main St. east. Turn right (south) onto South 300 East, and follow it through the tunnel beneath I-70. Or take I-70 east to exit 61, about 6.1 miles from the junction of I-70 and U.S. 89.

REST STOPS: Gooseberry Campground. On your way into Salina you will pass pretty Salina City Park.

THE DRIVE: The road, which some folks want paved, takes you along Sevenmile Creek through meadows bordered by aspens and pines. As you continue north you will pass verdant riparian (streamside) areas that have been fenced off to protect them from damage by cattle, and to study their recovery from the effects of grazing. This pastoral mountain valley lies at about 9,500 feet. The serene naturalness of its appearance — lush meadows and wetlands flanked by aspen forest — is striking. The road narrows to a single lane at the end of the valley, and soon takes you past 11,547-foot Mt. Terrill. You're climbing now, and at mile 10.2 the road crosses Niotche-Lost Creek Divide, at 10,550 feet. From here it descends via switchbacks toward another picturesque valley, passing the Gooseberry guard station and campground. In the distance far below lies the massive hump of the San Rafael Swell. As you descend, notice how the high-elevation vegetation is giving way to species common to drier climates. At mile 25.3, as you look out over Gooseberry Valley, you will see a small dirt road, No. 037, branching left into scenic Soldier Canyon. You can go straight 4 miles to I-70, but I recommend the pretty 7-mile drive between the high, eroded cliffs of Soldier Canyon. Salina is 10 miles from the Soldier Canyon turnoff.

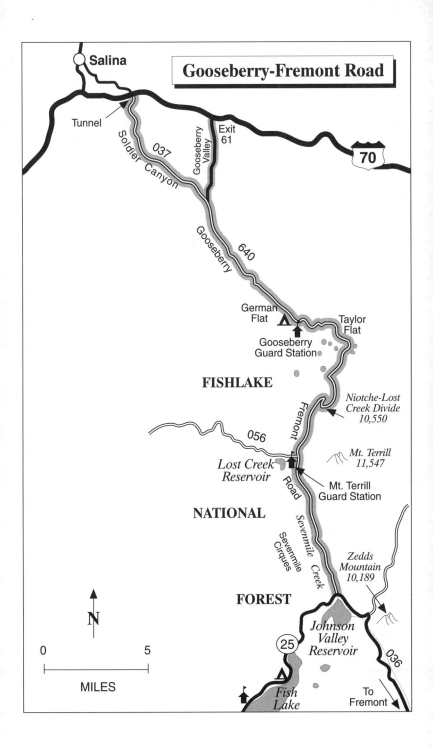

Gooseberry-Fremont Road

Golden Spike National Historic Site (Tour 1)

Old road cut along the Transcontinental Railroad Byway (Tour 1)

North Slope Road (Tour 6)

McKee Spring petroglyphs, Dinosaur National Monument (Tour 11)

Hermit's house, House Range (Tour 14)

Pony Express and Overland Stage Byway (Tour 15)

Overland Station, Pony Express & Overland Stage Byway (Tour 15)

Little Grand Canyon from the Wedge Overlook (Tour 23)

Temple Mountain, San Rafael Swell (Tour 25)

San Rafael Swell (Tour 25)

Flint Trail Overlook (Tour 26)

Delicate Arch, Arches National Park

Glass Mountain, Capitol Reef National Park (Tours 33, 34 & 35)

Cathedral Valley, Capitol Reef National Park (Tours 33, 34 & 35)

River Ford (Tour 35)

Bentonite Hills, Capitol Reef National Park (Tour 35)

Notom-Bullfrog Road and Waterpocket Fold (Tour 36)

Strike Valley Overlook, Capitol Reef National Park (Tour 36)

White Rim Road (Tour 42)

Canyon country camping

Lockhart Basin Road (Tour 44)

Pictographs, Canyonlands National Park

Tower Ruins, Horse Canyon (Tour 46)

Paul Bunyan's Potty, Horse Canyon (Tour 46)

DANCE HALL ROCK
THE ROUTE FROM ESCALANTE TO THIS SPOT WAS
RELATIVELY EASY. THE PIONEERS CAMPED ABOUT
ONE MILE SOUTH AT FORTY MILE CAMP WHILE THE
ROUTE AHEAD WAS BEING EXPLORED. SPIRITS WERE
HIGH BEFORE NEWS OF WHAT LIE AHEAD ARRIVED.
SQUARE DANCES WERE HELD WITHIN THIS HUGE
SANDSTONE AMPITHEATER KNOWN AS "THE HALL".
U.S. DEPARTMENT OF THE INTERIOR

Dance Hall Rock, Hole-In-The-Rock Road (Tour 56)

Lake Powell viewed through Hole-In-The-Rock (Tour 56)

Thousand Lake Mountain
to Cathedral Valley

LOCATION: Northeast of Fremont, in Fishlake National Forest and the northern end of Capitol Reef National Park.

HIGHLIGHTS: This loop plunges 3,000 feet from forested Thousand Lake Mountain into the high desert of Upper Cathedral Valley and the Waterpocket Fold, then it climbs back up the mountain. Best in late spring or early summer, and fall.

DIFFICULTY: Easy, although these roads can be impassable when wet, even with 4wd. There are some rocky stretches. Lower desert areas are hot in summer, when storms and flash floods occur. Snow and mud usually close the mountain roads from late October to June.

TIME & DISTANCE: 2.5 hours; 39 miles.

MAPS: Fishlake National Forest's *Fillmore, Richfield, Beaver and Loa Ranger Districts*. Recreational Map of Utah. At the park visitor center get a copy of *The Valley of Cathedrals*. DeLorme pp. 27, 28.

INFORMATION: Fishlake NF, Loa District. Capitol Reef National Park. See the park's Web site, listed at the back of the book.

SPECIAL NOTES: In the park, pets must be kept on leashes and are restricted to road corridors. Camp only in designated sites. Wood gathering is prohibited. Fires are allowed only in receptacles provided by the park. Removing anything from the park is illegal.

GETTING THERE: About 5.5 miles north of Fremont on Utah Hwy. 72, turn east onto road 206. Reset your odometer.

REST STOPS: Elkhorn Campground on Thousand Lake Mountain. Waterless Cathedral Valley Campground, near Hartnet Junction, has 5 sites and a toilet. The overlooks are great places to stop, but they have no toilets. Primitive camping is not allowed in the park.

THE DRIVE: There are a few small lakes on Thousand Lake Mountain, but it's possible that someone mistook it for the Aquarius Plateau and Boulder Mountain to the south, where there are indeed many lakes. At a Y at mile 4.5, at Heart Lake, go right toward Cathedral Valley. (The road to the left, 020, will be your return route.) Here you're at about 9,500 feet. At mile 5 turn left onto road 022, and soon you will begin the descent to Cathedral Valley. Note the contrast of aspen forest in the foreground and the great expanse of restless desert rolling into the distance. At mile 5.5 pass road 211, on the left. The tour enters the park at mile 10.8, and in another mile you will reach Hartnet Junction. You will go left here a bit later, passing Cathedral Valley Campground and continuing down the switchbacks to Upper Cathedral Valley. But for now, continue ahead to the fantastic views at Upper Cathedral Valley Overlook and Upper South Desert Overlook. In Cathedral Valley, the road passes high, intricately fluted walls, cliffs, spires and monoliths of relatively soft Entrada Sandstone capped by harder Curtis Sandstone, both from Jurassic time (135-190 MYA). Go left at Cathedral Valley Junction, along vertical slabs of upthrusting volcanic rock and up to a bench. At mile 21.7, after leaving the park, go left at the Y toward Thousand Lake Mountain, which looms beyond the oasis of rustic Baker Ranch. Soon you will re-enter the national forest, ascending the mountain on road 020, which will return you to road 206 and the highway.

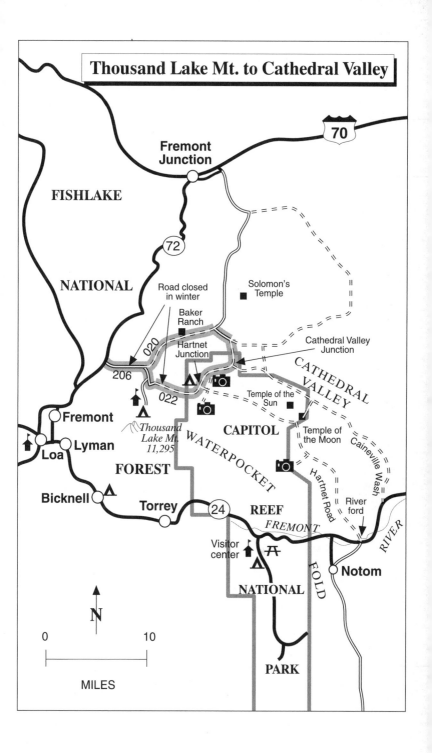

Thousand Lake Mt. to Cathedral Valley

70

Fremont Junction

FISHLAKE

72

NATIONAL

Solomon's Temple

Road closed in winter

Baker Ranch

020

Hartnet Junction

Cathedral Valley Junction

206

022

CATHEDRAL VALLEY

Temple of the Sun

Thousand Lake Mt. 11,295

CAPITOL

Temple of the Moon

Fremont

Lyman

Loa

WATERPOCKET

Caineville Wash

FOREST

Hartnet Road

Bicknell

Torrey

24

REEF

River ford

FREMONT

Visitor center

RIVER

Notom

NATIONAL

N

FOLD

0   10

MILES

PARK

Caineville Wash to I-70

LOCATION: Goes north from Utah Hwy. 24 near Caineville through Cathedral Valley in Capitol Reef NP to I-70 near Fremont Junction.

HIGHLIGHTS: Rainbow-colored hills; fascinating sandstone formations; Cathedral Valley's imposing cliffs, fins and monoliths; remote Last Chance Desert; North Caineville Reef. Best in spring and fall.

DIFFICULTY: Easy. The roads can be impassable when wet even with 4wd. It's hot in summer, when storms and floods can occur.

TIME & DISTANCE: 3 hours; 51 miles. Follows part of Tour 35.

MAPS: At the park get *Valley of Cathedrals*, a detailed guide to the route. Recreational Map of Utah. DeLorme pp. 28, 38.

INFORMATION: BLM's Henry Mountains Field Station and the Price Field Office. Capitol Reef NP. Refer to the park's Web site.

SPECIAL NOTES: In the park, pets must be kept on leashes and are restricted to roads. Camp only in designated sites. Wood gathering is prohibited. Fires are allowed only in receptacles provided by the park. Removing anything from the park is illegal. There are no services.

GETTING THERE: From Hwy. 24 (the way I take you): Drive 18.7 miles east of the park visitor center. About 0.2 mile west of Caineville, turn north at the sign for Cathedral Junction, and reset your odometer to 0. **From I-70:** About 37 miles east of Salina, or about 72 miles west of Green River, take exit 89 south and continue directly south, toward Baker Ranch and Hwy. 24.

REST STOPS: Primitive camping is allowed on BLM land, but use established sites and don't make wood fires. The park's waterless Cathedral Valley Campground has a toilet and only five sites, which are first come, first served. (A portable toilet can come in handy in this country.) There are picnic sites along Caineville Wash as well.

THE DRIVE: Driving up Caineville Wash, you will be surprised by the array of rock textures and colors: pink hues of the wash, saffron cliffs, beige ravines. On the right is upthrusted North Caineville Reef, which, like Capitol Reef and San Rafael Reef, were named after the marine reefs that were obstacles to travel. At mile 5.2 is Queen of the Wash, a large hill of colorful bentonite, a crumbly (and incredibly slick when wet) blend of volcanic ash, mud and silt deposited about 140 MYA. By mile 11, in the Middle Desert, Cathedral Valley presents its fluted cliffs, spires, fins and monoliths of Entrada Sandstone, relatively soft rock capped by harder, more erosion-resistant Curtis Sandstone. Temple of the Moon and Temple of the Sun preside near a knob of gypsum with an exaggerated name, Glass Mountain. (Don't take a piece.) At 24.8 is Cathedral Valley Junction. Turn right (north) here at a sharp, vertical volcanic rock exposure, and climb to a bench. From here, the eastern slopes of Thousand Lake Mountain and the rest of Utah's high spine melt into the eastward repose of the Last Chance Desert. Beyond Solomon's Temple, a butte east of the road some 7 miles north of Cathedral Valley Junction, the Earth's surface rises gradually toward the San Rafael Swell. High cliffs form an abrupt escarpment to the west. Go right at a Y at mile 29.4, and continue northward. A long cruise (watch for washed out spots) toward bluffs and through a broad expanse ends at a climb up Last Chance Anticline. Before arriving in pinyon-juniper woodland, you will cross flats strewn with volcanic boulders washed down from high lava fields thousands of years ago by melting ice-age glaciers. At mile 51.5 you're at I-70, at exit 89.

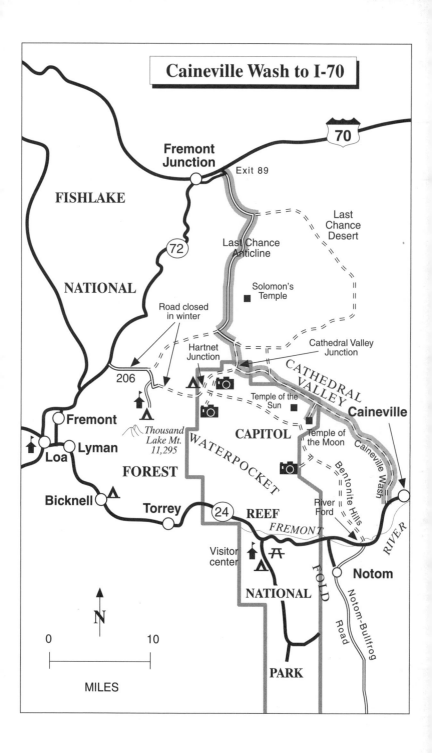

Caineville Wash to I-70

70

Fremont Junction

Exit 89

FISHLAKE

Last Chance Desert

72

Last Chance Anticline

NATIONAL

Solomon's Temple

Road closed in winter

Hartnet Junction

Cathedral Valley Junction

206

CATHEDRAL VALLEY

Temple of the Sun

Caineville

Thousand Lake Mt. 11,295

Fremont

CAPITOL

Temple of the Moon

Lyman

Loa

WATERPOCKET

FOREST

Bicknell

Torrey

24

REEF

FREMONT

River Ford

Bentonite Hills

Caineville Wash

RIVER

Visitor center

Notom

FOLD

NATIONAL

Notom-Bullfrog Road

N

0   10

MILES

PARK

River Ford to Cathedral Valley

LOCATION: North of Utah Hwy. 24. Capitol Reef National Park.

HIGHLIGHTS: Fording the Fremont River is a unique desert experience, and the moonscape of the Bentonite Hills is a strange sight indeed. The overlooks at Cathedral Valley are spectacular, and the subtle hues and eroded rocks of Caineville Wash are fascinating, especially in the golden light of late afternoon. Best in late spring and fall.

DIFFICULTY: Easy when dry, but possibly impassable when wet even with 4wd. The Fremont River has a rocky bed, and is rarely more than a foot deep. But it can be deeper after summer storms and during spring runoff. (When in doubt, walk across first. If it's too deep or fast, go up Caineville Wash, Tour 34, instead.) Avoid the Bentonite Hills when wet. There's flash-flood danger in summer due to storms.

TIME & DISTANCE: 5-6 hours; 68 miles. The drive retraces part of Caineville Wash to I-70 (Tour 34).

MAPS: Get *The Valley of Cathedrals* and the park brochure at the visitor center. Trails Illustrated's No. 707 (Fishlake National Forest & Capitol Reef National Park). DeLorme p. 28.

INFORMATION: BLM, Henry Mountains Field Station. Capitol Reef National Park. Also see the park's Internet home page.

SPECIAL NOTES: In the park, pets must be leashed and are restricted to road corridors. Camp only in designated sites. No wood gathering. Fires are allowed only in provided receptacles. Removing anything from the park is illegal. There are no services along this route.

GETTING THERE: Start at River Ford so you can check the river's level first. Take Hwy. 24 east for 11.7 miles from the park visitor center, or 7 miles west of Caineville. Turn north onto a dirt road among cottonwood trees just east of milepost 91. (You may see a sign for River Ford, Hartnet Road and other points north.) Zero the odometer and follow the road to either of two fording places.

REST STOPS: The overlooks are great, but there are no toilets. Waterless Cathedral Valley Campground, near Hartnet Junction, has a toilet and five first-come-first-served sites. There are primitive picnic areas along Caineville Wash. A portable toilet can come in handy.

THE DRIVE: Beyond the river, Hartnet Road climbs past colorful hills and Dry Wash Drop-Off. It crosses North Blue Flats, strewn with volcanic rocks washed down from high volcanic fields by melting ice-age glaciers. By mile 9 you're in the moonscape of the Morrison Formation Bentonite Hills, crumbly sediments deposited in the Jurassic Period about 140 MYA. The color-banded material is composed of volcanic ash, mud, silt and sand. Cross them to enter The Hartnet's low cliffs and sandy flats. At mile 14.1 is the turnoff to Lower South Desert Overlook. In 13 miles turn to Upper South Desert Overlook for the sight of a red trough paralleling the Waterpocket Fold. Go on to Upper Cathedral Valley Overlook and Hartnet Junction. Turn right. Take the switchbacks to the upper valley's great walls, fins, spires and monoliths of relatively soft Entrada Sandstone capped by a protective layer of younger, harder Curtis Sandstone, both from Jurassic time (135-190 MYA). Detour to gaping Gypsum Sink Hole, then follow the cliffs down Middle Desert past Layercake Wall's thin laminations. Visit Temples of the Sun and Moon, isolated sandstone siblings, then detour to Glass Mountain, a mound of gypsum (don't take a piece). Cruise along the widening desert presided over by Wood Bench and Queen of the Wash, a color-banded hill of bentonite, and finally along Caineville Wash Road to Hwy. 24.

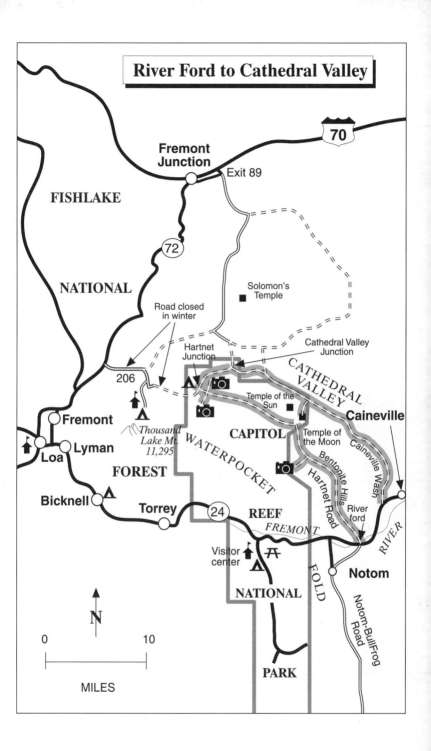

River Ford to Cathedral Valley

Notom-Bullfrog Road

LOCATION: South of Utah Hwy. 24, between the Waterpocket Fold and the Henry Mountains. It parallels and passes through Capitol Reef NP, and ends at Bullfrog, on Lake Powell in Glen Canyon NRA.

HIGHLIGHTS: This road courses down Strike Valley, between the Henry Mountains (Tour 37) and Waterpocket Fold, a spectacular 100-mile-long north-south wrinkle in the Earth's crust. It is named for depressions in the sandstone that collect water. The road links up with Burr Trail Road, where switchbacks climb 800 feet to the top of the Fold. Don't miss Upper Muley Twist Canyon's salmon-pink arches, cliffs and domes, and Strike Valley Overlook's head-spinning vista.

DIFFICULTY: Easy, on a 2wd dirt road that is impassable when wet. Summer storms often cause flooding and washouts; late spring and fall are best. The 4.9 miles south of Hwy. 24 are paved. The 24.9 miles north of Bullfrog are paved or graveled. The maintained Burr Trail Road is unpaved to the park boundary. The washbottom Strike Valley Overlook Road in Upper Muley Twist Canyon is 2wd for the first 0.5 mile. High clearance and possibly 4wd are required for the next 2.4 miles to the overlook trailhead. The overlook trail is easy.

TIME & DISTANCE: It's 1 hour and 33 miles from Hwy. 24 to Burr Trail Road; 36 miles and 45 minutes from Burr Trail Road to Bullfrog. 2.9 mile Strike Valley Overlook Road is a mile west of the top of the Burr Trail switchbacks. The hike is a quarter-mile one-way. The Halls Creek Overlook loop is 9.6 miles; allow an hour.

MAPS: At the visitor center get *The Waterpocket Fold*. The BLM's *General Recreation Map, The Henry Mountains & Surrounding Deserts*. ACSC's *Indian Country*. DeLorme pp. 20-21, 28.

INFORMATION: BLM, Henry Mountains Field Station. Capitol Reef National Park. See the park's Internet site, listed in the back.

GETTING THERE: 9 miles east of the Capitol Reef National Park visitor center, turn south from Hwy. 24 onto Notom-Bullfrog Road.

REST STOPS: Waterless Cedar Mesa CG, 21.4 miles south of Hwy. 24, has five sites. In the park, camp only in designated sites.

THE DRIVE: 65 million years ago, when geologic forces lifted the Colorado Plateau, sediments that had been laid down over hundreds of millions of years by ancient seas, tidal flats, deserts and rivers were lifted and folded. An estimated 7,000 feet of rock once lay atop what you see today, but it has eroded away. Now, the Waterpocket Fold's domes, cliffs, spires and upthrusting "reefs" only hint at its original size. The scenery is dominated by its gray-white peaks and domes of Navajo Sandstone, then the Kayenta Formation's ledges of river and stream deposits and, finally the cliffs of reddish Wingate Sandstone. Navajo and Wingate are the hardened sands of Triassic-Jurassic (144-208 MYA) deserts. Notom, at the north end, has been a ranching community for more than a century. Nearby, where the pavement ends, a fenced grave is west of the road. In it lie the remains of a 14-year-old boy killed in a horse accident in the 1880s. 13.6 miles south of Hwy. 24 is the turnoff for the drive into the Henry Mountains. 19.4 miles farther south is the west turn for Burr Trail Road. Drive up the switchbacks, then take the Strike Valley Overlook Road to the trailhead. The overlook provides an inspiring vista from atop the Fold. Notom-Bullfrog Road continues south, then bends east. 0.9 mile from where it branches south again from Clay Point Road, watch for the west turnoff for the Halls Creek (Grand Gulch) Overlook loop, which returns to Notom-Bullfrog Road 6 miles farther south.

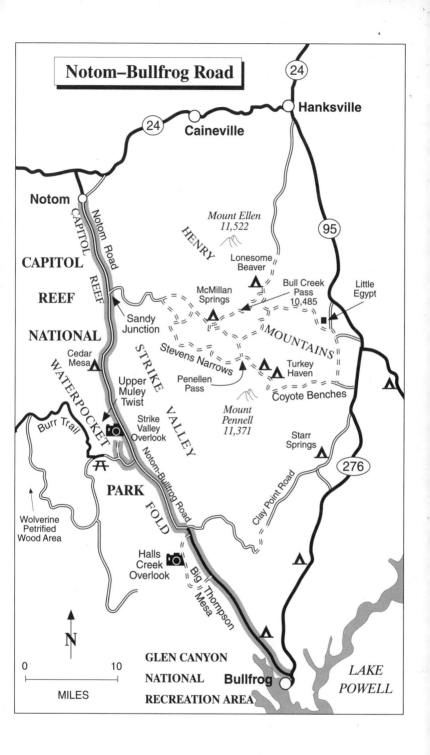

Notom–Bullfrog Road

Henry Mountains

LOCATION: South of Hanksville, east of Capitol Reef National Park and west of Utah Hwy. 95.

HIGHLIGHTS: This is the BLM's Bull Creek Pass National Back Country Byway. It goes into the soaring, granitic Henry Mountains, which rose millions of years ago through layers of sedimentary rock. Often said to be the last range in the Lower 48 to be explored and named, they rise more than 6,000 feet above the desert. In addition to vistas across the Colorado Plateau, including Capitol Reef National Park, the tour includes 10,485-foot Bull Creek Pass and the Little Egypt Geologic Site, with sphinx-shaped rocks of Entrada sandstone. Curiously, the Henrys are home to bison descended from 18 animals transplanted from Yellowstone National Park in 1941.

DIFFICULTY: Moderate. The roads are rocky, and flat tires are likely. Bull Creek Pass is generally snow-free July through October. But October's general hunting season is not the time to go.

TIME & DISTANCE: 5 hours; 68 miles.

MAPS: The BLM's *General Recreation Map, The Henry Mountains & Surrounding Deserts* is excellent. Its *Bull Creek Pass Byway* brochure is also good. ACSC's *Indian Country*. DeLorme pp. 28-29.

INFORMATION: BLM, Henry Mountains Field Station.

GETTING THERE: If you look at your map, you will see that there are a number of roads leading into and out of the Henry Mountains. To follow the official BLM Byway, the way I take you, follow Hwy. 95 south from Hanksville for 21 miles, then turn right (west) onto a dirt road. Look for signs for Little Egypt, North Wash, Crescent Creek and other points. Another way in: Take Notom-Bullfrog Road (Tour 36) south from Utah Hwy. 24 for 13.6 miles, to Sandy Junction, then turn east onto Bull Mountain Road (descending on this road lets you gaze out at the spectacular Waterpocket Fold).

REST STOPS: There are developed campgrounds at Lonesome Beaver, McMillan Springs and Starr Springs, and undeveloped campgrounds at Penellen Pass, Turkey Haven. Dandelion Flat Picnic Area is 0.5 mile north of Lonesome Beaver on the north side of the range.

THE DRIVE: At mile 1.4 is Little Egypt's curious sandstone figures. Go right at mile 3.7 to climb through hills dotted with pinyons and junipers, and by mile 12 you're among scrub oak, aspens and pines. Pass through the site of Eagle City, marked by a collapsed building, then make a hard right at 13.2. Edge along the mountainside toward Wickiup Pass. By about mile 16 you're at an intersection; go left, toward Notom. In 2.6 miles you're on Bull Creek Pass, looking across the Waterpocket Fold. This is the trailhead for a 5-mile (round-trip) hike north up 11,522-foot Mt. Ellen. Descend on a narrow road with switchbacks to McMillan Springs. At mile 26.8 there's an optional turnoff to the left that goes 8.1 miles along Salt Creek Ridge to Penellen Pass. I recommend continuing ahead, down the mountains. At 33.6, at the T at Sweetwater Creek, go left toward King Ranch. (Going right will take you on a gorgeous drive to Notom-Bullfrog Road.) In 1.9 miles go right at the Y, toward Stevens Narrows. Now you're in a colorful landscape of sandstone monoliths that are presided over by the range's five peaks. Go through Stevens Narrows. At a Y at 45.4, turn left. The road climbs 3.8 miles to Penellen Pass and The Horn. Keep right. At Straight Creek Junction go left, descending to Coyote Benches, Trachyte Ranch and Hwy. 95.

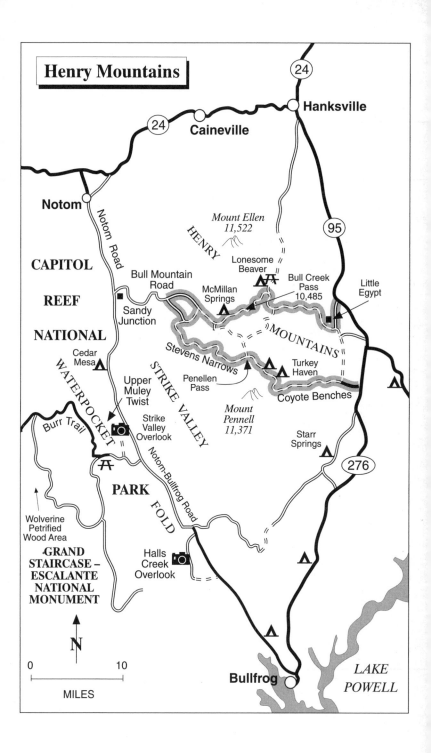

Henry Mountains

24 · Hanksville

24 · Caineville

Notom

HENRY

Mount Ellen 11,522

CAPITOL

Bull Mountain Road

Notom Road

95

REEF

Lonesome Beaver

McMillan Springs

Bull Creek Pass 10,485

Little Egypt

NATIONAL

Sandy Junction

MOUNTAINS

Cedar Mesa

WATERPOCKET

Stevens Narrows

Penellen Pass

Turkey Haven

Upper Muley Twist

STRIKE VALLEY

Coyote Benches

Burr Trail

Strike Valley Overlook

Mount Pennell 11,371

Starr Springs

Notom-Bullfrog Road

PARK

276

FOLD

Wolverine Petrified Wood Area

GRAND STAIRCASE – ESCALANTE NATIONAL MONUMENT

Halls Creek Overlook

N

0   10

MILES

Bullfrog

LAKE POWELL

Page 133

Sego Canyon

LOCATION: North of Thompson Springs and I-70.

HIGHLIGHTS: If you're traveling on I-70 west of the Utah/Colorado line, this is a convenient and rewarding side trip through the historic and prehistoric human presence in Utah. There are excellent prehistoric rock art panels from Archaic and Fremont peoples, as well as historic Ute Indian figures. The remains of the old coal town of Sego cap the tour. Spring and fall are best.

DIFFICULTY: Easy, on a high-clearance 2wd road.

TIME & DISTANCE: 1.5 hours; 10 miles round-trip.

MAPS: Recreational Map of Utah. DeLorme p. 40.

INFORMATION: Green River Visitor Center, in the John Wesley Powell History Museum. BLM, Moab Field Office.

GETTING THERE: Exit I-70 at Thompson Springs (exit 185), about 5.3 miles east of Crescent Junction/U.S. 191. Drive north through the hamlet, crossing the railroad tracks. Continue north on Thompson Canyon Road (a.k.a. Sego Canyon Road) toward the Book Cliffs and Thompson Canyon.

REST STOPS: You can get food and fuel at Thompson Springs. There are toilets and tables at the rock art site.

THE DRIVE: Once an important shipping point for cattle, Thompson Springs is now a quiet village of dusty memories. It's about 3.4 miles from town to the rock art site, which will be on the left. Three distinct styles can be seen on the rocks, from three separate cultures known to have been in this area over several thousand years. Interpretive signs will help you locate the figures (some later figures were created on top of much older figures), and identify the styles. But no one really knows what the petroglyphs (figures pecked into the rock's surface) and pictographs (painted figures) meant to the artists who created them. (**Note:** Never touch or disturb rock art.) Pavement ends just beyond the site. (On a rock face to the right, as the road crosses a cattle guard, are more pictographs.) Beyond the rock art site are the remains of trestles for the railroad that once hauled hard anthracite coal from mines in the area for use in steam-powered railroading. Continuing on Thompson Canyon Road, take the second right (a half-mile beyond the rock art site) onto Sego Canyon Road (there may be a sign). Soon you will see the old cemetery, on the right. About a mile from Thompson Canyon Road you will reach the ruins of Sego, which is private property. Founded in 1910, it once had as many as 500-600 people. It was named after Utah's state flower, the Sego lily. Sego was actually its third name. Its first was Ballard, and Neslin its second. The shells of the old American Fuel Co. store and a wood-frame boarding house still stand, and the hillsides are marked by various structures. The town existed until the mid-1950s. By then railroads had switched to diesel power, and demand for Sego's coal had waned. Most of the houses were hauled to Moab and sold. (The road continues up scenic Sego Canyon, onto the East Tavaputs Plateau, and ends in about 9.5 miles at a locked gate at the Uintah and Ouray Indian Reservation). On the return, angle left before the cemetery, and go through a railroad cut in a hill. Soon you will be back at Thompson Canyon Road. Turn left to return to I-70.

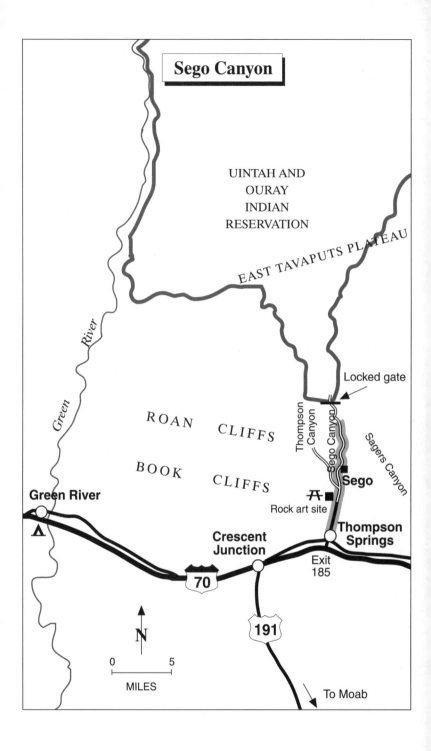

Sego Canyon

Tower Arch Loop

LOCATION: Arches National Park, north of Moab.

HIGHLIGHTS: Klondike Bluffs, Marching Men, Tower and Eye of the Whale arches, views of the La Sal Mountains. Best spring and fall.

DIFFICULTY: Salt Valley Road is easy, but impassable when wet. The rest is easy to moderate. There are rocky spots, long sandy stretches, some slickrock and ledges. It's very hot in summer.

TIME & DISTANCE: 2 hours; 22.5 miles. Allow perhaps 2 hours more to visit Tower and Eye of the Whale arches.

MAPS: The park brochure, obtained at the entrance station, is adequate. Trails Illustrated's No. 211 (Arches National Park) is best. DeLorme p. 40.

INFORMATION: Arches National Park.

SPECIAL NOTES: Pets aren't advised. They must be kept on leashes and cannot leave the road corridor. No backcountry camping is permitted along the roads. If you explore on foot or bike, stick to slickrock and washes. Never step or ride on cryptobiotic crust, the fragile topsoil you will see everywhere in canyon country. Vital to the ecology, it takes decades to recover. Check out the park's excellent Web site, listed under "Information Sources" in the back of the book.

GETTING THERE: From the park entrance follow the main park road 16.3 miles to Salt Valley Road, past Fiery Furnace. Turn onto Salt Valley Road and set your odometer to 0.

REST STOPS: Tower Arch. Picnic at Balanced Rock. Devil's Garden Campground.

THE DRIVE: Below Salt Valley is a shifting salt bed thousands of feet thick, deposited by an evaporating sea 300 million years ago. Its movement has lifted and distorted the Jurassic (144-208 MYA) salmon-hued Entrada Sandstone and buff-colored Navajo Sandstone deposited on top of it by floods, winds and oceans. That movement and erosion created the park's famous arches. On the left at mile 7.1 is the 4wd road to Tower Arch, Herdina Park and Balanced Rock. The Klondike Bluffs/Tower Arch hiking trail is a mile ahead. Go left. To the southeast rise the La Sal Mountains, once magma that pushed up against overlying sedimentary rock, creating a dome. The magma cooled, and the sedimentary cap eroded away, exposing the mountains. Soon you will see on the left the road south to Balanced Rock; you will return to it. On the right are the humps of Klondike Bluffs and the fins and spires of Marching Men. Dip into the wash ahead and go up the hill on the other side. Angle north around the bluffs' west side. You will soon reach a parking area from which you can hike to huge Tower Arch. The route to Balanced Rock follows sandy washes and crosses broad flats, with some slickrock to traverse. In the area called Herdina Park, you will descend on a stretch of soft sand.(Look right for Eye of the Whale.) Go left at Willow Flats Road to Balanced Rock and the paved park road.

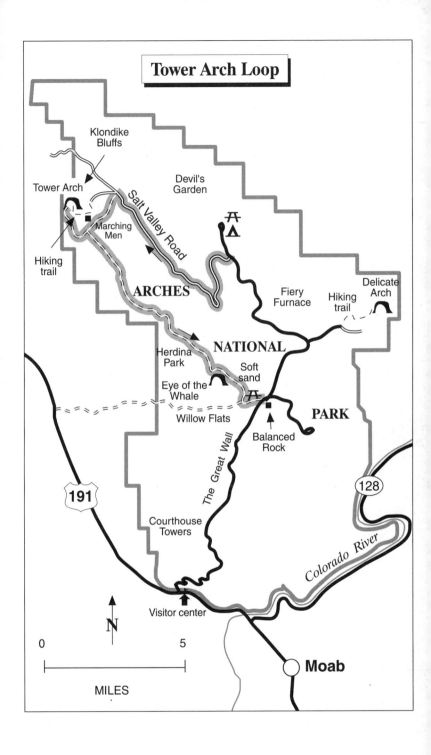

Tower Arch Loop

Klondike
Bluffs

Tower Arch

Devil's
Garden

Salt Valley Road

Marching
Men

Hiking
trail

ARCHES

Fiery
Furnace

Hiking
trail

Delicate
Arch

NATIONAL

Herdina
Park

Soft
sand

Eye of the
Whale

Willow Flats

PARK

Balanced
Rock

The Great Wall

Courthouse
Towers

128

Colorado River

191

N

Visitor center

0   5

MILES

Moab

Potash Road

LOCATION: Southwest of Moab.

HIGHLIGHTS: There are dinosaur tracks, Indian rock art sites and an arch (Jug Handle) on the way to the starting point. Watch for the signs. The scenery from the terraces and benches above the river is outstanding, and the Shafer Trail switchbacks never fail to thrill. Visit in spring or fall.

DIFFICULTY: Easy. The Shafer Trail switchbacks are exciting, with long drop-offs and views across the White Rim, but not difficult. Watch for mountain bikers. It's best spring and fall, but in a mild winter the shaded switchbacks may be driveable, though slick and dangerous.

TIME & DISTANCE: 2 hours; 24 miles.

MAPS: Trails Illustrated's No. 210 (Needles & Island In The Sky/Canyonlands National Park). DeLorme pp. 30, 40.

INFORMATION: Canyonlands National Park, Island in the Sky District. (See the park's Web site, listed at the back of the book.) BLM, Moab Field Office. Moab/Green River Information Center.

GETTING THERE: 1.3 miles north of the Colorado River bridge north of Moab, turn west off U.S. 191 toward Potash, on Utah Hwy. 279. Follow the Colorado River canyon, watching for petroglyphs and a pullout where you can look through a pipe aimed at dinosaur tracks imprinted on slabs of cliffside sandstone. The pavement ends, and the drive begins, in 16.9 miles. Set your odometer at 0.

REST STOPS: There is a small, waterless campground at Shafer Canyon (a national park permit is required), and a toilet at the White Rim Road junction.

THE DRIVE: The road climbs above the river onto a bench below towering sandstone cliffs, buttes and mesas. Ahead is 5,715-foot Pyramid Butte. At mile 3.1 follow a fence line at Moab Salt Production & Packaging's evaporation ponds. At mile 5.3 go through a gate, and in a half-mile you will see a spur going left to Pyramid Butte. It goes around the butte to a spectacular bench high above the river. 2.7 miles beyond this spur, the road angles right, around a rock outcrop. Here you can walk to a point with a head-spinning view. Other vista points will provide similar opportunities to watch the Colorado River loop around a meander called the Goose Neck. 0.9 mile from the point, the road edges between red cliffs of the Permian (245-286 MYA) Cutler Formation and the river canyon. 2 miles farther, as you continue across a limestone bed of the Elephant Canyon Formation, the road enters the park and climbs through the Middle Fork of Shafer Canyon to the junction with the White Rim Road (Tour 42). Here you will get a close-up view of ancient reddish-brown stream deposits, and then the namesake layer of White Rim Sandstone. At the junction, go right toward the head of Shafer Canyon. Yes, there's a road up the face of the cliff, narrow and steep with tight switchbacks. The old uranium haul road will take you to the top of Island in the Sky, a broad mesa, at Utah Hwy. 313.

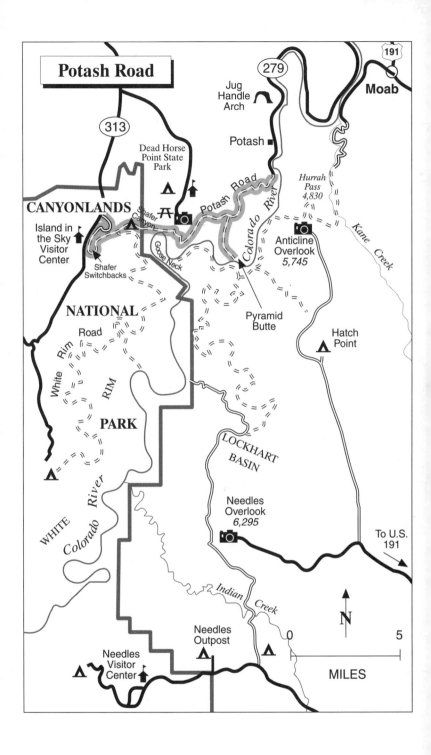

Potash Road

191

279

Moab

Jug
Handle
Arch

313

Potash

Dead Horse
Point State
Park

Potash Road

Hurrah
Pass
4,830

Colorado River

Kane Creek

CANYONLANDS

Shafer
Canyon

Anticline
Overlook
5,745

Island in
the Sky
Visitor
Center

Shafer
Switchbacks

Goose Neck

NATIONAL

Pyramid
Butte

Hatch
Point

Road

White Rim

RIM

PARK

LOCKHART
BASIN

Colorado River

Needles
Overlook
6,295

WHITE

To U.S.
191

Indian Creek

N

Needles
Outpost

0

5

Needles
Visitor
Center

MILES

La Sal Mountains

LOCATION: These mountains are just east of Moab.

HIGHLIGHTS: You will see great vistas of Canyonlands and the Colorado Rockies as you reach 10,700 feet in these lofty mountains. June through October are pleasant, but October's general hunting season might make this a place to avoid.

DIFFICULTY: Easy, on high-clearance 2wd roads.

TIME & DISTANCE: 4 hours; 106 miles (54 on dirt).

MAPS: Manti-La Sal National Forest's *Moab and Monticello Ranger Districts*. DeLorme pp. 30-31, 40-41.

INFORMATION: Moab/Monticello Ranger Districts, Moab Office.

GETTING THERE: I start at the Colorado River bridge north of Moab, on Hwy. 128. Set your odometer at 0.

REST STOPS: Big Bend Recreation Area, 7 miles from Moab on Utah Hwy. 128.

THE DRIVE: Take the highway along the Colorado River for 15.5 miles, then turn right (south) to Castle Valley at the sign. Besides the La Sals, the valley is dominated by the sandstone cliffs of Porcupine Rim and Castle Rock, which rises 2,000 feet above the valley floor. At mile 26.2 continue ahead toward Gateway Road. 0.6 mile farther you'll enter the national forest, where the road becomes No. 207. Bid asphalt farewell by mile 32, and continue east above Fisher Valley and Bull Canyon into stands of ponderosa pine. At about mile 33.9, at the turnoff to Gateway, Colo., stay on road 207, which bends south through dense scrub oak. Go right at mile 38.6, toward Sally's Hollow. About 9.8 miles later, after crossing Taylor Flat, go right again. The road climbs gently here through grassy hills, sagebrush and scrub oak. At the next Y keep left on a rocky single-lane road. If you look east, you will see Colorado's snowy San Juan Mountains far in the distance. Go right at the turnoff for Buckeye Reservoir, and 3.9 miles later pass through Canopy Gap. When you re-enter the national forest the road is 208; 1.5 miles later turn north on road 129 toward Geyser Pass. La Sal peaks dominate now. The highest, 12,721-foot Mt. Peale, looms ahead. This island range began as magma rising against the overlying sedimentary rock, creating a dome. The magma cooled before breaking through, and erosion wore the overlying sedimentary layers away, exposing the laccolithic mountains we see today. 4 miles from where you turned onto road 129, keep right at the Y. 4.7 miles farther a two-track, 723, goes a half-mile to a pretty basin. From here the main road becomes a shelf with vistas to the east. In another half-mile you will reach 10,700 feet and 3.5 miles later the road crosses Geyser Pass, 100 feet lower. Here the road, 071, becomes two-lane dirt and gravel. When you reach semi-paved La Sal Loop Road you can go left toward Moab, about 20 miles. Better yet, go right to take in the spectacular view from Castle Valley Overlook, and complete a loop by returning via Castle Valley (15 miles).

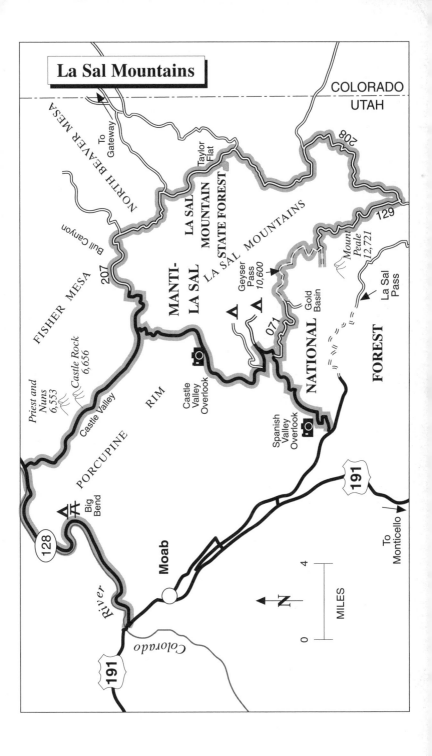

La Sal Mountains

White Rim Road

LOCATION: Canyonlands National Park, Island in the Sky District.

HIGHLIGHTS: This is one of North America's most beautiful landscapes, an eroded and incised sandstone world that rivals the Grand Canyon. It includes towering cliffs and buttes, the gorges of the Colorado and Green rivers, the pinnacles of Monument Basin, Musselman Arch and desert bighorn sheep. Best in spring and fall.

DIFFICULTY: Easy, on what is mostly a 2wd high-clearance road with some rocky stretches, narrow ledges and steep climbs. The road can be very slick when wet, so use caution if it rains.

TIME & DISTANCE: 2 1/2 days; 110 miles with spurs. Or just take day trips along segments of the road.

MAPS: Trails Illustrated's No. 210 (Needles & Island in the Sky/Canyonlands National Park), or the cheaper No. 1003 (Canyonlands-Island Recreation Map). DeLorme p. 30.

INFORMATION: Canyonlands National Park, Island in the Sky District. See the park's Web site, listed at the back of the book.

SPECIAL NOTES: Camp only in designated sites. Pets are not allowed in the backcountry. Wood fires are prohibited. Watch for mountain bikers. You will find no water, fuel or services. Summers are hot. Spring and fall are busy. Winter is a beautiful and quiet time.

GETTING THERE: From U.S. 191 north of Moab take Utah Hwy. 313 to the park entrance. Go left 0.2 miles beyond it.

REST STOPS: There are 10 camping areas (a backcountry permit & $25 reservation fee are required; reserve sites 6 months in advance, or even earlier for spring and fall). Lathrop Canyon has picnic sites.

THE DRIVE: From Island in the Sky Mesa you will plunge 1,400 feet in 4.5 miles on the Shafer Trail switchbacks, an old Indian and stock trail that was improved by prospectors and the Atomic Energy Commission during the 1950s uranium boom. You can see the White Rim Road, another boom relic, threading along a rim of white coastal sandstone left over from the Permian Period, 245-286 MYA. Above the trail is the Moenkopi Formation, brown sandstone created by tidal mud flats that existed 240-245 MYA. Far below all this, the Colorado River meanders through its breathtaking gorge. By mile 5.2 you're at Potash Road (Tour 40), on the White Rim. At 6.5 walk to a view of the river snaking around the Goose Neck. The living cryptobiotic soil crust is vital to the desert ecology, so stay off it. You will also see "potholes," depressions in the rock that teem with life after rains. Leave them alone, too. Soon you're walled in by imposing red-brown cliffs of Wingate Sandstone from a Jurassic-Triassic desert's sands. At 8.6 is Musselman Arch. 8 miles farther, go 3.7 miles down Lathrop Canyon to an oasis with tables and river access. 15 miles farther are the pillars of Monument Basin, where caps of White Rim Sandstone are perched atop eroding pedestals of softer brown Organ Shale Rock. Beyond White Crack veer north at Junction Butte, above the Green River's Stillwater Canyon. (The Green and Colorado meet south of here.) Climb up Murphy Hogback, then drop into Soda Springs Basin. Beyond Potato Bottom are more switchbacks, then a viewpoint overlooking Fort Bottom. There you can hike up the point to ancient Puebloan (Anasazi) Fort Ruin. In 4.5 miles take the 5-mile spur up Taylor Canyon to the monoliths Zeus & Moses. About 2.5 miles farther you'll leave the park. Mineral Bottom switchbacks take you to Horsethief Point. It's 13 miles more to Utah Hwy. 313.

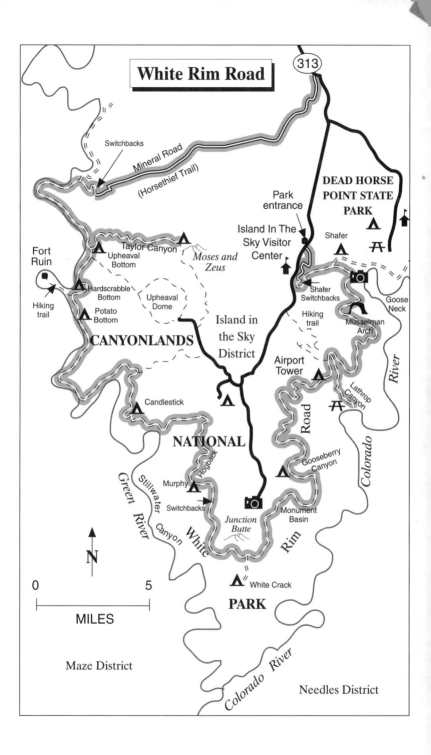

White Rim Road

313

Switchbacks

Mineral Road

(Horsethief Trail)

Park entrance

Island In The Sky Visitor Center

DEAD HORSE POINT STATE PARK

Shafer

Fort Ruin

Taylor Canyon

Upheaval Bottom

Moses and Zeus

Hardscrabble Bottom

Hiking trail

Potato Bottom

Upheaval Dome

CANYONLANDS

Shafer Switchbacks

Hiking trail

Goose Neck

Musselman Arch

Island in the Sky District

Airport Tower

Lathrop Canyon

Candlestick

Colorado River

NATIONAL

Hogback

Gooseberry Canyon

Green River

Stillwater Canyon

Murphy

White

Switchbacks

Junction Butte

Monument Basin

Rim

N

0   5

MILES

White Crack

PARK

Maze District

Colorado River

Needles District

Chicken Corners

LOCATION: BLM's Canyon Rims Recreation Area, southwest of Moab.

HIGHLIGHTS: You will have spectacular views of the Colorado River gorge and the La Sal Mountains, to the east. There are roadside petroglyphs on the way. At the end, narrow Chicken Corners, where the road is pinched between a cliff and the river canyon, is a thrill. Spring and fall are best.

DIFFICULTY: Easy to moderate. The first 4.7 miles from Moab are paved, then the road becomes gravel to Kane Creek. It's native dirt, rock and sand beyond that. Don't attempt to cross if the creek is running high, which can occur with spring runoff and during summer storms. There's a nasty spot just below Hurrah Pass, on the west side of the anticline. The road from the pass down to the benchlands above the river is quite rocky.

TIME & DISTANCE: 4 hours; about 52 miles round-trip from Moab.

MAPS: F.A. Barnes' *Canyon Rims & Needles Areas*. DeLorme p. 30 (depicts the route only as far as Lockhart Basin Road).

INFORMATION: The Moab/Green River Information Center, where you can pick up a copy of the helpful brochure, *Moab Area Jeep Trails*. BLM, Moab Field Office.

GETTING THERE: I start in downtown Moab, at Kane Creek Road and Main Street (at the McDonald's restaurant). Reset your odometer.

REST STOPS: There are no water, toilets or services of any kind. Picnic on the benchlands overlooking the river.

THE DRIVE: Take Kane Creek Road along the Colorado River through its magnificent high-walled canyon. The pavement ends at mile 4.6, where the road veers away from the river to wind up Kane Creek Canyon. At mile 6, walk down to a large boulder below the road to the right. It bears the "birthing scene" petroglyph. (Never touch or disturb rock art.) At mile 11 ford Kane Creek, then curve right and drive up the anticline to Hurrah Pass, at 4,830 feet. The high bluff to the south is Anticline Overlook. Far below are benches overlooking the river. In the distance you'll see Moab Salt Production & Packaging's evaporation ponds. There's a bad spot in the road just below the pass. In a ravine at mile 17.4, the road angles sharply right. Beyond the ravine the road becomes smooth, packed sediments as it angles south on the bench among reddish-brown Wingate Sandstone cliffs and side canyons. At mile 18.9 continue south toward Lockhart Basin Road (Tour 44), which you will reach at mile 21.4. As you continue along the bench, cliffs gradually force the road closer to the rim of the canyon, with the river some 400 feet below. Soon it's squeezed between boulders and cliffs on the left and the long, sheer drop-off to the river on the right. This is Chicken Corners. Just beyond the ledge is a turnaround area where you can enjoy the outstanding scenery directly below Dead Horse Point, at the start of the river's much-photographed meander around a hook of land called the Goose Neck. The road ends about 1.5 miles beyond Chicken Corners.

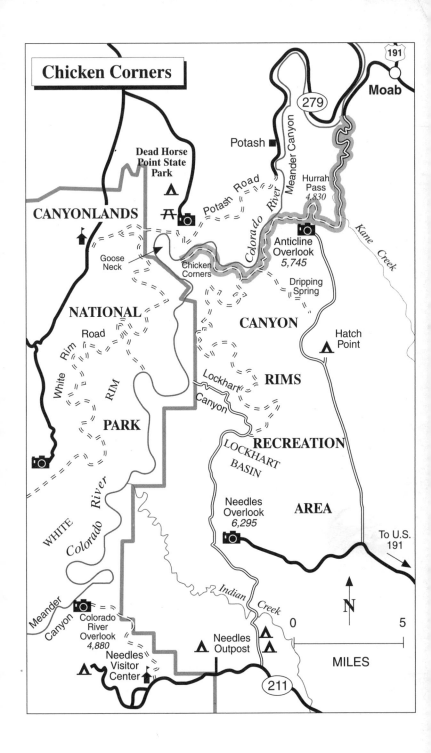

Chicken Corners

Lockhart Basin Road

LOCATION: BLM's Canyon Rims Recreation Area, just east of Canyonlands National Park.

HIGHLIGHTS: From serpentine Kane Creek Canyon to the vistas across Canyonlands, this is a red-rock adventure that will immerse you in the remote beauty of canyon country. Best in spring and fall.

DIFFICULTY: The first mile from the Hurrah Pass-Chicken Corners road (Tour 43) involves a difficult climb up a very rocky ravine. (With my wife and daughter as spotters, I maneuvered a new Toyota Land Cruiser through without a scratch.) The 20-mile journey from the top of the ravine along the bench to Lockhart Basin is slow and tedious because of the rocky roadbed and numerous small washes across the road. The segment from Lockhart Basin to Utah Hwy. 211 is on county-maintained road. Indian Creek, which you will ford at the south end, can be high in spring or after summer storms.

TIME & DISTANCE: 11 hours at least (this is a slow drive, so it's best to camp along the way); 57 miles from Moab to Hwy. 211. The dead-end segment down Lockhart Canyon adds 10.7 miles.

MAPS: F.A. Barnes' *Canyon Rims & Needles Areas*. Trails Illustrated's No. 210 (Needles & Island in the Sky/Canyonlands National Park). DeLorme p. 30.

INFORMATION: BLM, Moab Field Office. Moab/Green River Information Center.

GETTING THERE: Begin at Moab and go south to decide if you want to attempt the ravine. Take the Chicken Corners route (Tour 43) 21.4 miles from Main Street in Moab over Hurrah Pass and down to the signed junction with Lockhart Basin Road. Then go left, up the ravine. If you only want to go to Lockhart Basin, take the maintained dirt road north from Hwy. 211, east of the Needles District entrance.

REST STOPS: There are only barren, rocky and primitive campsites until you get south of Indian Creek, where there are many primitive sites and where the BLM maintains picnic tables and pit toilets at two locations. Indian Creek is a pleasant place. (Scan the cliffs on the north side for a tiny ruin.) There are no water, services or toilets until you reach the BLM sites. I recommend bringing a portable toilet.

THE DRIVE: Once you leave the Hurrah Pass-Chicken Corners road, plan your course up the rocky ravine carefully. Beyond it you will have views across the Colorado River canyon to the White Rim (Tour 42), Dead Horse Point and countless other features. About 3.6 miles beyond the ravine is a divide with a sweeping view of the sandstone remains of great deserts, seas and rivers. To the west is Island in the Sky Mesa; to the south, the pinnacles of the Needles District; to the east, the La Sal Mountains. Ahead lie miles of rocky roadbed and small washes as you drive below Hatch Point. About 14 long, tedious miles farther the amphitheater of boulder-strewn Lockhart Basin, where the road improves, appears below. In another 3.3 miles is the right turn for the spur down Lockhart Canyon to the river (access is poor). It ends at a nice spot just inside Canyonlands National Park where cliffs are etched with petroglyphs. South of the basin, you will see the glint of the kiosk at Needles Overlook high atop Wingate Sandstone cliffs formed of an ancient desert's dunes. In the distance to the south rise North and South Six Shooter Peaks. Hwy. 211 is about 15 miles south of Lockhart Basin.

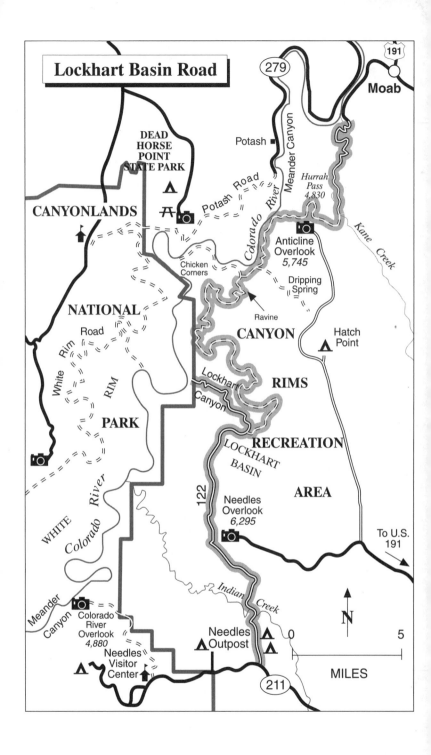

Lockhart Basin Road

191

279

Moab

DEAD
HORSE
POINT
STATE PARK

Potash

CANYONLANDS

Potash Road

Colorado River

Meander Canyon

Hurrah
Pass
4,830

Kane Creek

Chicken
Corners

Anticline
Overlook
5,745

Dripping
Spring

NATIONAL

Road

Ravine

CANYON

Hatch
Point

White Rim

RIM

CANYON

RIMS

Lockhart

PARK

Canyon

RECREATION

LOCKHART
BASIN

122

AREA

Needles
Overlook
6,295

WHITE

Colorado River

To U.S.
191

Meander
Canyon

Colorado
River
Overlook
4,880

Indian Creek

Needles
Outpost

N

0   5

Needles
Visitor
Center

211

MILES

Colorado River Overlook

LOCATION: Needles District, Canyonlands National Park.

HIGHLIGHTS: This drive provides a convenient and rewarding sampling of the Needles District's beguiling geology, including one of the district's few views of the Colorado River. Along the way are vistas that include the dramatic lower segment of Salt Creek Canyon, the Needles, the Abajo (a.k.a. Blue) and La Sal mountains. At the end, you will gaze at the gorge of the Colorado River, near the confluence with Salt Creek.

DIFFICULTY: Easy to moderate for the first six miles, with a crossing of Salt Creek wash and rocky spots to get over. I rate the last mile or so moderate to somewhat difficult because it's very rough, with ledges and roadbed rocks. Scars left on the rocks by undercarriages suggest that driving to the end isn't worth the effort. In fact, I think this final stretch is too rocky even for biking, although the park cites the road as one of the best in the district for mountain bikes. I recommend parking at mile 6 and walking the remaining mile. This road is often closed after storms. If Salt Creek is flooding, do not attempt to cross. There are no guardrails at the overlook, so be careful and do not let children get close to the edge. Pets are not allowed.

TIME & DISTANCE: Allow about 2.5 hours with time at the overlook. It's 14 miles round-trip.

MAPS: If you're planning to spend time in the Needles District, buy Trails Illustrated's No. 210 (Needles & Island in the Sky). Otherwise, the maps you receive at the entrance station will suffice for this easy-to-follow route. This road isn't shown in the DeLorme map book.

INFORMATION: Needles Visitor Center. The park has important rules about backcountry travel, so be sure to inquire. Its Internet home page, listed in the back of the book, is very good.

GETTING THERE: From U.S. 191, take Utah Hwy. 211 west to Canyonlands' Needles District visitor center. The road begins at the gate at the northwest corner of the parking lot. You will see a sign.

REST STOPS: Stop at the visitor center, the overlook, and almost anywhere else along the way that appeals to you. Fuel and other supplies are available at the Needles Outpost, just outside the park. Camping is not allowed along the road or at the overlook.

THE DRIVE: From the visitor center parking lot, the sandy single-lane road meanders gently across grassy flats and past sculpted Cedar Mesa sandstone. To the east, you can see the peaks of the La Sals. At mile 2.6 the road enters the wash of Salt Creek, where you will see little jeep signs indicating the route. The road will climb to a sandstone flat, and continue northwest, paralleling Salt Creek. Soon it will angle right (north), just upstream from Lower Jump, where the creek spills into the gorge of lower Salt Creek Canyon, which you will see as you look west toward the sandstone spires called the Needles (there is a scenic pullout at mile 4.8). At mile 6 the road becomes very rocky. You can park among the pinyon pines and junipers, or continue on if you don't mind the bumping and grinding. At road's end you will have to scramble across the jumbled sandstone to reach the overlook area, a breathtaking vantage point more than 1,000 feet above the Colorado River.

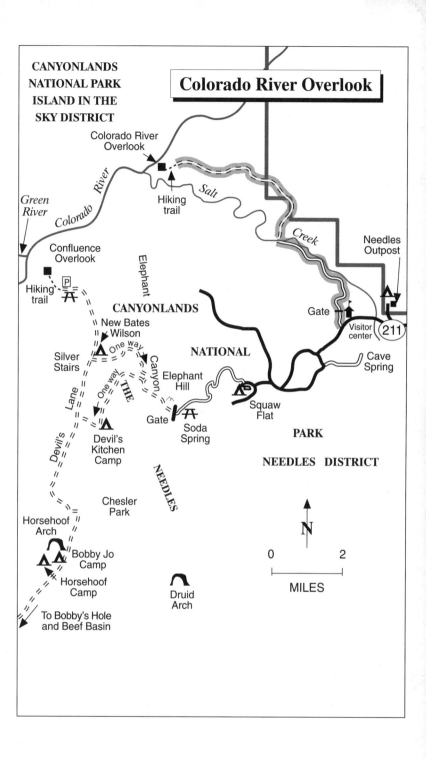

CANYONLANDS NATIONAL PARK ISLAND IN THE SKY DISTRICT

Colorado River Overlook

Colorado River Overlook

Green River

Colorado River

Salt

Creek

Hiking trail

Confluence Overlook

Needles Outpost

Hiking trail

Elephant

P

CANYONLANDS

New Bates Wilson

One way

NATIONAL

Gate

Visitor center

211

Silver Stairs

One way

THE

Canyon

Elephant Hill

Cave Spring

Devil's Lane

Gate

Squaw Flat

Devil's Kitchen Camp

Soda Spring

PARK

NEEDLES

NEEDLES DISTRICT

Chesler Park

N

Horsehoof Arch

0   2

Bobby Jo Camp

MILES

Horsehoof Camp

Druid Arch

To Bobby's Hole and Beef Basin

Horse Canyon

LOCATION: Canyonlands National Park, Needles District.

HIGHLIGHTS: Tower Ruins; Paul Bunyan's Potty; Fortress and Castle arches. There are many ancient structures and rock art sites here in the Salt Creek Archaeological District, which is listed on the National Register of Historic Places. Drive slowly and stop often to carefully scan the cliffs (bring binoculars). You can explore side canyons on foot to find them as well. Just don't trample the fragile soil crust. Best in spring and fall.

DIFFICULTY: Moderate, with stretches of soft sand. Air down your tires (15 psi or so). It's rocky for the last 200 yards. Summer storms often cause flash floods and quicksand; cancel if storms are in the area. There is a stretch of deep water on the way to Peekaboo Camp (see p. 30).

TIME & DISTANCE: 4-5 hours; about 21.2 miles round-trip from the gate.

MAPS: Trails Illustrated's No. 210 (Needles & Island in the Sky/Canyonlands National Park). DeLorme p. 30.

INFORMATION: Canyonlands National Park, the Needles District, or the park's general information number. The park's excellent Internet Web site has a great deal of information.

SPECIAL NOTES: A $5 vehicle day-use permit is required; a maximum of 10 are issued daily. Reservations are recommended for spring, fall and holiday weekends. Don't touch or in any way disturb rock art or structures. Do not enter ruins, disturb or remove artifacts. Walking near ruins can cause damage, so view them from a distance. Artifacts, archaeological sites and rock art are protected by federal law. Camp only at Peekaboo. Pets and wood fires are not allowed.

GETTING THERE: Take Utah Hwy. 211 to the Needles Visitor Center to get information, a permit and the combination to the locked gate. Turn left just past the visitor center. Follow the paved road a short distance, then go left at the sign for Salt Creek and Cave Springs. In 0.8 mile go right, onto the road to Salt Creek and Horse canyons. Unlock the gate, then lock it behind you. In 2.3 miles the road splits. Horse Canyon is left. Salt Creek Canyon, which is closed to motor vehicles beyond Peekaboo Camp to protect the riparian area from damage, is to the right. Reset your odometer.

REST STOPS: There are two campsites at Peekaboo Camp, which require a $25 reservation fee. There's a toilet at Paul Bunyan's Potty.

THE DRIVE: Archaic and ancestral Puebloan (Anasazi) Indians inhabited this area for at least 7,600 years, leaving silent buildings and mysterious rock art panels. You will be fascinated by the color-banded and complex canyons, amphitheaters and arches eroded into the Cedar Mesa sandstone, dune and sandbar deposits from the Permian Period (245-286 MYA). You will see reddish riverbed deposits as well. The canyon's marbled cliffs gradually close in. Soon you will see the arch that is appropriately named Paul Bunyan's Potty (see p. 121). A mile farther is the turn to Tower Ruins (see p. 120), Puebloan ruins tucked in a cave (don't climb up to them). At mile 7.6, pass below a cliff overhang, where your vehicle must squeeze between the overhang and a boulder. The washbottom road becomes rocky by mile 8.2. Watch on the right for the short trail to a view of Castle Arch. The road ends soon, at the start of the half-mile trail to Fortress Arch.

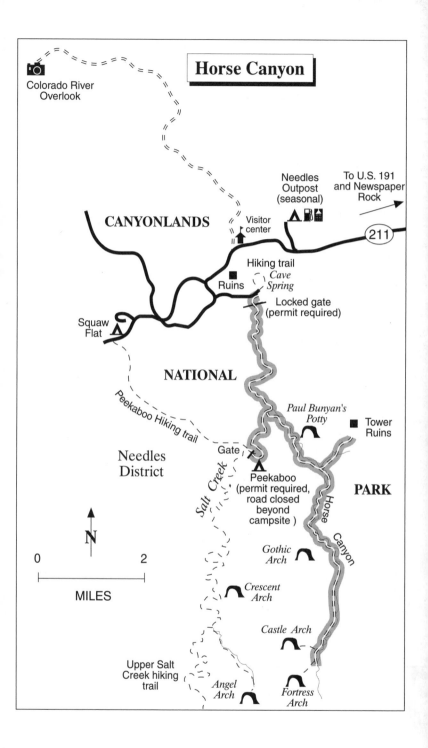

Horse Canyon

Colorado River Overlook

CANYONLANDS

Needles Outpost (seasonal)

To U.S. 191 and Newspaper Rock

Visitor center

211

Hiking trail

Cave Spring

Ruins

Locked gate (permit required)

Squaw Flat

NATIONAL

Peekaboo Hiking trail

Paul Bunyan's Potty

Tower Ruins

Gate

Needles District

Salt Creek

Peekaboo (permit required, road closed beyond campsite)

PARK

Horse Canyon

N

0   2

MILES

Gothic Arch

Crescent Arch

Castle Arch

Upper Salt Creek hiking trail

Angel Arch

Fortress Arch

Confluence Overlook

LOCATION: Needles District, Canyonlands National Park.

HIGHLIGHTS: The is the most difficult route in the book. It follows the one-way Elephant Hill Loop Road, dozed by ranchers in pre-park days and now one of Utah's most famous 4wd roads. From the rock-walled troughs called grabens to the Cedar Mesa sandstone spires of the Needles and the confluence of the Colorado and Green rivers, the sights you will encounter are unsurpassed in beauty and scale. If you're observant, you might even spot prehistoric rock art. This route can be used to access BLM-managed Beef Basin (Tour 48).

DIFFICULTY: Difficult in many places, with easy two-track segments, this route requires substantial 4wd experience. Vehicle damage is possible. The road includes washes, a narrow passage between rock walls, ledges, tight switchbacks, steep rocky grades and even a switchback that must be taken in reverse. A locking rear differential would be a great help. Air down the tires for better grip.

TIME & DISTANCE: 5-6 hours. My odometer read 15.1 miles; the Park Service map says 16.6 miles. It's a half-mile hike to the overlook.

MAPS: The route is well-marked, but bring Trails Illustrated's No. 210 (Needles & Island in the Sky). DeLorme p. 30.

INFORMATION: Needles Visitor Center. Inquire about restrictions and prohibitions on pets, wood fires, camping, etc., before you go. The park's Internet site, listed in the back of the book, is very useful.

GETTING THERE: From U.S. 191 south of Moab, take Utah Hwy. 211 to the Needles District and Squaw Flat CG. Where the paved road bends left into Campground B, follow the gravel road ahead to a picnic area. Elephant Hill Loop Road begins at a gate directly ahead.

REST STOPS: Tables and toilets are available at the starting point. There are waterless campsites (a camping permit is required and a $25 fee is charged) at Devil's Kitchen and New Bates Wilson. There are toilets at Devil's Kitchen and the overlook trailhead, but you must bring your own to New Bates Wilson. The overlook has no guardrail.

THE DRIVE: Once you've scaled the steep and rough segment at the start and reached the top, you can enjoy the view. Then comes a rocky descent, involving backing down a switchback (signs will direct you). At about mile 1.4 from the start, keep left at the fork. The route is one-way (clockwise) from here. (You will come out via the road on the right.) At 3.2 is Devil's Kitchen, where the road passes between very narrow rock walls to emerge near campsites tucked among massive sandstone outcrops. Follow the sign for Devil's Lane, about 0.6 mile farther. When you reach it, go right at the intersection (Chesler Park and Beef Basin are left) and follow the easy two-track road along the grassy graben. It will take you through more, but wider, rock narrows, then down the steps called the Silver Stairs. 0.3 mile farther is another intersection, near New Bates Wilson Camp. (The one-way road on the right is your return route to Elephant Hill.) Continue ahead to reach the short foot trail to the overlook, where you can gaze 1,200 feet down at the confluence of the Green River (on the left) and the Colorado River (on the right). The return to Elephant Hill involves another rocky downhill segment, followed by rocky streambed. When you reach the road over Elephant Hill, go left, and do the hill again.

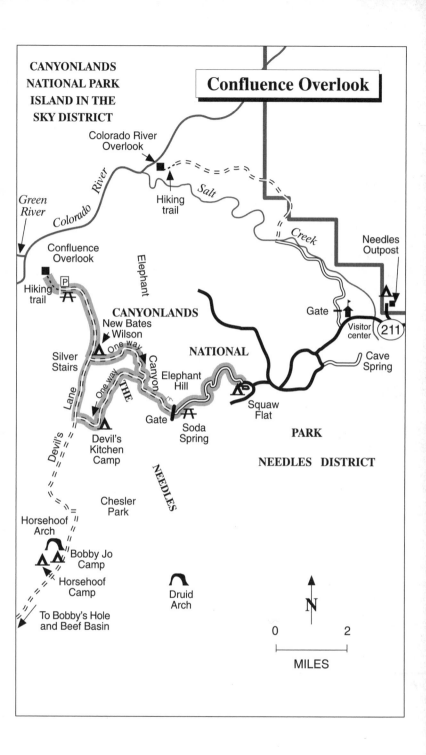

Confluence Overlook

CANYONLANDS NATIONAL PARK ISLAND IN THE SKY DISTRICT

Colorado River Overlook

Green River

Colorado River

Salt

Creek

Needles Outpost

Confluence Overlook

Hiking trail

Hiking trail

Elephant

P

CANYONLANDS

New Bates Wilson

One way

Gate

Visitor center

211

Silver Stairs

Lane

THE

One way

Canyon

NATIONAL

Elephant Hill

Cave Spring

Devil's

Devil's Kitchen Camp

Gate

Soda Spring

Squaw Flat

PARK

NEEDLES DISTRICT

NEEDLES

Chesler Park

Horsehoof Arch

Bobby Jo Camp

Horsehoof Camp

To Bobby's Hole and Beef Basin

Druid Arch

N

0   2

MILES

Beef Basin

LOCATION: BLM's Canyon Rims Recreation Area, between Canyonlands National Park's Needles District and the Abajo Mountains.

HIGHLIGHTS: There are many ancestral Puebloan (Anasazi) structures and rock art sites in this scenic basin, some close to the Beef Basin loop road. Others are up side roads. On the way to Beef Basin, which has a long history in the cattle business, are magnificent views of Cottonwood Canyon and upper Salt Creek Canyon, in the Needles District. View archaeological sites from a distance. Do not enter or climb on structures, or disturb these irreplaceable sites in any way.

DIFFICULTY: Easy. But these roads can quickly become impassable and dangerous when wet, even with 4wd.

TIME & DISTANCE: I recommend a full day. Starting from Utah Hwy. 211, expect to drive 100 miles or more round-trip. If you stick to the main loop road, it's about 80 miles round-trip. From Elk Ridge Road (Tour 50), it's about 30 miles round-trip for the loop alone.

MAPS: F.A. Barnes' *Canyon Rims & Needles Areas* is best. Trails Illustrated's No. 210 (Needles and Island In The Sky/Canyonlands National Park). Manti-La Sal National Forest's *Moab and Monticello Ranger Districts*. DeLorme p. 30.

INFORMATION: BLM, Monticello Field Office.

GETTING THERE: From Utah Hwy. 211, about 13.6 miles from the Needles entrance station or 20.3 miles from U.S. 191, turn west onto County Road 104 at the sign for Beef Basin and Elk Mountain. This is the direction I describe. Another access is from Canyonlands' Needles District via the difficult Elephant Hill 4wd road (Tour 47).

REST STOPS: Refer to your map for campgrounds in the vicinity.

THE DRIVE: The Navajo Indian word "Anasazi" has long been applied to the native people who, after occupying the Colorado Plateau for more than a thousand years, mysteriously abandoned the region by about 1300 A.D. Yet they were not Navajo, but ancestors of today's Pueblo Indians. Thus, the term Anasazi, which means "the ancient enemies" or "the ancient ones," is giving way to "ancestral Puebloan." Relics of their culture, from rock art to cliffside structures, exist throughout the Four Corners region, including Canyonlands and Beef Basin. From Hwy. 211, County Road 104 climbs gradually above North Cottonwood Creek, skirting the cliffs of Bridger Jack Mesa and entering pinyon-juniper woodland on the slopes of the Abajo Mountains. The road passes Cathedral Butte and runs along Salt Creek Mesa, above upper Salt Creek Canyon. At about mile 20.3 the road enters Manti-La Sal National Forest. Beef Basin Road, still 104, branches to the right about five miles farther, and soon enters BLM-managed land. It descends past terraced, color-banded Cedar Mesa sandstone cliffs to the signed intersection at Middle Park, where there is a registration box. From there, you can follow the road to the right (north) to Ruin Park (and even Canyonlands), where there are structures among the rocks. Or you can follow the easy but fun loop road around Beef Basin, watching for spurs that may go to ruins.

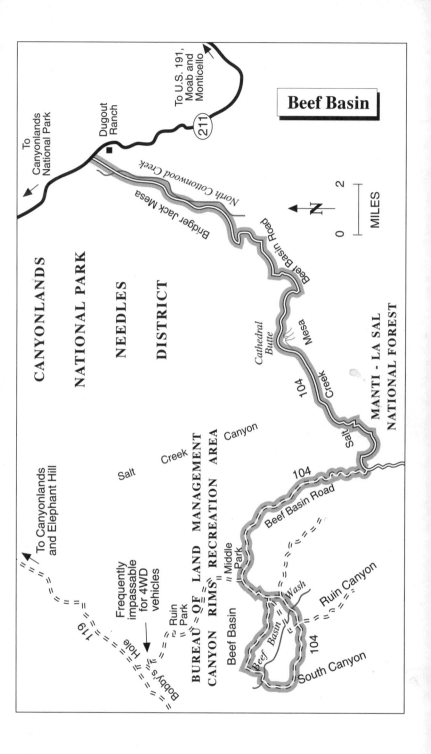

Beef Basin

Peavine Corridor

LOCATION: Northeast of Natural Bridges National Monument, in Manti-La Sal National Forest and Dark Canyon Wilderness.

HIGHLIGHTS: For those seeking a more rugged wilderness experience, this tour provides access to a deep, beautiful and forested sandstone canyon on a legal 4wd motor-vehicle corridor through Dark Canyon Wilderness. It's a great place to mix hiking and backcountry driving. You will see an arch and terraced cliffs, and you can hike to a historic cowboy cabin and oil drilling site. Best June through October.

DIFFICULTY: Easy to Little Notch; moderate to difficult in the Peavine Corridor on an unmaintained 4wd road. There are many wash crossings, and possibly washed-out sections.

TIME & DISTANCE: 6 hours; 62.5 miles round-trip from Utah Hwy. 95; or 2.5-3 hours and 17 miles round-trip from Elk Ridge Road (Tour 50). I stop at Dark Canyon, where road 089 splits.

MAPS: Manti-La Sal National Forest's *Moab and Monticello Ranger Districts*. Trails Illustrated's No. 703 (Manti-La Sal National Forest). Canyonlands Natural History Association's *Dark Canyon Trail Guide*. DeLorme 22, 30.

INFORMATION: Moab and Monticello Ranger District, Monticello Office.

SPECIAL NOTE: In the wilderness area mechanized travel is restricted to the designated corridor, which extends 66 ft. from the center of the road.

GETTING THERE: Follow the Elk Ridge Road directions (see Tour 50) to Little Notch. Or, from Hwy. 95 6.3 miles west of the Hwy. 95/U.S. 191 junction, take county road 268 to forest road 092, then Elk Ridge Road, No. 088, to Little Notch. I start at Hwy. 95.

REST STOPS: There are primitive campsites in the canyon. Natural Bridges NM has developed campsites and other facilities.

THE DRIVE: Keep right at a Y at mile 0.9 mile, where road 268 becomes dirt and gravel. You will see Elk Ridge to the west and north. At mile 11.3, in the national forest, the road narrows and becomes rougher. As you make the 3,000-foot climb to Elk Ridge, trading pinyon-juniper woodland for pine forest, the Colorado Rockies will rise to the east. Keep right at the Y at mile 19.8, taking road 088/225 toward Big Notch, a.k.a. The Notch. 2 miles farther, at Little Notch, road 089 branches left. Take it. You will soon see a sign-in box. Descend 1,300 feet in 2 miles along Kigalia Canyon on a narrow, rocky road to Peavine Canyon, amid Dark Canyon Wilderness' mix of ponderosa pines, oak, cottonwoods, and white and pink sandstone cliffs dotted with pinyons and junipers. At canyon bottom the route crosses the wash often. At 30.6, the route splits at Dark Canyon. Stop and scan the cliffs ahead for a large arch. I end the drive here, but you have two choices for easy hikes. Ahead, the old, brushy road to the left goes 1.2 miles up Rig Canyon, to a late-1920s oil drilling site. The narrow track to the right, which may be badly eroded and too dangerous to drive on, goes almost 2 miles to Scorup Cabin, a historic cowboy cabin that was moved from Rig Canyon when drilling for oil there ended in 1930.

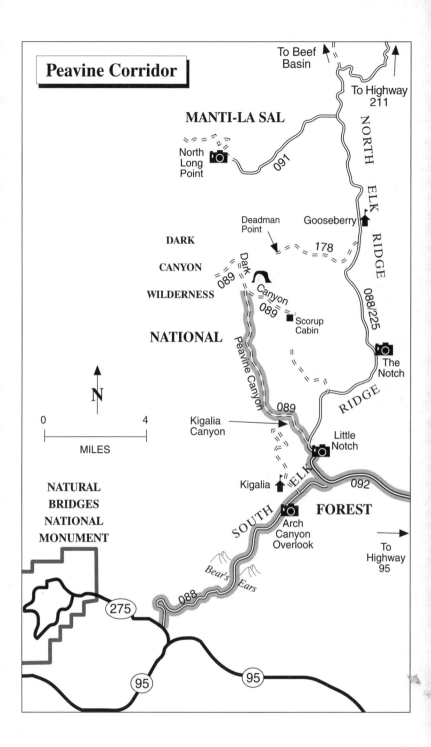

Peavine Corridor

MANTI-LA SAL

North Long Point

091

To Beef Basin

To Highway 211

NORTH ELK RIDGE

DARK

CANYON

WILDERNESS

NATIONAL

Deadman Point

Gooseberry

178

Dark Canyon 089

089

Scorup Cabin

088/225

The Notch

Peavine Canyon

089

RIDGE

Kigalia Canyon

Little Notch

Kigalia

SOUTH ELK

092

NATURAL
BRIDGES
NATIONAL
MONUMENT

Arch Canyon Overlook

FOREST

To Highway 95

N

0   4

MILES

Bear's Ears

088

275

95

95

Elk Ridge Road

LOCATION: In Manti-La Sal National Forest, north of Natural Bridges National Monument, south of Canyonlands National Park.

HIGHLIGHTS: A ridge with views of Canyonlands, Dark Canyon Wilderness, Arch and Salt Creek canyons, the Abajo, La Sal and Henry mountains. Natural Bridges NM. Best June through October.

DIFFICULTY: Easy when dry. But the roads in this country can quickly become impassable when it rains.

TIME & DISTANCE: 3-4 hours; 58 miles.

MAPS: Manti-La Sal National Forest's *Moab and Monticello Ranger Districts*. ACSC's *Indian Country*. DeLorme 22, 30.

INFORMATION: Moab and Monticello Ranger District, Monticello Office.

GETTING THERE: I go north to end at Hwy. 211. Take Hwy. 275 northwest from Hwy. 95, toward Natural Bridges. 0.7 mile from Hwy. 95 go north onto South Elk Ridge Road (forest road 088/San Juan County Road 228).

REST STOPS: There are many primitive campsites, as well as developed campgrounds at Natural Bridges National Monument, Canyonlands National Park and Newspaper Rock State Park.

THE DRIVE: The graded road climbs up Maverick Point through pinyon-juniper woodland, passing between two peaks called the Bear's Ears. Rising from the sandstone desert to the west are the Henry Mountains, igneous "island" mountains. You will pass ponderosa pines, scrub oak and aspen, and meadows. Keep right at mile 7.9. At mile 9.6, stop and gaze down into Arch and Texas canyons. At mile 11.8 go left to North Elk Ridge. When you reach the head of Hammond Canyon, at Little Notch, you will have views of the Abajo Mountains, another island range, to the east. (4wd Peavine Corridor, Tour 49, into Dark Canyon Wilderness, branches left here.) As you continue on road 088, you will have excellent views of the wilderness area's sandstone terraces. Elk Ridge Road narrows to a ledge, and at mile 19.4 you will reach The Notch, a.k.a. Big Notch. Look down into Dark Canyon to the west and Notch Canyon to the east. At 26.7, at Sego Flat, go left at the Y, toward Beef Basin. About 3.3 miles farther you can take easy 091 west to North Long Point (about 6 miles one-way) for a terrific view of Dark Canyon and Canyonlands. Forest road 088/county road 224 continues to the right, providing views of North and South Six Shooter Peaks in the distance. At 32.8 is the left turn onto Forest Road 093/County Road 104 to Beef Basin (Tour 48), famous for its abundant ancestral Puebloan (Anasazi) ruins. From here, road 93/088/104 (take your pick of designations) takes you about 25 miles to Hwy. 211, providing inspiring views of canyons, buttes and mesas. In 2 miles you're on Salt Creek Mesa, at the head of labyrinthine Salt Creek Canyon. Soon the road takes you past marbled Cathedral Butte and the soaring cliffs of Bridger Jack Mesa, then down to Hwy. 211 by mile 57.8.

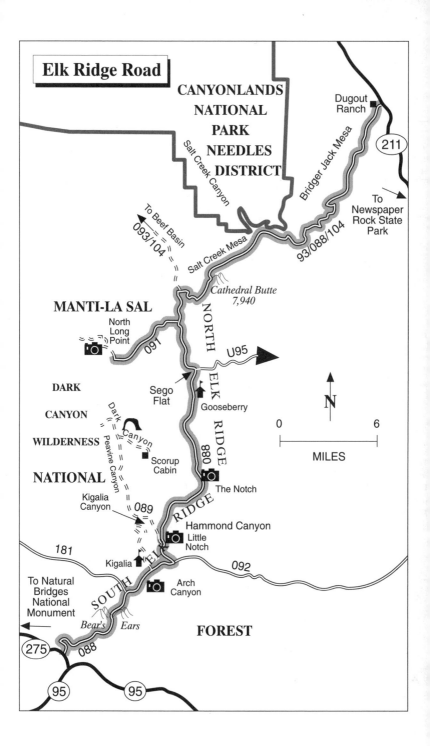

Elk Ridge Road

CANYONLANDS
NATIONAL
PARK
NEEDLES
DISTRICT

Dugout
Ranch

211

Salt Creek Canyon

Bridger Jack Mesa

To
Newspaper
Rock State
Park

To Beef Basin
093/104

Salt Creek Mesa

93/088/104

Cathedral Butte
7,940

MANTI-LA SAL

North
Long
Point

091

NORTH

U95

ELK

N

DARK

CANYON

WILDERNESS

NATIONAL

Dark
Canyon

Peavine Canyon

Sego
Flat

Gooseberry

RIDGE

880

0   6

MILES

Scorup
Cabin

The Notch

Kigalia
Canyon

089

RIDGE

Hammond Canyon

Little
Notch

181

Kigalia

092

To Natural
Bridges
National
Monument

SOUTH

ELK

Arch
Canyon

Bear's   Ears

FOREST

275

088

95   95

Abajo Mountains

LOCATION: West of Monticello, in Manti-La Sal National Forest.

HIGHLIGHTS: This is a beautiful summer-to-fall mountain drive off U.S. 191 that returns you to the highway after climbing to about 10,500 feet. You'll go through pine forest, grassy slopes and dramatic mountains on a road that at times runs along a mountainside ledge. It provides a fine view of the southern Utah desert as well.

DIFFICULTY: Easy, but the roads can be impassable after heavy rains. It's rocky and steep in places, with some switchbacks and narrow ledges.

TIME & DISTANCE: 1 hour; 21.4 miles from where the asphalt ends to where it resumes.

MAPS: Manti-La Sal National Forest's *Moab and Monticello Ranger Districts*. Trails Illustrated's No. 703 (Manti-La Sal National Forest). ACSC's *Indian Country*. DeLorme pp. 22, 30-31.

INFORMATION: Moab and Monticello Ranger District, Monticello Office.

GETTING THERE: In Monticello, go west off U.S. 191 on 2nd South toward Hart's Draw Loop Road. In 5.3 miles turn left (south) onto road No. 079, toward Blanding.

REST STOPS: You can camp at Buckboard and Dalton Springs campgrounds, near the start. The Dinosaur Museum and Edge of the Cedars State Park in Blanding are worth visiting.

THE DRIVE: Like the laccolithic La Sal and Henry mountains, the Abajos (a.k.a. Blue Mountains) are igneous laccolithic mountains that tower above the Colorado Plateau's sandstone expanse. They began as magma (molten rock) pushing up through faults and layers of sedimentary rock. The upper sedimentary layers formed a dome as the rising magma pressed against it, but the magma cooled before breaking through, and over eons the sedimentary layers were eroded away, exposing the igneous rock beneath. Abajo is Spanish for *down, below* or *underneath*. The road immediately climbs through pines and grassy slopes as you drive up North Creek Canyon to North Creek Pass, at almost 10,500 feet the high point of the route 3.9 miles from the start. Around you are peaks that exceed 11,000 feet, including 11,360-foot Abajo Peak (Tour 52) to the southeast. The road winds along a ledge high above a forested canyon, then descends along a mountainside into the canyon. By mile 7.3 you will reach Indian Creek, at the bottom of the canyon. The roadbed is loose and rocky as you climb out. After another 3 miles, as you drive through stands of ponderosa pine, you can gaze across the vast desert expanse to the south. At mile 16 the serpentine road begins to straighten out, and at mile 17.2 the Elk Ridge Road turnoff (Tour 50) will be on the right. Asphalt resumes in 4.2 miles. It's 7.8 miles to Blanding.

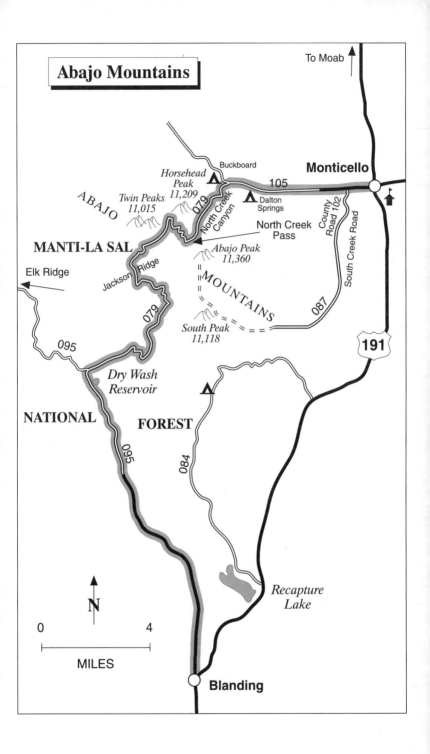

Abajo Mountains

To Moab

Buckboard

Monticello

Horsehead Peak 11,209

Twin Peaks 11,015

ABAJO

North Creek Canyon

Dalton Springs

105

North Creek Pass

County Road 102

South Creek Road

MANTI-LA SAL

079

Jackson Ridge

Abajo Peak 11,360

MOUNTAINS

Elk Ridge

095

079

South Peak 11,118

087

191

Dry Wash Reservoir

NATIONAL

095

FOREST

084

N

0   4

MILES

Recapture Lake

Blanding

Abajo Peak

LOCATION: In the Abajo Mountains west of Monticello. Manti-La Sal National Forest.

HIGHLIGHTS: 11,360-foot Abajo Peak is the highest in the Abajo Mountains, which also are known as the Blue Mountains due to the bluish hue they have when seen from a distance. The Abajo Mountains were named by the Spanish in the 1700s ("abajo" means "lower"). Abajo Peak provides an outstanding panoramic view of southeastern Utah, Colorado, and the Four Corners region where Utah, Arizona, Colorado and New Mexico meet. Another tour of these mountains is No. 51, *Abajo Mountains*.

DIFFICULTY: Easy, on a gravel road that becomes a one-lane shelf.

TIME & DISTANCE: About 45 minutes and 12.7 miles each way.

MAPS: Manti-La Sal National Forest's *Moab and Monticello Ranger Districts*. DeLorme pp. 30-31.

INFORMATION: Manti-La Sal National Forest, Moab and Monticello Ranger District, Monticello Office.

GETTING THERE: In Monticello, go west from U.S. 191 on 2nd South (North Creek Road) toward Dalton Springs and the Hart's Draw Loop Road. Just outside of town, turn left (south) onto County Road 102 (South Creek Road), at the sign for Lloyd's Lake. The road will become Forest Road 87, a.k.a 087 on the Forest Service map.

REST STOPS: There are campgrounds in the vicinity; refer to your map. Monticello has all services.

THE DRIVE: Many visitors are drawn to southeastern Utah by its breathtaking canyons, sculpted sandstone monoliths and other-worldly expanses of slickrock. But it doesn't take long to notice something else: isolated laccolithic mountain ranges, the Abajos, La Sals and Henrys, that rise thousands of feet above the Colorado Plateau. They are beautiful and unique places, yet one hears relatively little about them. Millions of years ago they were magma (molten rock), pushing up through faults and layers of sedimentary rock. The magma pressed against the overlying rock, creating great domes, but before breaking through it began to cool. Over eons, the more erodable sedimentary rock above was worn away, gradually exposing what had become harder igneous rock. The road climbs steadily, first southwest, then north below 11,118-foot South Peak, and on to Abajo Peak, the highest point in these mountains. It passes through forest of scrub oak, aspen and pine, and the views are inspiring indeed. At mile 8 the road becomes a shelf below a high slope of loose, broken rock. As you climb, you will see stands of aspen below that promise autumn color. Beyond mile 11, the road crosses several narrow saddles, including Dickson Pass. Just below the summit's electronic towers, on the right, is a spot where you can pull off the road, have lunch and take in another of Utah's great views.

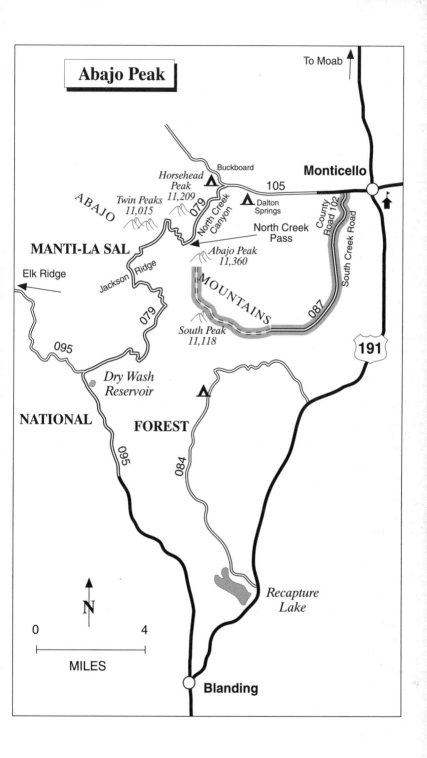

Abajo Peak

To Moab

Buckboard

Monticello

105

Horsehead Peak 11,209

Twin Peaks 11,015

079

Dalton Springs

ABAJO

North Creek Canyon

North Creek Pass

County Road 102

South Creek Road

MANTI-LA SAL

Elk Ridge

Jackson Ridge

Abajo Peak 11,360

MOUNTAINS

087

079

South Peak 11,118

191

095

Dry Wash Reservoir

NATIONAL

FOREST

084

095

Recapture Lake

N

0   4

MILES

Blanding

Posey Lake Road

LOCATION: On the Aquarius Plateau between Bicknell and Escalante. Dixie National Forest.

HIGHLIGHTS: This is an enchanting cruise across a high plateau with countless lakes to almost 10,000 feet, followed by the 4,000-foot descent into the red desert of the Escalante region. The road is closed in winter. Summer and fall are best.

DIFFICULTY: Easy, on a maintained dirt and gravel road.

TIME & DISTANCE: 2 hours; 50 miles.

MAPS: Dixie National Forest's *Escalante and Teasdale Ranger Districts*. ACSC's *Indian Country*. DeLorme pp. 19, 27.

INFORMATION: Dixie National Forest, Escalante and Teasdale Ranger Districts. Escalante Interagency Visitor Center, on Utah Hwy. 12 at Escalante's west end.

GETTING THERE: Take this north-south route either way. I go south from Bicknell, on Utah Hwy. 24. Turn south off the highway at the Utah Scenic Backway sign. The road is No. 154 in Dixie National Forest. Reset your odometer.

REST STOPS: Posey Lake. Escalante Petrified Forest State Park. The towns of Bicknell and Escalante.

THE DRIVE: The pavement ends soon, as you roll through undulating farmlands and foothills, climbing toward forested mountains on a good dirt and gravel road across the sparsely vegetated Awapa Plateau. At mile 15 you will see a two-track road up Smooth Knoll, on the right (west). It provides a panorama from about 9,350 feet of pink cliffs to the north, mountain ridges to the west and the volcanic plateau below. When the road enters the national forest, it passes alternately through woodlands and open areas, with expansive, inspiring vistas. The road passes a number of wetlands, and eventually comes to see the right turn for Griffin Top Road (Tour 54, Escalante Mountains). About 4 miles farther you will see grassy Cyclone Lake, pretty when autumn sets the aspens around it alight. The road ahead provides glimpses of the sandstone cliffs and canyons of Capitol Reef and Escalante country. Then comes the turnoff to Posey Lake, where you can picnic, camp and fish. 1.7 miles farther, pass Hell's Backbone Road, a scenic graveled road above craggy Box-Death Hollow Wilderness. As you descend from the plateau, pines largely give way to pinyon-juniper woodlands. But tall ponderosa pines grow in cracks in the Triassic-Jurassic Period Navajo Sandstone (144-208 MYA) of the spectacular Antone Bench, the high ridge to the east (left) along Pine Creek Road. Pavement is at mile 48.1. Hwy. 12 is a couple of miles farther.

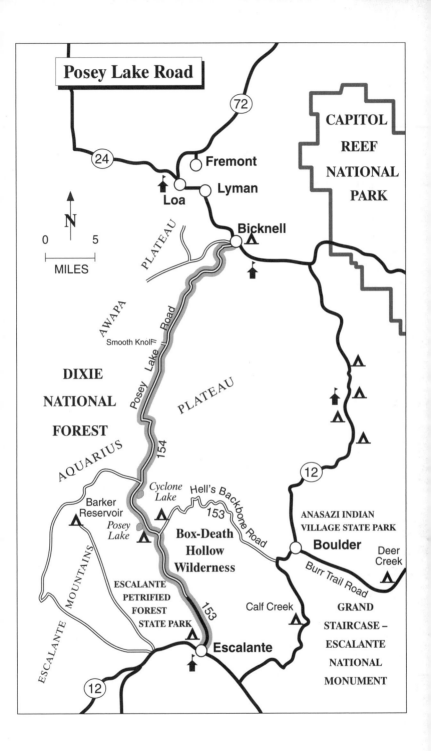

Posey Lake Road

72

24

Fremont

Lyman

Loa

Bicknell

PLATEAU

N

0 — 5
MILES

AWAPA

Smooth Knoll

Posey Lake Road

DIXIE

NATIONAL

FOREST

PLATEAU

AQUARIUS

154

12

Cyclone Lake

Hell's Backbone Road

Barker Reservoir

153

Posey Lake

Box-Death Hollow Wilderness

ANASAZI INDIAN VILLAGE STATE PARK

Boulder

Deer Creek

Burr Trail Road

ESCALANTE PETRIFIED FOREST STATE PARK

153

Calf Creek

GRAND STAIRCASE – ESCALANTE NATIONAL MONUMENT

ESCALANTE MOUNTAINS

Escalante

12

CAPITOL REEF NATIONAL PARK

Escalante Mountains

LOCATION: Dixie National Forest, northwest of Escalante.

HIGHLIGHTS: This tour will take you through high meadows and forest as it climbs to 10,500 feet. Vistas take in the Escalante River Basin, Capitol Reef National Park and Glen Canyon National Recreation Area. You may also see antelope, deer, elk and waterfowl. Box-Death Hollow Wilderness offers outstanding hiking in deep, high-walled canyons. Best in summer and fall.

DIFFICULTY: This is an easy loop on maintained dirt and gravel roads.

TIME & DISTANCE: 2.5 to 3 hours; 58 miles.

MAPS: Dixie National Forest's *Powell, Escalante and Teasdale Ranger Districts*. ACSC's *Indian Country*. DeLorme pp. 19, 27.

INFORMATION: Dixie National Forest, Escalante Ranger District. Escalante Interagency Visitor Center, on Utah Hwy. 12 (Main Street) at Escalante's west end.

GETTING THERE: In Escalante, turn north off Utah Hwy. 12 onto Pine Creek Road/Hell's Backbone Road. It becomes road 153 when it enters the national forest, then 154 as it climbs toward Posey Lake and Bicknell. Reset your odometer.

REST STOPS: Posey Lake.

THE DRIVE: For the first 21.6 miles, follow the southern leg of the Posey Lake route (Tour 53). To the east (right) rise the Antone Bench's gray-orange Navajo Sandstone cliffs, capped by rock of the Jurassic (144-208 MYA) Carmel Formation. The bench separates The Box and Death Hollow areas of Box-Death Hollow Wilderness. The road climbs about 3,700 feet onto the volcanic Aquarius Plateau, through a forest of spruce, fir and aspen. At mile 21.6, past Cyclone Lake, turn left (west) onto road 140, the Griffin Top Road. The mountain it traverses is named for sheep rancher Charles Griffin. Climb gradually through long, open meadows bordered by pine and aspen forest. At mile 28.3 you will pass through an area where large boulders have been left in fields to keep people from driving across them. Through the trees you will glimpse Escalante country's expanses of deeply carved Navajo Sandstone. At mile 35 you've peaked at about 10,500 feet on Griffin Top. In another 5 miles the views change from rolling meadows and hilltops to rugged, mountainous terrain. At mile 42 are vistas to the south and east of Capitol Reef National Park, Glen Canyon National Recreation Area and the Henry Mountains. Eventually the road reaches a T, at road No. 17 at 9,200-foot Escalante Summit. From there you can go right to John's Valley, past the remains of the old farm town of Widtsoe. I think it's more scenic to go left down Main Canyon Road (Forest Hwy. 17), along Birch Creek past terraced white and yellow cliffs whiskered with pinyon pines and junipers to reach Hwy. 12 at mile 58.5.

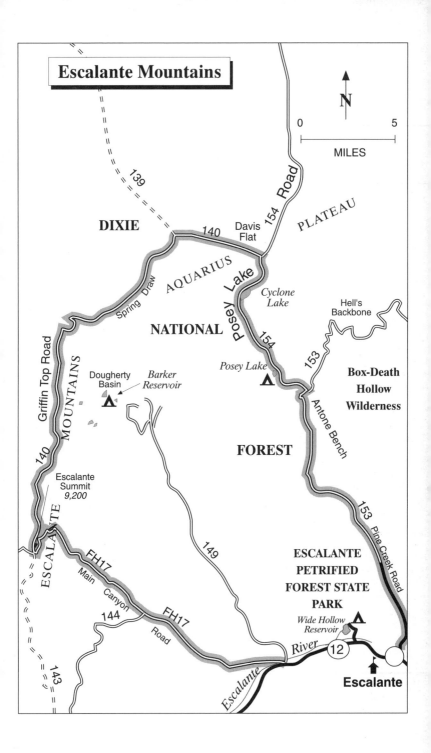

Escalante Mountains

Wolverine Loop Road

LOCATION: Grand Staircase-Escalante National Monument, southeast of Boulder. West of Capitol Reef National Park.

HIGHLIGHTS: This is a spur off the once-wild Burr Trail Road, a.k.a. Boulder to Bullfrog Road, tamed by asphalt in 1990 to the park boundary. Among the attractions are the Circle Cliffs and the Wolverine Petrified Wood Natural Area, all of it located amid one of the largest and most remote wildlands remaining in the Lower 48.

DIFFICULTY: Easy (when dry), with a high-clearance vehicle. But it can be impassable when wet, and can wash out during or after storms. There are washbottom segments as well. The hike through the petrified wood area is easy. Burr Trail Road is chip-sealed for 31 miles from Boulder to the boundary of Capitol Reef National Park. Best in spring and fall.

TIME & DISTANCE: Wolverine Loop Road is 27.8 miles; allow about 2 hours. The petrified wood area hike is about a mile, and a half-hour, each way.

MAPS: Trails Illustrated's No. 710 (Canyons of the Escalante). PLIA's *Grand Staircase-Escalante National Monument*. ACSC's *Indian Country*. DeLorme pp. 20, 28.

INFORMATION: GSENM. Escalante Interagency Visitor Center, at the west end of Escalante on Utah Hwy. 12. GSENM visitor contact station at Anasazi Indian Village State Park in Boulder. See the monument's informative Web site, listed in the back of the book.

GETTING THERE: From Boulder, on Hwy. 12: Take Burr Trail Road (a.k.a. Boulder to Bullfrog Road) 18.4 miles through Long Canyon. After you exit Long Canyon, go right (south) onto Wolverine Loop Road, and take the loop counterclockwise. (This is the direction I take you.) **From Capitol Reef National Park:** Take Burr Trail Road west from Notom-Bullfrog Road (Tour 36) for 7 miles, then turn left (south) onto Wolverine Loop Road and take the drive clockwise.

REST STOPS: The developed campgrounds at Deer Creek (7 sites; no water), along the Burr Trail Road; and at Calf Creek (13 sites, water spring through fall), on Hwy. 12 are first come, first served. Primitive campsites are listed on GSENM's Internet Web site.

THE DRIVE: Asphalt is to backcountry roads what dams are to wild rivers. Like dammed rivers, paved roads can have tributaries that recall the main stem's wild past. So it is with Wolverine Loop Road. It courses beneath the soaring Wingate Sandstone Circle Cliffs, once the dunes of a Triassic-Jurassic (144-208 MYA) desert, then crosses a grassy valley. 4 miles from Burr Trail Road, canyon walls on either side close in as the roadbed becomes sandy. (About 1.2 miles farther you will pass the 12.4-mile washbottom road down Horse Canyon. The BLM has closed it to mechanized public use, but it's still a great hike through a spectacular canyon.) 4.5 miles farther along the loop road, the Wolverine Petrified Wood Natural Area will be on the right. There, hike a mile or so up the wash of Wolverine Creek to an area in the Chinle Formation with large petrified stumps and logs, which were living trees when dinosaurs roamed the region. (No collecting is allowed.) Farther down the road, to the left, is an expanse of white sandstone that has been eroded into a maze of narrow slots and gullies. The loop road eventually reaches a T. Go left to reach Burr Trail Road in about 8.2 miles.

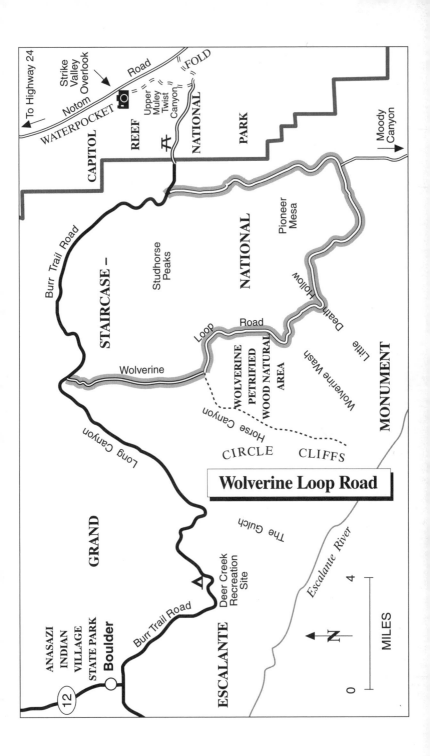

Wolverine Loop Road

Hole-In-The-Rock Road

LOCATION: Grand Staircase-Escalante National Monument and Glen Canyon NRA, between the town of Escalante and Lake Powell.

HIGHLIGHTS: Retrace the general route taken in 1879-80 by the expedition of Mormon pioneers who settled at Bluff. As you skirt the edge of the famous Escalante River canyons, ponder the sandstone figures at Devil's Garden, gaze at Chimney Rock and imagine the pioneers' music at Dance Hall Rock. At road's end, you will peer down at Lake Powell through the crack, or "hole," in the rock wall of Glen Canyon that the pioneers had to widen. Best in spring and fall.

DIFFICULTY: Most of the road is an easy (when dry), maintained 2wd road. But it can become dusty, rutted and severely washboarded. The last 5 miles are on a very rocky, moderately difficult 4wd road. The climb up to, and the descent from, Fiftymile Bench are both steep and rough (the grade at the north end is especially so). I rate them moderately difficult. I found the segment on the bench fairly easy with high clearance. All roads here are impassable when wet.

TIME & DISTANCE: 8 hours or longer; 106 miles round-trip. Chimney Rock adds 6.5 miles and 40 minutes. Fiftymile Bench, which parallels Hole-In-The-Rock Road, is 11 miles and an hour.

MAPS: Trails Illustrated's No. 710 (Canyons of the Escalante). PLIA's *Grand Staircase-Escalante National Monument.* ACSC's *Indian Country.* DeLorme pp. 19, 20.

INFORMATION: GSENM & Glen Canyon NRA. Escalante Interagency Office, at the west end of Escalante on Hwy. 12. Also see the Internet Web sites for GSENM and GCNRA, particularly the site for the Hole-In-The-Rock Road at www.nps.gov/glca/hitrdrv.htm.

GETTING THERE: 4.6 miles east of Escalante on Hwy. 12 turn southeast near the scenic turnout. Reset your odometer.

REST STOPS: Devil's Garden day-use area. Contact GSENM and Glen Canyon NRA for camping rules, regulations and sites.

THE DRIVE: Pioneer lore is replete with tales of false "shortcuts." Thus it was for the Hole-In-The-Rock expedition, 250 men, women and children with 83 wagons and 1,000 head of cattle that set out to settle at the mouth of Montezuma Creek, on the San Juan River. The road generally follows their route along the edge of the Escalante River canyons below the Straight Cliffs, at the eastern rim of Fiftymile Mountain/Kaiparowits Plateau. 12.3 miles from Hwy. 12 is the short spur to Devil's Garden; and 1.6 miles beyond that is the right (west) turn for beautiful, moderately difficult Left Hand Collet Canyon, which connects to Smoky Mountain Road (Tour 57). At mile 33.4 from the highway, a two-track goes left (east) about 2.5 miles to the spire Chimney Rock. Continue to Dance Hall Rock, a huge sandstone block hollowed by wind erosion, about 32.6 miles from Hwy. 12. The pioneers held dances here while expedition members scouted a route ahead. In Carcass Wash, 3 miles farther, seven Boy Scouts and six adults died in a road accident in 1963. Four miles farther, on the right, is the southern leg of the spur up to Fiftymile Bench, a 2,000-foot climb. (Use the rough north access for the descent.) Hole-In-The-Rock Road requires 4wd and high clearance in GCNRA. At Hole-In-The-Rock itself, ponder the pioneers who widened the crack until they could lower their wagons almost 2,000 feet to the Colorado River. To return via Fiftymile Bench, take the spur noted earlier up to the bench, then go right at the T for the 10-mile drive north and the descent on rough and steep Willow Tank Slide to Hole-In-The-Rock Road.

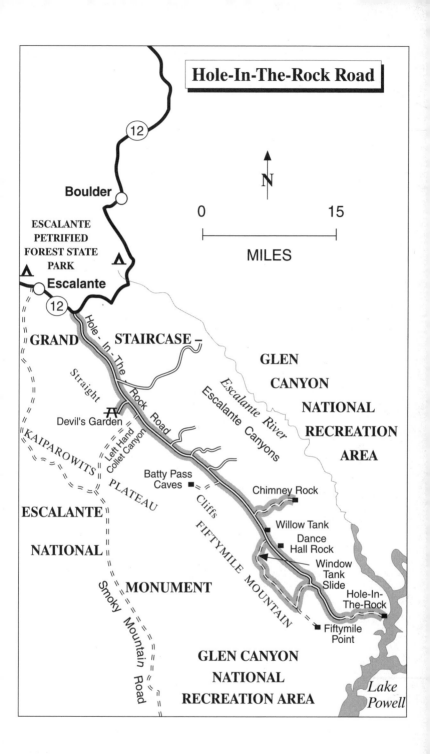

Hole-In-The-Rock Road

N

0   15

MILES

Boulder

12

ESCALANTE
PETRIFIED
FOREST STATE
PARK

Escalante

12

GRAND   STAIRCASE –

Hole- In -The- Rock Road

Straight

GLEN

CANYON

NATIONAL

RECREATION

AREA

Escalante River

Escalante Canyons

Devil's Garden

Left Hand Collet Canyon

KAIPAROWITS

PLATEAU

Batty Pass
Caves

Chimney Rock

Willow Tank

Dance
Hall Rock

ESCALANTE

NATIONAL

Cliffs

FIFTYMILE MOUNTAIN

Window
Tank
Slide

Hole-In-
The-Rock

MONUMENT

Smoky Mountain Road

Fiftymile
Point

GLEN CANYON

NATIONAL

RECREATION AREA

Lake
Powell

Smoky Mountain Road

LOCATION: This north-south road between Escalante, on Utah Hwy. 12, and Big Water, on U.S. 89 at Lake Powell, crosses the Kaiparowits Plateau, in 1.9-million-acre Grand Staircase-Escalante National Monument, created in 1996. A few miles of the drive, at the road's south end, are in Glen Canyon NRA.

HIGHLIGHTS: This road traverses one of the most remote regions in the Lower 48. The 1,400-foot ascent/descent on the switchbacks and shelf of the Kelley Grade, at the south end, is fun and the scenery awesome. Near the northern end, narrow, high-walled Left Hand Collet Canyon is a terrific adventure. There are views of Lake Powell, Bryce Canyon and Navajo Mountain as well. Spring and fall are best.

DIFFICULTY: Easy, high-clearance 2wd when dry; impassable when wet, even with 4wd. Hot, dusty in summer. Left Hand Collet Canyon is a slow washbottom 4wd route that is subject to flash floods during and after summer storms. I rate it moderately difficult. There are no facilities or services. Help will be far away. Junctions are signed, but signs often don't last long in the wild. Go well-prepared.

TIME & DISTANCE: 4-5 hours and 78 miles from Big Water to Escalante via Alvey Wash. Left Hand Collet Canyon, from Collet Top to Hole-In-The-Rock Road, is about 1.5 hours and 12.7 miles.

MAPS: PLIA's *Grand Staircase-Escalante National Monument.* ACSC's *Indian Country.* DeLorme pp. 19, 20.

INFORMATION: GSENM, including its informative Web site. The Escalante Interagency Office, at the west end of Escalante.

GETTING THERE: You can go north or south. To go south from Escalante: Turn south off Hwy. 12 at the Utah Scenic Backway sign. To go north (the way I describe): At Big Water, on U.S. 89 just west of Glen Canyon NRA, turn onto Ethan Allen Street, and follow the Utah Scenic Backway sign, and the signs for GCNRA and Hwy. 12.

REST STOPS: Check with GSENM for locations of primitive camp-sites and for fire restrictions.

THE DRIVE: From the south, the asphalt ends 2.1 miles from U.S. 89, and the roadbed becomes graded two-lane dirt and gravel. This red and yellow desert, the Warm Creek badlands, is forbidding, harsh and barren. Yet its stark beauty is overwhelming, the hues infinitely varied. To the left (north) rises Nipple Bench. To the south is Lake Powell. Ahead is Smoky Mountain, named for its burning underground coal deposits, and the 600,000-acre Kaiparowits Plateau, a high, wedge-shaped block of mesas and incised canyons. The Kaiparowits is the middle of three components of the monument. To the east are the Canyons of the Escalante. To the west is the Grand Staircase, a series of cliffs that rise north of the Grand Canyon, and which are named for their colors, e.g. Vermilion, White, Gray and Pink. At mile 3.7 the road passes through bentonite hills featured in a number of sci-fi films, including "Planet of the Apes." At 12.9 go right at a Y. At mile 13.9, pass a spur on the right. At 16.7 begin the climb onto the plateau via the Kelly Grade. By mile 21.7 you're on Smoky Mountain. The road winds around canyons amid pinyon-juniper woodland, climbing steadily, and by mile 35.7 you're at Last Chance Creek. At Collet Top (6,410 feet), at mile 47.3, either continue north to Escalante, about 32 easy miles via Alvey Wash, or go right (east) for 1.5 miles, then turn left (northeast) into Left Hand Collet Canyon for the descent to Hole-In-The-Rock Road (Tour 56), near the Escalante Canyons. Then go north for 13.6 miles to Hwy. 12.

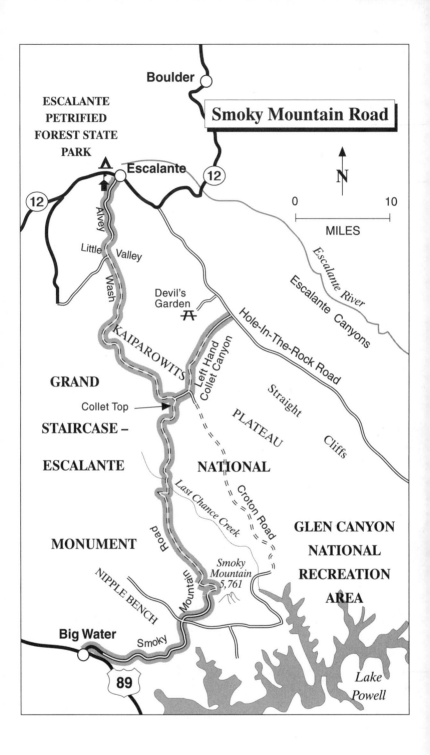

Smoky Mountain Road

Cottonwood Canyon Road

LOCATION: Grand Staircase-Escalante National Monument, between U.S. 89 (northeast of Kanab) and Hwy. 12 at Cannonville.

HIGHLIGHTS: This tour is a rainbow-hued geologic showcase that includes Kodachrome Basin State Park, Grosvenor Arch (a rare double arch), and Cottonwood Canyon, along a skyward-thrusting, saw-toothed flexure in the Earth's crust, The Cockscomb, a geologic divide between two of the monument's three components, the Grand Staircase and the Kaiparowits Plateau. Spring and fall are best

DIFFICULTY: This maintained 2wd dirt road is easy with a high-clearance vehicle when conditions are good. But weather changes its condition often, and quickly. It's dusty and washboarded after dry periods, and impassable when wet. Flash floods are possible during and after summer storms. Major washouts can occur, as in September 1998, when entire sections were washed away. It's used as a shortcut between Bryce Canyon and Glen Canyon, so it gets busy in summer.

TIME & DISTANCE: 2 hours; 46 miles, including the 2-mile (round-trip) spur to Grosvenor Arch. Add 4.6 miles and additional time to visit beautiful Kodachrome Basin.

MAPS: PLIA's *Grand Staircase-Escalante National Monument.* ACSC's *Indian Country.* Recreational Map of Utah. DeLorme p. 19.

INFORMATION: Grand Staircase-Escalante National Monument's visitor contact station in Cannonville. See the monument's Internet Web site, where you can check road conditions and get other important and useful information. Also contact Kodachrome Basin State Park. The BLM's Paria Contact Station (no telephone) is on U.S. 89 about 3 miles west of the Cottonwood Canyon Road turnoff.

GETTING THERE: Travel either north from U.S. 89 east of Kanab, or south from Hwy. 12 at Cannonville. I describe it going north.

REST STOPS: Kodachrome Basin has camping, showers, picnic tables and supplies. Contact GSENM, or see its Web site, for locations of primitive campsites. There are picnic areas at Grosvenor Arch. There's also a day-use area and some Western movie set buildings a few miles north of U.S. 89, not far from the old Pahreah townsite.

THE DRIVE: From soaring arches and colossal sandstone domes to fanciful hoodoos and spires, serpentine canyons and the upthrusting points of the "cockscomb," this tour takes you through a colorful geologic wonderland sculpted by geologic forces, wind, water and time. From the south, the undulating road passes below the cliffs of Brigham Plain as it meanders toward the Paria River. As you drive through and along The Cockscomb, which resembles a long line of jagged lower teeth, you're following a "strike valley" of relatively soft, more easily eroded shale and clay flanked by high "hogbacks," or humps, of harder Navajo, Page and Straight Cliff sandstones. To the east, the Kaiparowits Plateau rises to more than 7,000 feet. To the west is the Grand Staircase, geologic "steps" that rise north of the Grand Canyon, and which are named for their colors, e.g. Vermilion, White, Gray and Pink. At mile 26.4 north of U.S. 89, the road enters narrows of fanciful salmon-pink and white hoodoos, domes and cliffs. Stop here and walk into the narrows of Cottonwood Creek just west of the road. In another 3.3 miles turn right (east) to see Grosvenor Arch. Back on the main road, ford Rock Springs Creek, and in 2 miles pavement resumes near Kodachrome Basin. Hwy. 12 is 7.3 miles farther.

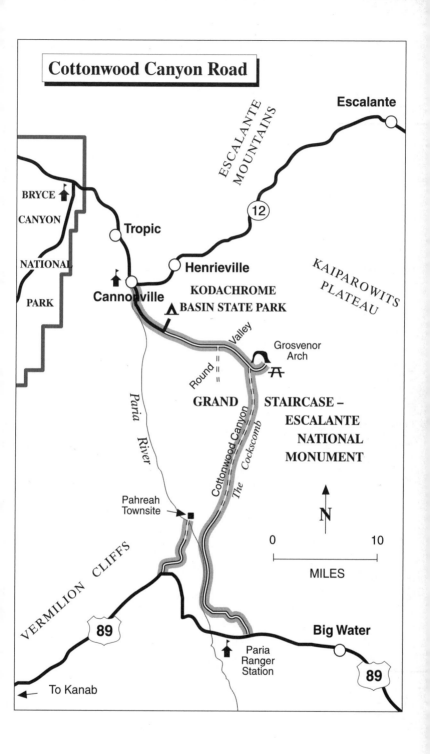

Cottonwood Canyon Road

Escalante

ESCALANTE MOUNTAINS

BRYCE CANYON NATIONAL PARK

Tropic

12

Henrieville

KAIPAROWITS PLATEAU

KODACHROME BASIN STATE PARK

Cannonville

Valley

Grosvenor Arch

Round

GRAND STAIRCASE – ESCALANTE NATIONAL MONUMENT

Paria River

Cottonwood Canyon

The Cockscomb

N

0   10

MILES

Pahreah Townsite

VERMILION CLIFFS

89

Big Water

Paria Ranger Station

To Kanab

89

Dry Lakes/Summit Canyon

LOCATION: East of Cedar City and I-15.

HIGHLIGHTS: This is a particularly beautiful drive, especially in autumn, with outstanding views of the Great Basin and the pink cliffs of Cedar Breaks National Monument. There are pretty stretches through stands of aspen and pine as well as you climb more than 3,000 feet. It's best June through October.

DIFFICULTY: Easy, but steep and somewhat rocky in places. Closed in winter. Watch for logging trucks and deer.

TIME & DISTANCE: 1 hour; 20.6 miles.

MAPS: The 1982 edition of Dixie National Forest's *Pine Valley and Cedar City Ranger Districts* more clearly and accurately depicts the road than the 1995 edition. ACSC's *Indian Country* is good as well. DeLorme pp. 17, 18.

INFORMATION: Iron County. Cedar City Ranger District.

GETTING THERE: From I-15, exit at Summit, north of Cedar City. A half-mile north of Summit go east on the dirt and gravel road toward Hurricane Cliffs. Reset your odometer to 0.

REST STOPS: Brian Head Ski Area. Cedar Breaks National Monument.

THE DRIVE: As you drive east toward the escarpment of the Hurricane Cliffs, which rise from the Hurricane Fault, you're crossing a geologic frontier. Behind you, the Great Basin spreads westward. Directly ahead, to the east, the Hurricane Cliffs welcome you to the Colorado Plateau and the many smaller plateaus that comprise Utah's spectacular plateau country. Beyond the cliffs rise the Markagunt (Paiute for *highland of trees*) Plateau and the Paunsaugunt (Paiute for *home of the beaver*) Plateau. The road climbs steadily up Summit Canyon, then steeply as it angles south through mostly private land. You'll be amazed by the view west across the checkerboard fields of the Parowan and Cedar valleys and the Escalante Desert, where the southernmost evidence of ice age Lake Bonneville is found. At mile 5.3 the road takes you past Summit Mountain. At mile 10.8, the road enters Dixie National Forest, where it becomes No. 265. (You will leave and enter the national forest several times.) By mile 12.3 the road climbs above 9,700 feet as it crosses Sugarloaf Mountain. At mile 12.4 is a pullout where you can gaze at the ancient lakebed deposits that formed Cedar Breaks. Descend along Dry Lakes Creek to reach Hwy. 143 at 20.6. Brian Head Ski Area is 4 miles south.

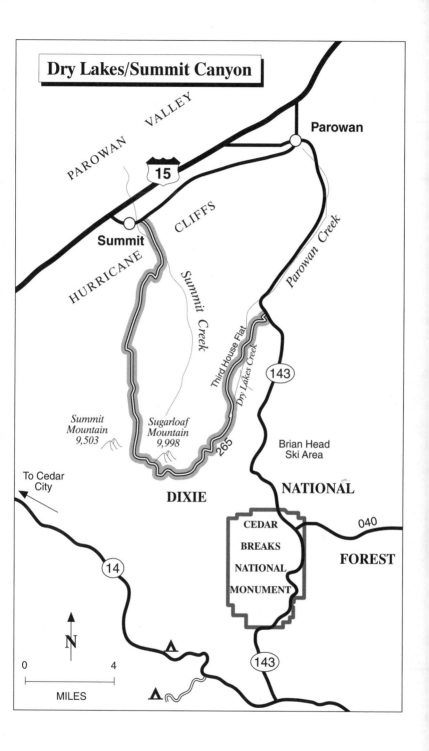

Dry Lakes/Summit Canyon

Pink Cliffs

LOCATION: West of Bryce Canyon National Park, along the East Fork of the Sevier River.

HIGHLIGHTS: The brilliant pink cliffs you will see are much like those in the park, but smaller and without the crowds. The cruise along Podunk Creek is very pretty as well. I suggest going June through October.

DIFFICULTY: Easy to moderate.

TIME & DISTANCE: 3 hours; 56 miles.

MAPS: Dixie National Forest's *Powell, Escalante and Teasdale Ranger Districts*. Trails Illustrated's No. 705 (Paunsaugunt Plateau, Mt. Dutton, Bryce Canyon). DeLorme p. 18.

INFORMATION: Dixie National Forest's Powell Ranger District.

GETTING THERE: Take Utah Hwy. 12 about 10.8 miles east from U.S. 89. Turn south onto wide, graveled East Fork of the Sevier River Road (a Utah Scenic Backway) that becomes No. 087 in Dixie National Forest.

REST STOPS: There's camping at Tropic Reservoir, and many fine picnic spots along the way as well.

THE DRIVE: For miles the road resembles an unpaved highway as it parallels the East Fork of the Sevier River, the longest river entirely in Utah. It goes up a valley on the Paunsaugunt (a Paiute Indian word for *home of the beaver*) Plateau. Here and there you will see eroded pink and white rock, Tertiary (1.6-66.4 MYA) lakebed deposits suggestive of the sights in Bryce Canyon. Pass Tropic Reservoir, and at mile 15.2 pass road 099, which branches left up Podunk Creek to the park boundary (a locked gate blocks access). Soon you will see the Podunk guard station. At Dairy Hollow, mile 17.7, go left toward Crawford Creek on road 092. Climb 2.2 miles to 8,511-foot Crawford Pass. Turn right here onto a rougher road, No. 203. It climbs 3.6 miles to the rim of dramatically eroded pink cliffs. Just beyond them is a Y. The tour goes left, following road 203 down Pipeline Canyon. Road 215 goes right; take it 0.5 mile, then go left on a spur. About a mile from 215 the road ends atop a flat with a panoramic view, from almost 9,400 feet, of more brilliant cliffs, Bryce Canyon and much of canyon and plateau country. Descend Pipeline Canyon for views of the pink cliffs you looked down on earlier. In 4.3 miles road 203 reaches rougher road 092, at Meadow Canyon. Go left to Crawford Pass. There, turn right on road 098 (there might be a sign saying it's No. 1211) and follow it down to Podunk Creek and road 092. Turn right (north), and return to Hwy. 12.

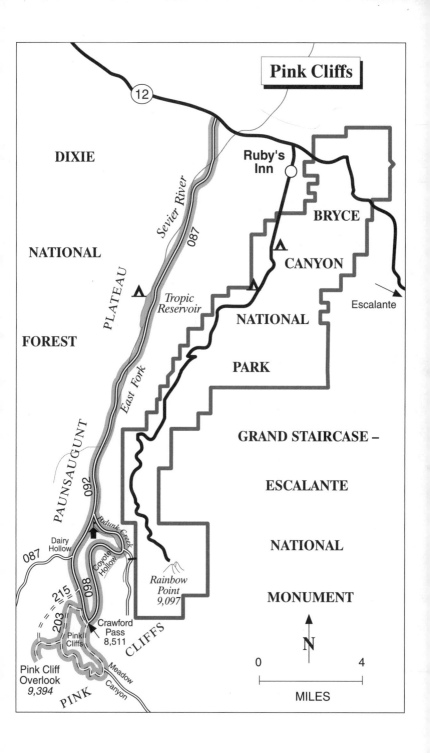

Pink Cliffs

Kolob Terrace Road

LOCATION: East of I-15 between Utah Hwys. 14 and 9. The road passes through a portion of Zion National Park.

HIGHLIGHTS: This is a picturesque drive through a range of plant zones, including grassy hills, pinyon-juniper woodlands and forests of aspen, fir and towering ponderosa pine. There are some fantastic views of the Great Basin and Zion National Park's west side as well. It's best in spring and fall.

DIFFICULTY: Easy. The road surface ranges from maintained dirt and gravel to two-lane asphalt. The dirt segments can be impassable in wet weather. The road is closed from late November to May or June.

TIME & DISTANCE: 2 hours; 48.4 miles.

MAPS: ACSC's *Indian Country*. Dixie National Forest's *Pine Valley and Cedar City Ranger Districts*. DeLorme p. 17.

INFORMATION: Iron County. Washington County. Zion National Park.

GETTING THERE: I go south, but you can take this north-south road (a.k.a. Kolob Road and Kolob Reservoir Road) in either direction, beginning or ending at Virgin. Take Hwy. 14 east from Main Street in Cedar City for 4.9 miles. Turn south at the sign for Kolob Reservoir. Reset the odometer to 0.

REST STOPS: Fish at Kolob Reservoir. Tour Zion National Park. Springdale has all services.

THE DRIVE: Most of the road passes through private land. The first 8 miles coming from the north are paved and forested as you ascend Kolob Terrace, a plateau of Cretaceous (66.4-144 MYA) seabed deposits. The name Kolob derives from the star in the center of the universe which, according to Mormon Church doctrine, is closest to the throne of God. As you curve around the west side of Lone Tree Mountain and cross Cedar Mountain, you will have tremendous views of the vast Great Basin, with its waves of mountain ranges and expanse of pale desert. Rolling hills, aspen groves, grazing sheep and log fences add to the charm of this undulating country road as it climbs to over 9,300 feet. It narrows to a single serpentine dirt lane at mile 19.1 as it descends through a pretty canyon. By mile 23 you're approaching Kolob Reservoir, where the road improves. About 3 miles farther asphalt resumes. Then the road takes you into Zion National Park, at mile 30 (only to leave, re-enter and leave again), passing through meadows and aspen stands. You'll have views of Kolob Canyons' red walls in Zion's northwestern corner. Continuing south, gaze across the park's beige and salmon-pink Navajo Sandstone canyons, cliffs and domes, once the dunes of a great desert in late Triassic-early Jurassic time (190-136 MYA). By mile 36 you're on a two-lane paved road, descending through pinyon-juniper woodland to Hwy. 9 at Virgin.

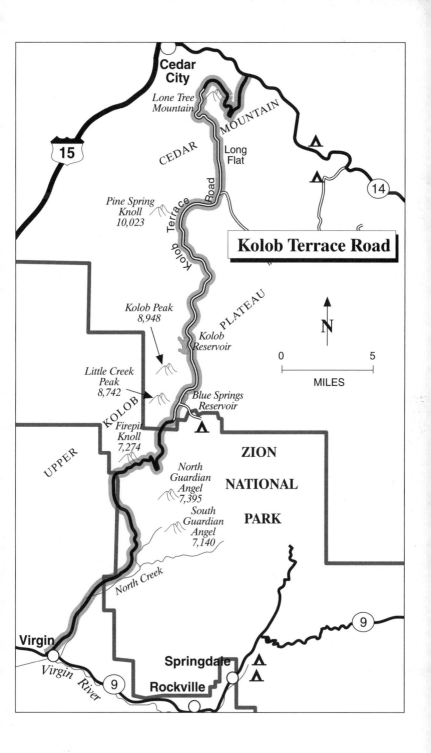

Mojave Desert & Joshua Tree Road

LOCATION: Near the Arizona border in Utah's southwest corner, in the Beaver Dam Mountains west of St. George.

HIGHLIGHTS: This road winds through semi-arid mountains in the region where the Mojave Desert, Great Basin and Colorado Plateau meet. Here, not far from Utah's lowest point (Beaver Dam Wash, 2,350 feet, southwest of the Beaver Dam Mountains) is the northern-most place where Joshua trees grow in large numbers. In fact, 1,000 acres have been designated a national landmark. The road also passes the Woodbury Desert Study Area, set aside for the birds, desert tor-toises, rattlesnakes (watch your step!) and other desert life.You will want to stop to take in the fantastic views of the brilliant red cliffs in the distance, and of Zion National Park.

DIFFICULTY: Easy, on a 2wd high-clearance road.

TIME & DISTANCE: An hour; 19 miles.

MAPS: ACSC's *Indian Country*. Recreational Map of Utah. DeLorme p. 16.

INFORMATION: Interagency Offices & Information Center in St. George.

SPECIAL NOTE: The northern 3 miles or so of this county-main-tained road cross the Shivwits Indian Reservation, so avoid trespass-ing off the road corridor.

GETTING THERE: You can take this basically north-south route in either direction, beginning or ending on old U.S. 91. I go south. In St. George, take St. George Blvd. west to Bluff Street; go right. Turn left on Sunset Blvd. toward the Shivwits Indian Reservation. Drive through Santa Clara. On the reservation, on old U.S. 91 almost 2 miles from the turnoff to Gunlock, take the dirt and gravel road that branch-es left toward the Apex gold mine.

REST STOPS: St. George has all services.

THE DRIVE: Drive up a broad valley bordered by desert mountains vegetated with sagebrush, pinyon pines and junipers. Deep shades of gray mixed with hues of red make these metamorphic mountains quite pretty. By mile 5, as you skirt the base of Jarvis Peak, you'll have out-standing views to the north of vaulting red cliffs made of Jurassic (144-208 MYA) desert sands. By mile 6.5 a panorama of brilliant red desert, the pale Navajo Sandstone monoliths of Zion and the endless sprawl of southern Utah opens up before you. At mile 7.9, at Cedar Wash, pass the road to Apex Mine, on the right. Here the route dimin-ishes to a single rocky lane. At mile 9.6 you'll cross Bulldog Pass, then descend to Bulldog Canyon. A couple of miles farther you will begin to see Joshua trees, named by Mormon pioneers who thought they resembled the prophet's outstretched arms, and other Mojave Desert plants. Soon the Mojave Desert spreads out to the south, dotted with countless Joshua trees. From here you will descend along the edge of the Beaver Dam Mountains Wilderness (to the south) and through the Woodbury area. About 3 miles east of the highway, the unsigned and decidedly low-key Joshua Tree National Landmark lies to the north of the tour route. The road brings you to the highway by mile 19.

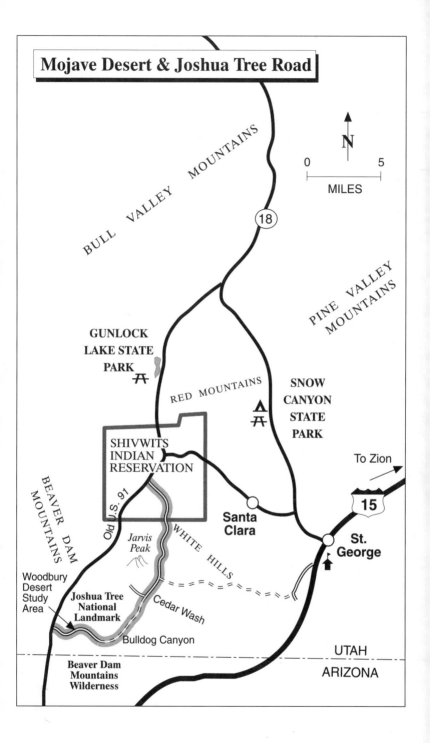

Mojave Desert & Joshua Tree Road

BULL VALLEY MOUNTAINS

PINE VALLEY MOUNTAINS

N

0 — 5

MILES

18

GUNLOCK LAKE STATE PARK

RED MOUNTAINS

SNOW CANYON STATE PARK

To Zion

15

SHIVWITS INDIAN RESERVATION

BEAVER DAM MOUNTAINS

Old U.S. 91

Jarvis Peak

WHITE HILLS

Santa Clara

St. George

Woodbury Desert Study Area

Joshua Tree National Landmark

Cedar Wash

Bulldog Canyon

UTAH

ARIZONA

Beaver Dam Mountains Wilderness

Smithsonian Butte

LOCATION: South of Zion National Park, east of I-15. Between Utah Hwy. 9 at the north end and Utah Hwy. 59 at the south end.

HIGHLIGHTS: Views include the park's Zion Canyon and East and West Temple, the Virgin River Valley, Canaan Mountain and the Vermilion Cliffs. Smithsonian Butte, named by explorer John Wesley Powell, rises to 6,632 feet along this BLM National Back Country Byway. The ghost town of Grafton, used in the film *Butch Cassidy and the Sundance Kid,* and its nearby pioneer cemetery add interest. Spring and fall are best.

DIFFICULTY: Easy when dry, but the roads here can be impassable when wet.

TIME & DISTANCE: Half an hour to an hour; 13.1 miles including the 4-mile (round-trip) spur to Grafton.

MAPS: Recreational Map of Utah. ACSC's *Indian Country.* DeLorme p. 17.

INFORMATION: BLM, Cedar City Field Office.

GETTING THERE: To go south, take Hwy. 9 to Rockville, 3 miles west of Zion National Park, then go south on Bridge Road. Cross the Virgin River on Old Rockville Bridge, a one-lane steel truss bridge built in 1926. To go north (for the best views) turn north onto the byway from Hwy. 59 about 14.2 miles southeast of Hurricane or 7.8 miles northwest of Hildale. I describe it going south.

REST STOPS: Primitive camping is allowed on BLM land. You will find developed campgrounds in Zion National Park. Springdale has all services.

THE DRIVE: After crossing the old bridge the road bends right (west) and parallels the river valley through fields and orchards. The pavement ends 0.9 mile from Hwy. 9. Views across the scoured red, white and tan sandstone world of Zion begin to expand. At mile 1.6 the route angles left (south), but go right toward Grafton. In 1.5 miles go left at a Y to see the old cemetery, where the dead include settlers killed by Indians in 1866. Grafton, founded that year, was abandoned in 1907. An adobe schoolhouse, a brick house and the ruins of log buildings are all that remain. (It's private property.) The main road climbs steeply through red beds of the Moenkopi and Chinle formations (Triassic Period, 208-245 MYA) whiskered with pinyon pines and junipers along a ridge between two washes, toward the Vermilion Cliffs. Soon Smithsonian Butte looms to the left. Once atop a broad flat you'll see the turnoff for the optional 10-mile (round-trip) spur along Gooseberry Mesa, to a point overlooking the Virgin River region. Continue south to Hwy. 59.

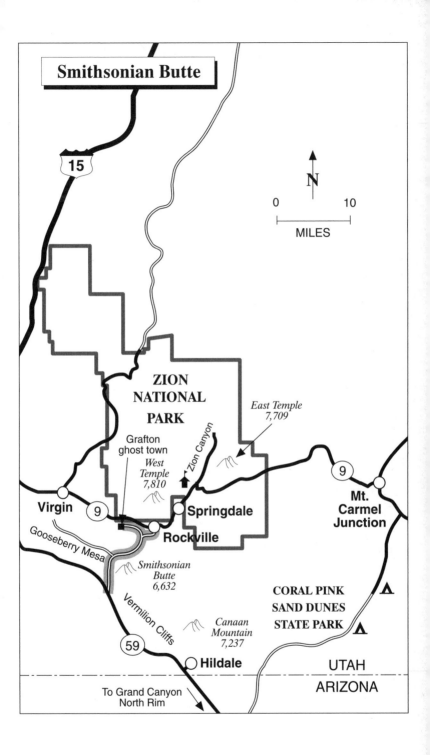

Smithsonian Butte

San Juan River Goosenecks

LOCATION: Just north of the San Juan River; northwest of Mexican Hat off U.S. 163; east end of Glen Canyon National Recreation Area.

HIGHLIGHTS: The San Juan River's deep, meandering gorge; petroglyphs; the high cliffs of Cedar Mesa. This is a good mountain-bike road as well. Monument Valley is to the south. Spring and fall are best.

DIFFICULTY: Easy for the 15 miles that I cover; moderate beyond that.

TIME & DISTANCE: 2 hours; 15 miles one-way. I end at John's Canyon. Beyond that the scenery is repetitive and the road is rougher, although there are more roadside petroglyphs. It ends at a trailhead.

MAPS: Trails Illustrated's No. 706 (Grand Gulch Plateau). ACSC's *Indian Country*. DeLorme p. 22.

INFORMATION: BLM, San Juan Field Office.

GETTING THERE: North of Mexican Hat, take Utah Hwy. 316 a half-mile west of Hwy. 261 toward Goosenecks State Park. Turn north onto dirt San Juan County road 244.

REST STOPS: Picnic at the creek at the mouth of John's Canyon. You'll find dry camping and toilets at Goosenecks State Park. There is a great vista from Muley Point off Hwy. 261, near the top of Moki Dugway.

THE DRIVE: The first 3.5 miles cross a broad bench below Muley Point, atop the saffron-colored cliffs of Cedar Mesa to the right. To the left are the deeply entrenched meanders, or loops, carved by the San Juan River. The river snakes through a gorge in Pennsylvanian (280-320 MYA) rock deposited in shallow seas, with the Honaker Trail Formation on the upper slopes and the Paradox Formation below. Deep side canyons force the road to the base of Cedar Mesa, and by mile 5.5 you're on a dramatic terrace. At 6.8, at the brink of a side canyon, go through a gate and close it. 1.7 miles farther scan the boulders to the right about 75 yards from the road for a horizontal slab with a blue-black patina, or varnish. It bears wonderful petroglyphs, including triangular human-like figures with bird heads. (Don't touch them.) As you continue, watch carefully for more petroglyphs on similar flat surfaces. At 11.3 a spur branches left. It ends shortly, but you can walk to a rocky point overlooking the gorge. Soon the main road angles right, up John's Canyon along a gorge. At mile 14.9 or so you will reach a creek at the gorge at the mouth of John's Canyon. This is a good place to stop. The road continues along the opposite side of the gorge, ending in 7.5 miles at a trailhead to the Grand Gulch Wilderness Study Area, where mechanized travel is prohibited.

ALSO TRY: The easy and beautiful 16.9-mile drive through Valley of the Gods, to the north.

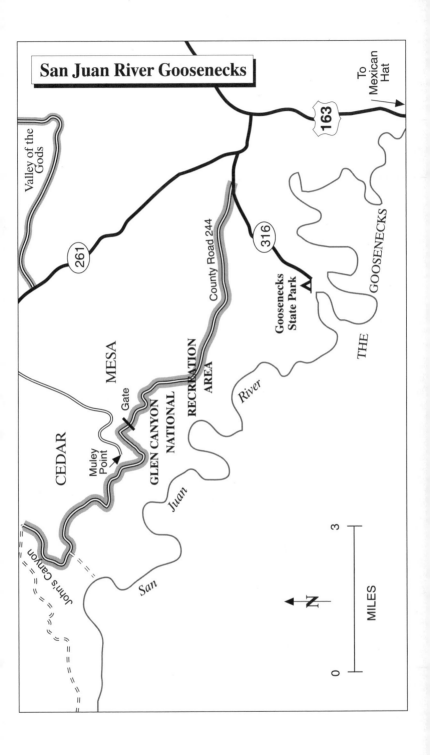

San Juan River Goosenecks

Comb Wash

LOCATION: Southeastern Utah, southwest of Blanding and northwest of Bluff. Between Hwys. 95 and 163.

HIGHLIGHTS: The wash courses along the base of a spectacular north-south ridge with 800-foot-high cliffs bursting from the Earth's crust. In this area, once populated by ancestral Puebloan Indians (Anasazi), occurred what may have been the last skirmish in the U.S. between Indians and white settlers. Comb Wash also is where writer Edward Abbey's fictional "Monkey Wrench Gang" sabotaged road-building heavy equipment (Chapter 6, *The Raid At Comb Wash*). It's best in spring and fall.

DIFFICULTY: Easy. This is a periodically maintained dirt road.

TIME & DISTANCE: 1 hour; 18.6 miles.

MAPS: ACSC's *Indian Country*. Trails Illustrated's No. 706 (Grand Gulch Plateau). Recreational Map of Utah. DeLorme p. 22.

INFORMATION: BLM, San Juan Field Office.

GETTING THERE: You can go north or south. I take you north. So, turn north off U.S. 163 onto San Juan County road 235 about 2.8 miles west of the junction with U.S. 191 southwest of Bluff. The turn is just west of the bridge over Comb Wash.

REST STOPS: There's a waterless BLM campground near the north end. Don't miss nearby Butler Wash Anasazi Ruins.

THE DRIVE: The dramatic humps (hogbacks) of Comb Ridge mark the eastern edge of the Monument Upwarp, a huge arched fold in the Earth's crust, or anticline, that extends west to Glen Canyon. Comb Ridge runs north from Kayenta, Ariz., for about 90 miles to the Abajo Mountains. At Comb Ridge, the upwarp's strata suddenly nosedive deep into the Earth. The dramatic cliffs are mostly dune Wingate sandstone, with stream-deposited Kayenta Formation sediments, and a crest of Navajo sandstone from what may have been the Earth's greatest desert. All are from the early Jurassic (144-208 MYA)-late Triassic (208-245 MYA) periods. In 1923, friction between whites and Paiute Indians flared into armed conflict. Chief Posey and another Paiute were killed. The other Paiutes were jailed. Following the wash north, 2.3 miles from U.S. 163, road 237 goes left (west) along the route of the 1879-80 Mormon Hole-In-The-Rock expedition (Tour 56). Follow Comb Wash north.

ALSO TRY: The 21-mile Butler Wash Road along the east side of Comb Ridge is also a great drive. More avid four-wheelers can try long (about 8 miles one-way) and serpentine Arch Canyon (moderate to difficult), famous for its namesake arches and Anasazi ruins. To get there, at Hwy. 95 go west for about 100 yards, then north 2.25 miles. Go left at the campground just before the creek, dip into the wash, angle left and proceed to the sign-in box.

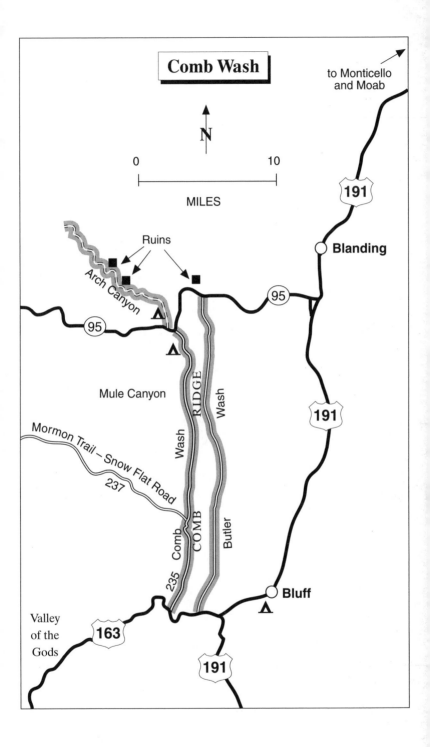

Grand Staircase-Escalante National Monument
(Tours 55, 56, 57 & 58)

APPENDIX

Information Sources

NOTE: Telephone numbers, mailing addresses and Internet addresses can change. Utah is in the Mountain Time zone.

4X4NOW.com & 4X4BOOKS.com

AAA Utah
560 E. 500 S.
Salt Lake City, UT 84102
(801) 364-5615

**Anasazi Indian Village
State Park**
P.O. Box 1329
Boulder, UT 84716-1329
(435) 335-7308

Arches National Park
P.O. Box 907
Moab, UT 84532
(435) 259-8161 (voice)
TTY: (435) 259-5279
www.nps.gov/arch
archinfo@nps.gov

**Arizona Strip
Interpretive Association
Visitor Information Center**
345 E. Riverside Dr.
St. George, UT 84790
(435) 688-3246

Ashley National Forest
www.fs.fed.us/r4/ashley

>   **Duchesne/Roosevelt
>   Ranger District**
>   Duchesne Office
>   85 W. Main St.
>   P.O. Box 981
>   Duchesne, UT 84021
>   (435) 738-2482
>
>   **Duchesne/Roosevelt
>   Ranger District**
>   Roosevelt Office
>   244 W. Hwy. 40
>   P.O. Box 333-6
>   Roosevelt, UT 84066
>   (435) 722-5018
>
>   **Flaming Gorge National
>   Recreation Area**
>   Highways 43 & 44

P.O. Box 279
Manila, UT 84046
(435) 784-3445

>   **Supervisor's Office**
>   355 N. Vernal Avenue
>   Vernal, UT 84078
>   (435) 789-1181
>   daugustus/r4_ashley@fs/fed/us
>
>   **Vernal Ranger District**
>   353 N. Vernal Avenue
>   Vernal, UT 84078
>   (435) 789-1181

**Brown's Park
National Wildlife Refuge**
1318 Hwy. 318
Maybell, CO 81640
(970) 365-3613

Bryce Canyon National Park
P.O. Box 170001
Bryce Canyon, UT 84717-0001
(435) 834-5322
www.nps.gov/brca
brca_reception_area@nps.gov

Bryce Canyon Natural History Assoc.
Bryce Canyon National Park
P.O. Box 17001
Bryce Canyon, UT 84717
(435) 834-5322

Bureau of Land Management
www.ut.blm.gov

>   **Arizona Strip District Office**
>   345 E. Riverside Drive
>   St. George, UT 84790
>   (435) 688-3246
>
>   **Browns Park/Green River &
>   Jarvie Historic Property**
>   Site ranger: (435) 885-3307
>   BLM Vernal Field Office
>   170 S. 500 East
>   Vernal, UT 84078
>   (435) 781-4400
>   www.blm.gov/utah/vernal
>   /rec/john.html
>
>   **Cedar City Field Office**
>   176 E. D.L. Sargent Drive
>   Cedar City, UT 84720
>   (435) 586-2401

Fillmore Field Office
P.O. Box 778
35 E. 500 North
Fillmore, UT 84631
(435) 743-6811

Grand Staircase-Escalante National Monument
Contact the Kanab Field Office
Escalante Office:
(435) 826-5499
Boulder Contact Station:
(at Anasazi Indian Village SP)
(435) 335-7308
Cannonville Contact Station:
(435) 679-8981
www.ut.blm.gov/monument

Henry Mountains Field Station
P.O. Box 99
Hanksville, UT 84734
(435) 542-3461

Kanab Field Office
318 N. First East
Kanab, UT 84741
(435) 644-2672

Moab Field Office
82 E. Dogwood
Moab, UT 84532
(435) 259-2100

Monticello Field Office
P.O. Box 7
435 N. Main
Monticello, UT 84535
(435) 587-1502

Paria Contact Station
Highway 89
44 miles east of Kanab
Hours vary; no telephone

Price Field Office
125 South 600 West
Price, UT 84501
(435) 636-3601

Richfield Field Office
150 East 900 North
Richfield, UT 84701
(435) 896-1523

Salt Lake Field Office
2370 South 2300 West
Salt Lake City, UT 84119
(801) 977-4300

St. George Field Office
345 E. Riverside Drive
St. George, UT 84720
(435) 688-3200

State Office
324 S. State St., Suite 301
P.O. Box 45155
Salt Lake City, UT 84145-0155
(801) 539-4001

Vernal Field Office
170 South 500 East
Vernal, UT 84078
(435) 781-4400

Camp Floyd-Stagecoach Inn State Park
P.O. Box 446
Riverton, UT 84065-0446
(801) 768-8932

Canyonlands National Park
2282 S. West Resource Blvd.
Moab, UT 84532-3298
(435) 259-7164 (general information)
www.nps.gov/cany
canyinfo@nps.gov

Note: The park's free official publica-
tion, *Canyonlands National Park Trip
Planner* (published by the Canyonlands
Natural History Association), is an
excellent source of information.
Camping reservations must be made by
mail or fax. Overnight backcountry
camping requires a permit. Other important rules apply to backcountry use, so
inquire ahead.

Reservations Office
2282 S. West Resource Blvd.
Moab, UT 84532-3298
(435) 259-4351; M-F 8 a.m.-12:30
p.m.)
(435) 259-4285 fax
Island in the Sky District
(435) 259-4712
Needles District
(435) 259-4711
Maze District
(Hans Flat Ranger Station)
(435) 259-2652

Canyonlands Natural History Assoc.
3031 S. Highway 191
Moab, UT 84532
(435) 259-6003
1-800-840-8978
www.cnha.org

Capitol Reef National Park
Superintendent
HC 70, Box 15
Torrey, UT 84775-9602
(435) 425-3791
www.nps.gov/care

Capitol Reef Natural History Assoc.
HC 70, Box 15
Torrey, UT 84775-9602
(435) 425-3791

Castle Country Travel Council
P.O. Box 1037
155 E. Main Street
Price, UT 84501
(800) 842-0789 or (435) 637-3009
www.castlecountry.com

Cedar Breaks National Monument
2390 W. Hwy. 56, Suite 11
Cedar City, UT 84720-4151
(435) 586-9451
www.nps.gov/cebr

**Coral Pink Sand Dunes
State Park**
P.O. Box 95
Kanab, UT 84741-0095
(435) 648-2800

Dixie Interpretive Association
P.O. Box 349
Santa Clara, UT 84765
(520) 347-5165

Dead Horse Point State Park
P.O. Box 609
Moab, UT 84532-0609
(435) 259-2614

Deer Creek State Park
P.O. Box 257
Midway, UT 84049-0257
(435) 654-0171

Dinosaur National Monument
4545 Hwy. 40
Dinosaur, CO 81610
(970) 374-3000
www.nps.gov/dino

Dinosaur Nature Association
1291 E. Highway 40
Vernal, UT 84078-2830
1-800-845-3466

Dixie National Forest
www.fs.fed.us/dxnf

>**Cedar City Ranger District**
>82 North 100 East
>Cedar City, UT 84720
>(435) 865-3200

>**Escalante Ranger District**
>755 W. Main
>P.O. Box 246
>Escalante, UT 84726
>(435) 826-5400

>**Pine Valley Ranger District**
>196 E. Tabernacle St.
>St. George, UT 84770
>(435) 652-3100

>**Powell Ranger District**
>225 East Center
>P.O. Box 80
>Panguitch, UT 84759
>(435) 676-8815

>**Supervisor's Office**
>82 North 100 East
>Cedar City, UT 84720
>(435) 865-3700

>**Teasdale Ranger District**
>P.O. Box 90
>Teasdale, UT 84773
>(435) 425-3702

Edge of the Cedars State Park
660 West 400 North
Blanding, UT 84511-0788
(435) 678-2238

Escalante Interagency Visitor Center
755 W. Main
Escalante, UT 84726
(435) 826-5499

Escalante State Park
710 N. Reservoir Road
Escalante, UT 84726-0350
(435) 826-4466

**Fish Springs National
Wildlife Refuge**
Dugway, UT 84022
(435) 831-5353
www.r6.fws.gov/REFUGES/FISHSPNG/

Fishlake National Forest
www.fs.fed.us/r4/fishlake

Beaver Ranger District
575 S. Main St.
P.O. Box E
Beaver, UT 84713
(435) 438-2436

Fillmore Ranger District
390 S. Main St.
P.O. Box 265
Fillmore, UT 84631
(435) 743-5721

Loa Ranger District
138 S. Main St.
P.O. Box 129
Loa, UT 84747
(435) 836-2811

Richfield Ranger District &
Forest Supervisor's Office
115 East 900 North
Richfield, UT 84701
(435) 896-9233

Flaming Gorge National
Recreation Area
Ashley National Forest
P.O. Box 279
Manila, UT 84046
(435) 784-3445

Forest Service, U.S.
Intermountain Region Office
324 25th Street
Ogden, UT 84401
(801) 625-5127
    Campground reservations:
    1-800-280-2267
    For the hearing-impaired:
    1-800-879-4496

Fremont Indian State Park
11550 W.t Clear Creek Canyon Road
Sevier, UT 84766-9999
(435) 527-4631

Glen Canyon National
Recreation Area
P.O. Box 1507
Page, AZ 86040
(520) 608-6404
www.nps.gov/glca

Note: All overnight backcountry use
requires a permit and a camping reservation. Reservation requests are handled
only by Canyonlands National Park.
Requests are accepted only by mail or

fax. For further information, call (435)
259-7164 or 4351. Important rules apply
to backcountry use, so inquire in
advance.

Carl Hayden Visitor Center
(520) 608-6404
Bullfrog Visitor Center
(435) 684-7400
Hans Flat Ranger Station
(435) 259-2652

Glen Canyon Natural History Assoc.
32 N. 10th Ave., Suite 9
P.O. Box 581
Page, AZ 86040
(520) 645-3532
www.pagelakepowell.org/

Goblin Valley State Park
P.O. Box 637
Green River, UT 84525-0637
(435) 564-3633

Golden Spike
National Historic Site
P.O. Box 897
Brigham City, UT 84302
(435) 471-2209, ext. 18 or 21
www.nps.gov/gosp

Goosenecks State Park
P.O. Box 788
Blanding, UT 84511-0788
(435) 678-2238

Grand County Roads Department
(435) 259-5308

Grand County Travel Council
P.O. Box 550
Moab, UT 84532
(800) 635-MOAB (6622)
(435) 259-8825

Grand Staircase-Escalante
National Monument
See Bureau of Land Management

Great Basin National Park
Baker, NV 89311-9702
(775) 234-7331
www.nps.gov/grba

Great Basin Natural History Assoc.
Great Basin National Park
Baker, NV 89311
(775) 234-7270

Green River State Park
P.O. Box 637
Green River, UT 84525-0637
(435) 564-3633
(800) 322-3770

Green River Visitor Center &
John Wesley Powell History Museum
P.O. Box 508
Green River, UT 84526
(435) 564-3526

GTR Mapping
(Recreational Map of Utah)
P.O. Box 1984
Canon City, CO 81215-1984
(719) 275-8948

Gunlock Reservoir State Park
P.O. Box 140
Santa Clara, UT 84765-0140
(435) 628-2255

Hovenweep National Monument
McElmo Route
Cortez, CO 81321
(435) 459-4344 (within Utah)
(970) 749-0510 cellular

Interagency Offices &
Information Center
(BLM & Forest Service)
345 E. Riverside Drive
St. George, UT 84790
(435) 688-3246

Iron Mission State Park
585 N. Main
Cedar City, UT 84720-1079
(435) 586-9290
Iron County
(435) 586-8652

James Q. Jacobs' Rock Art Pages
www.geocities.com/Athens/Olympus/48
44/rock_art.html

John Wesley Powell
River History Museum
885 E. Main
Green River, UT 84525
(435) 564-3526

Kodachrome Basin State Park
P.O. Box 238
Cannonville, UT 84718-0238
(435) 679-8562/8767

LNT (Leave No Trace), Inc.
(promotes responsible, minimum-
impact outdoor recreation)
P.O. Box 997
Boulder, CO 80306
or
2019 19th Street
Boulder, CO 80302
Fax: (303) 442-8217
www.lnt.org

Manti-La Sal
National Forest
www.fs.fed.us/r4/mantilasal

Ferron/Price Ranger District
Ferron Office
115 W. Canyon Road
P.O. Box 310
Ferron, UT 84523
(435) 384-2372

Ferron/Price Ranger District
Price Office
599 W. Price River Dr.
Price, UT 84501
(435) 637-2817

Moab/Monticello Ranger District
Moab Office
2290 S. West Resource Blvd.
P.O. Box 386
Moab, UT 84532
(435) 259-7155

Moab/Monticello Ranger District
Monticello Office
496 E. Central
P.O. Box 820
Monticello, UT 84535
(435) 587-2041

Sanpete Ranger District
540 N. Main
Ephraim, UT 84627-1117
(435) 283-4151

Supervisor's Office
599 W. Price River Dr.
Price, UT 84501
(435) 637-2817

Millsite State Park
P.O. Box 1343
Huntington, UT 84528-1343
(435) 687-2491

Minersville State Park
P.O. Box 1531
Beaver, UT 84713-1531
(435) 438-5472

Moab/Green River
Information Center
Center & Main
Moab, UT 84532
(435) 259-8825
1-800-635-6622

Monticello Multi-Agency
Visitor Center
117 S. Main Street
P.O. Box 490
Monticello, UT 84535
(435) 587-3235
or 1-800-574-4386

National Geographic Maps/
Trails Illustrated
P.O. Box 4357
Evergreen, CO 80437-4357
(303) 670-3457 or (800) 962-1643
www.trailsillustrated.com

National park campground
reservations
1-800-365-2267

National Park Reservation Service
http://reservations.nps.go/

National Parks by Name
www.nps.gov/parklists/byname.htm

Natural Areas Association
(Interagency Natural Areas of Utah)
P.O. Box 645
145 Zion Park Rd.
Springdale, UT 84767
(435) 772-2445

Natural Bridges National Monument
P.O. Box 1
Lake Powell, UT 84533
(435) 692-1234
www.nps.gov/nabr

Needles Outpost
P.O. Box 1349
Moab, UT 84532
(435) 979-4007 (store)
(435) 259-8545 (message)

Northeastern Utah
Visitor Center
(In the Utah Field House
of Natural History)

235 East Main
Vernal, UT 84078
(435) 789-7894
www.dinoland.com

Outdoor Recreation
Information Center
(Wasatch-Cache National Forest)
3285 East 3300 South
Salt Lake City, UT
(801) 466-6411
Located inside the R.E.I. store

Outdoor Recreation Network
www.outdoorwire.com

Public Lands Interpretive Association
(formerly Southwest Natural & Cultural
Heritage Association)
6501 4th St. NW
Albuquerque, NM 87107
(505) 345-9498

Quail Creek Reservoir State Park
P.O. Box 1943
St. George, UT 84770-1943
(435) 879-2378

Rainbow Bridge National Monument
P.O. Box 1507
Page, AZ 86040
(520) 608-6404
www.nps.gov/rabr

Recreation.Gov
An all-in-one Web site
for federal recreation areas.
www.recreation.gov

Red Fleet State Park
8750 N. Hwy. 191
Vernal, UT 84078-7801
(435) 789-4432

Red Rock 4-Wheelers, Inc.
P.O. Box 1471
Moab, UT 84532-1471
(435) 259-7625

San Juan County
Visitor Services
P.O. Box 490
Monticello, UT 84535
(800) 574-4386
(435) 587-3235

Scofield Reservoir State Park
P.O. Box 166
Price, UT 84501-0166
(435) 448-9449

Snow Canyon State Park
P.O. Box 140
Santa Clara, UT 84765-0140
(435) 628-2255

**Southwest Parks &
Monuments Assoc.**
221 N. Court Ave.
Tucson, AZ 85701
(520) 622-1999

Starvation State Park
P.O. Box 584
Duchesne, UT 84021-0584
(435) 738-2326

State of Utah Official Web Site
www.state.ut.us

Steinaker State Park
4335 N. Hwy. 191
Vernal, UT 84078-7800
(435) 789-4432

SUV OnLine
www.suv.com

Territorial Statehouse State Park
50 W. Capitol
Fillmore, UT 84631-0657
(435) 743-5316

T.I. Maps, etc.
29 E. Center
Moab, UT 84532
(435) 259-5529
maps@moab.net

**Timpanogos Cave
National Monument**
RR 3, Box 200
American Fork, UT 84003
(801) 756-5238
www.nps.gov/tica

Tooele County
(435) 843-3204

Tread Lightly!
298 24th Street, Suite 325
Ogden, UT 84401
1-800-966-9900
www.treadlightly.org

Uinta National Forest
www.fs.fed.us/r4/uinta

Heber Ranger District
2460 S. Hwy. 40
Heber City, UT 84032
(435) 654-0470
Nephi Sub-office
740 S. Main St.
Nephi, UT 84648
(435) 623-2735

Pleasant Grove Ranger District
390 North 100 East
Pleasant Grove, UT 84062
(801) 785-3563

Spanish Fork Ranger District
44 West 400 North
Spanish Fork, UT 84660
(801) 798-3571

**Strawberry Visitors
Information Center**
Heber, UT 84032
(435) 548-2321

Supervisor's Office
88 West 100 North
Provo, UT 84601
(801) 377-5780

U.S. Forest Service
Web site
www.fs.fed.us

**U.S. Geological Survey
Earth Science Information Center**
2300 South 2222 West
West Valley City, UT 84117
(801) 975-3742
1-800-872-6277 for the ESIC nearest
you.
www.usgs.gov

Utah State Parks & Recreation
1594 W. North Temple, Suite 116
Salt Lake City, UT 84114-6001
(801) 538-7220
  Campground reservations:
  (801) 322-3770 (in Salt Lake City) or
  1-800-322-3770
www.nr.state.ut.us/parks/utahstpk.htm

Utah Department of Transportation
4501 South 2700 West
Salt Lake City, UT 84119
(801) 965-4000
www.dot.state.ut.us

**Utah Field House of
Natural History State Park**
235 E. Main Street
Vernal, UT 84078-2605
(435) 789-3799

Utah Geological Survey
1594 W. North Temple
Salt Lake City, UT 84114
(801) 537-3320

Utah Idaho Supply/Map World
(They have a number of stores.)
1151 S. Redwood Rd. No. 104
Salt Lake City, UT 84104
(801) 974-3144

Utah Travel Council
P.O. Box 147420
Salt Lake City, UT 84114-7420
(801) 538-1030
1-800-200-1160
(801) 538-1399 fax
www.utah.com & travel@utah.com

Utah Tourism & Recreation Information Center
Council Hall/Capitol Hill
Salt Lake City, UT 84114
(801) 538-1467

Wasatch Mountain State Park
P.O. Box 10
750 W. Snake Creek Rd.
Midway, UT 84049-0010
(435) 654-1791

Wasatch-Cache National Forest
www.fs.fed.us/wcnf/

Evanston Ranger District
1565 Hwy. 150, Suite A
P.O. Box 1880
Evanston, WY 82930
(307) 789-3194

Kamas Ranger District
50 E. Center Street
P.O. Box 68
Kamas, UT 84036
(801) 783-4338

Logan Ranger District
1500 E. Highway 89
Logan, UT 84327
(435) 755-3620

Mountain View Ranger District
P.O. Box 129
Mountain View, WY 82939
(307) 782-6555

Ogden Ranger District
507 25th Street
Ogden, UT 84401
(801) 625-5112

Salt Lake Ranger District
6944 South 3000 East
Salt Lake City, UT 84121
(801) 943-1794

Supervisor's Office
8230 Federal Building
125 S. State Street
Salt Lake City, UT 84138
(801) 524-5030

Union Station Information Center
2501 Wall Avenue
Ogden, UT 84401
(801) 625-5306

Washington County
(435) 634-5736

Willard Bay State Park
900 West 650 North #A
Willard, UT 84340-9999
(435) 734-9494

Zion National Park
Superintendent
Springdale, UT 84767
(435) 772-3256
www.nps.gov/zion

Zion Natural History Assoc.
Zion National Park
Springdale, UT 84767
(435) 772-3265 or (435) 772-3264

References

A Collector's Guide to Rock, Mineral & Fossil Localities of Utah, by James R. Wilson. Utah Geological Survey, Salt Lake City, UT. (1995)

A Naturalist's Guide to the White Rim Trail, by David Williams & Damian Fagan. Wingate Ink, Moab, UT. (1994)

Canyon Country Off-Road Vehicle Trails; Arches & La Sals Areas, by F.A. Barnes. Wasatch Publishers, Salt Lake City, UT. (1978)

Canyon Country Off-Road Vehicle Trails; Canyon Rims & Needles Areas, by F.A. Barnes. Canyon Country Publications, Moab, UT. (1990)

Canyon Country Off-Road Vehicle Trails; Island Area, by F.A. Barnes. Wasatch Publishers, Salt Lake City, UT. (1978)

Canyonlands Country: The Geology of Canyonlands and Arches National Parks, by Donald L. Baars. University of Utah Press, Salt Lake City, UT. (1995)

Dark Canyon Trail Guide, Canyonlands Natural History Association, Moab, UT. (1994)

John Jarvie of Brown's Park, by William L. Tennent. U.S. Bureau of Land Management. No. 7, Cultural Resources Series. (1984)

Makin' Tracks: The Saga of the Transcontinental Railroad, by Lynne Rhodes Mayer & Ken Vose. Barnes & Noble Books (1995)

Mountain Biker's Guide to Utah, by Gregg Bromka. Menasha Ridge Press, Birmingham, AL, and Falcon Press, Helena, Montana. (1994)

National Geographic Maps/Trails Illustrated, Nos. 210, 211, 220, 246, 701-712, 1002, 1003.

Petroglyphs and Pictographs of Utah, Vols. 1 & 2, by Kenneth B. Castleton, M.D. Utah Museum of Natural History, Salt Lake City, UT. (1984 & 1987).

Rails East to Promontory: The Utah Stations, Anan S. Raymond & Richard E. Fike. U.S. Bureau of Land Management. No. 8, Cultural Resource Series. (1994)

Roadside Geology of Utah, by Halka Chronic. Mountain Press Publishing Co., Missoula, MT. (1990)

The Lincoln Highway: Main Street Across America, by Drake Hokanson. University of Iowa Press (1988)

The Monkey Wrench Gang, by Edward Abbey. Avon Books, New York. (1985)

The Sierra Club Guides to the National Parks: Desert Southwest, published by Stewart, Tabori & Chang. (1984)

Tour of The Waterpocket Fold, by Ward J. Roylance. Capitol Reef Natural History Association, Torrey, UT.

Tour of The Valley of Cathedrals, by Ward J. Roylance. Capitol Reef Natural History Association, Torrey, UT.

Utah Atlas & Gazetteer, DeLorme Mapping, Freeport, ME.

Utah Handbook, by Bill Weir & Robert Blake. Moon Publications, Inc., Chico, CA. (1995)

Utah's National Parks, by Ron Adkison. Wilderness Press, Berkeley, CA. (1996)

Utah Place Names, by John W. Van Cott. The University of Utah Press, Salt Lake City, UT. (1990)

Utah Scenic Byways & Backways, by the Utah Travel Council, U.S. Bureau of Land Management, U.S. Forest Service, Utah Department of Transportation, Utah Travel Regions, Associations of Governments, National Park Service.

4-Wheel Freedom: The Art of Off-Road Driving, by Dr. Brad DeLong, Paladin Press. (1996)

Glossary

Anthropomorphs — Rock art figures that resemble a human form.

Anticline — A convex, or arched, fold in layered rock.

Bentonite — A soft, colorful rock formed by the decomposition of volcanic ash.

BLM — Bureau of Land Management, an agency of the U.S. Department of Interior. It manages almost 23 million acres of publicly owned land in Utah.

Cairn — Rocks deliberately piled up to serve as a trail marker.

CG — Campground.

Desert varnish — A dark coating of iron and manganese that commonly covers desert rocks.

Fault — A fracture in the Earth's crust accompanied by a displacement of one side of the fracture with respect to the other and in a direction parallel to the fracture.

Flexure — the act of flexing or bending.

Fold — A curve or bend in rock strata, or layers.

Igneous rock — Rock formed of magma, or molten rock.

Laccolith — A mass of igneous rock formed from magma that spread laterally into a lenticular body, forcing overlying strata to bulge upward.

Magma — Molten rock.

Meander — A looping bend in a river channel.

Monocline — A fold in stratified rock in which all the strata, or layers, dip in the same direction.

NF — National forest.

NP — National park.

MYA — Million years ago.

Petroglyph — A design deliberately pecked into the thin, dark varnish that commonly covers desert rock.

Pictograph — A design deliberately painted on rock surfaces.

Reef — A ridge of sharply upturned rock that 19th century pioneers saw as obstacles to travel akin to marine reefs.

Sandstone — Rock composed of sand grains cemented together.

Sedimentary rock — Rock formed of accumulated sediments.

Shale — Solidified muds, clays and silts that can be split into sheets or slabs.

SP — State park.

Strata — Layers of sedimentary rock.

Stratified — Layered, or sheetlike, rock or earth of one kind lying between beds of other kinds.

Travertine — A light-colored porous calcite deposited from solution in ground or surface water.

Trilobite — A general term for a group of extinct marine invertebrates (anthropods) with three-lobed, oval-shaped bodies found as fossils in rocks from the Paleozoic (245-570 MYA) Era.

Upwarp — A broad area where layered rocks have been uplifted by internal forces.

Wash — A normally dry streambed that can fill with water during or after rain storms.

Wilderness — Once just a sparsely or unpopulated place dominated by nature, the 1964 Wilderness Act made it a legislative designation as well. It is now defined, in part, as land that appears to be in a natural state, where the impact of humans is essentially unnoticeable. They are protected from consumptive uses, such as mining and logging. Mechanized travel is not allowed in legislated wilderness areas.

Index

Moab

About The Author

Tony Huegel's *Backcountry Byways* guidebooks, as well as his adventure driving travel articles, have introduced thousands of travelers to some of the most scenic and historic backroads in the American West.

In addition to his regular, award-winning contributions to *Open Road* magazine, his writing and photography have appeared in *Mercedes Momentum* and *4Wheel Drive & Sport Utility* magazines, and the *San Jose Mercury News*, the *Sacramento Bee* and the *San Diego Union-Tribune* newspapers.

He grew up in the San Francisco Bay Area, spending his free time hiking in the East Bay hills and backpacking in the Sierra Nevada Mountains. His travels have taken him from Alaska to Central America, and from the Rocky Mountains to Europe and North Africa. After earning a bachelor's degree in journalism at the University of California, Berkeley, he worked as a journalist in California, Idaho and Wyoming, winning awards for legal affairs and government reporting as well as feature writing.

Whether bouldering in Wyoming, mountain biking in Utah, rock climbing in Yosemite, scuba diving in Mexico, sky diving in California or wandering the wilds of Montana, he has always taken the road less traveled. He and his family, who frequently accompany him on his journeys, live in Idaho.